# Changing Thymes

New Traditions in Texas Cooking

Austin Junior Forum

The objective of Austin Junior Forum is to create a greater interest among young women in civic, educational and philanthropic fields. Profits from the sale of *Changing Thymes* will be returned to the community through Austin Junior Forum projects and grants.

Library of Congress No. 93-074405
ISBN 0-9607152-2-3

Additional copies of Changing Thymes may be obtained by contacting:
Austin Junior Forum Publications, Inc.
P.O. Box 26628
Austin, TX 78755-0620

Phone: 800-661-2537    512-835-9233
Fax: 512-835-9178

Photography by Dennis Fagan
Austin, Texas
Background design on cover © Imperial Wallcoverings, Inc.

First Printing    March 1995    30,000

Printed in the USA by

**WIMMER**
The Wimmer Companies, Inc.
Memphis • Dallas

# About Changing Thymes

From AJF Publications, Inc.,
publisher of the successful
*Lone Star Legacy* & *Lone Star Legacy* II

*Changing Thymes* means something different to everyone. To many, it means spending less time in the kitchen and more time with our families, and for ourselves. We still want the delicious, mouth-watering meals our mothers prepared, but in about half the time. With this special collection of recipes, you can build menus that balance full, busy lives with a desire for elegant dining. Many of the recipes included can be on your table in less than thirty minutes!

Today, however, being fast and easy is not enough. The way we think about food has changed. To most of us, *Changing Thymes* means new awareness of our nutritional needs. We still desire tasty, satisfying meals, but also want them to be balanced and nutritious. With *Changing Thymes* you can have it all. The nutritional analysis included with each recipe takes the mystery out of calories, fat grams, cholesterol, sodium, carbohydrates, and protein.

Making informed choices allows you to enjoy splurging without the guilt. All it takes is a little ingenuity. Create a balanced breakfast by choosing Jamaican Baked Bananas to complement Belgian Brunch Sandwiches. Or, satisfy your cravings for dessert with Cappuccino-Chocolate Cheesecake after a sensible meal of Salsa Chicken, Santa Fe Citrus Salad, and Seasoned French Bread.

*Changing Thymes*, our third presentation of extraordinary, family-tested recipes collected from past generations and present friends, reflects the dynamic lifestyles and changing needs of Texas cooks. Just turn the page, and begin forming new traditions that capture the meanings of the past while fulfilling the needs of today's lifestyles.

This first printing of *Changing Thymes* is lovingly dedicated to the memory of Beverly Woldhagen James.
Thanks for the smiles!

# Austin Junior Forum Publications

## Changing Thymes Committee

### Chairman
Vicki Ashley Atkins

**Design**
Vera Dufour, chairman
Ann Armstrong
Kathy Gordon
Nanci Jordt
Sandy Niederstadt

**Bookkeeper**
Georgia Henrich
Barbara McEachern

**Writing**
Laura Pankonien, chairman
Vicki Atkins
Jeanne Cassidy
Beverly James

**Editing**
Cheryl Patton, chairman
Ann Armstrong
Ginny Ashley
Barbara Bump
Mary Lou Cindrich
Donna Crain
Mary Cheryl Dorwart
Rosemary Douglass
Ann Grote
Gwen Irwin
Beverly James
Janet Nash
Bryan N. Rumble
Jane Sanders
Patti Shields

### Publicity & Marketing
Laura Pankonien, coordinator
Ginny Ashley, marketing services
Mary Cheryl Dorwart, public relations
Cheryl Patton, sales

### Austin Junior Forum Cookbook Board
Kathy Marsh, chairman

Ginny Ashley
Vicki Atkins
Donna Crain
Denise Forwood

Georgia Henrich
Joyce Moeller
Wanda Rich
Bryan N. Rumble

## Collections, Testing, and Public Relations
Jeanne Cassidy, chairman, collections & testing
Vicki Atkins, coordinator

The Cookbook Committee of Austin Junior Forum sends a heart-felt thank you to each AJF member, her family and friends for the time spent collecting, submitting, preparing and testing recipes for *Changing Thymes*. It has been a terrifically successful, cooperative effort. Thanks!

| | | |
|---|---|---|
| Carla Annear | Liza Fox-Mills | Diane Olbert |
| Ann Armstrong | Mary Francis | Susie Olson |
| Ginny Ashley | Elizabeth Goodwin | Laura Pankonien |
| Vicki Atkins | Kathy Gordon | Cheryl Patton |
| Karen Ball | Rhonda Gracely | Jeanine Pettis |
| Tricia Barbee | Ann Grote | Suzanne Phillips |
| Randi Barrentine | Donna Hallett | Kelley Pickens |
| Tamra Bashaw | Debbie Harris | Renette Presti |
| Elaine Boozer | Janet Henegar | Rita Relyea |
| Barbara Bittner | Georgia Henrich | Karen Ressman |
| Shannon Boggus | Jennie Hentges | Wanda Rich |
| Vicki Bohls | Laura Hobby | Jan Richards |
| Pam Bommarito | Cindy Holcomb | Martha Rife |
| Barbara Boyd | Judy Holladay | Teresa Roberts |
| Jo Brown | Beverly Irick | Bryan N. Rumble |
| Pam Brown | Gwen Irwin | Jane Sanders |
| Rory Brown | Patty Jackson | Carol Schmidt |
| Barbara Bump | Beverly James | Mary Ellen Schmidt |
| Linda Bush | Debby Jenson | Patti Shields |
| Chris Bussell | Pam Johnson | Cynthia Simar |
| Betsy Campbell | Pamela Jones | Deborah Simmons |
| Jeanne Campbell | Nanci Jordt | Linda Simmons |
| Allyson Campsey | Michelle Just | Millie Skidmore |
| Colleen Cannon | Rosemary (Bunny) Kahler | Jennifer Smedley |
| Kathryn Cantilo | Linda Kelley | Sherrie Smith |
| Andrea Carter | Sue Kidwell | Debbie Smolik |
| Kathy Carlson | Cindy Kilmer | Ada Smyth |
| Marilyn Carlson | Lisa Koestner | Jill Spencer |
| Carol Cesaro | Jean Kreuz | Marcia Stiles |
| Rhonda Chapman | Llewellyn Lampley | Linda Stockton |
| Terre Churchill | Sue Loyd | Debi Stokes-Daughn |
| Mary Lou Cindrich | Carla Lott | Judy Strawmyer |
| Julie Clark | Sandra Lott | Maricela Sullivan |
| Donna Clay | Stephaney MacLeod | Kathy Sweigard |
| Kathy Clay | Ann McCoppin | Mary Tavcar |
| Lori Cooke | Barbara McEachern | Marilyn Taylor |
| Donna Crain | Kathy Marsh | Linda Uhl |
| Laurie Davis | Ginger Martin | Carol Verrengia |
| Mary Cheryl Dorwart | Lee Meeks | Linda Watson |
| Rosemary Douglass | Ann Mills | Julie Westcott |
| Vera Dufour | Joyce Moeller | Lisa White |
| Adele Ely | Eleece Moffatt | LaNyce Whittemore |
| Patsy Eppright | Joyce Moore | Betty Williams |
| Susie Erard-Coupe | Kathleen Moore | Carol Willis |
| Kathy Farley | Linda Moore | Cindy Willis |
| Judy Fincannon | Janet Nash | Ellin Wilson |
| Carla Fisher | Shermette Naumann | Kathleen Wimbish |
| Denise Forwood | Sandy Niederstadt | Michelle Zogas |

# About Austin Junior Forum

Austin Junior Forum (AJF), chartered in 1969, is a group of women supporting those in need across greater Austin, Texas, through gifts of time, talent and funds. About 125 active and 100 sustaining members provide in excess of 12,000 hours per year, and return an average 71 cents of every dollar earned back to the community through grants and in-kind gifts.

The ongoing publication and sales of cookbooks has been one of the largest contributors to AJF's grants effort. *Changing Thymes* joins earlier publications, *Lone Star Legacy* and *Lone Star Legacy II*, enabling us to continue giving to those less fortunate in Austin. It is fitting that its initial printing occur during our 25th anniversary year.

# About the Nutritional Analyses

Comprehensive nutritional analyses have been included with each recipe in *Changing Thymes*, through use of the ESHA Research software program, Food Processor Plus. These analyses allow you to make informed decisions about the food you prepare. However, remember that nutritional needs vary from person to person depending upon age, sex, health status and total diet.

The nutritional values given are approximate and we believe them to be correct, but they may vary depending upon the products you use. Also note that whenever a range or choice is included in the recipe ingredients, the first option was used as the basis of the nutritional analysis. For example:

If 8 to 10 potatoes are called for, eight have been used as the basis of the analysis.

If margarine or butter is called for, margarine has been used, as it is the first option. Likewise, if butter or margarine is called for, butter (because it is the first entry) will have been used as the basis of the analysis.

Any ingredients listed as optional have not been included in the analysis.

# Contents

# Appetizers and Beverages

At the first sign of wildflowers, Texans pack their picnic baskets and head for the Bluebonnet Trail, in anticipation of Bluebonnets, Indian Paintbrush, Primrose, Mexican Hats, Firewheels, and more. To make the experience even more memorable take along a cool pitcher of **Lemon Sangría**, with a sherry and walnut **Raspberry Cheese Ball**, a bowl of **Antipasto Dip** and corn chips, a **Creamy Clam Bake**, and a variety of gourmet crackers.

*Select serving pieces courtesy of Williams Sonoma, Inc., Austin, Texas.*

# Antipasto Dip
Carla Fisher

1 (4 ounce) can ripe olives
1 (4 ounce) can green chilies
2 ripe tomatoes, chopped
2 green onions, chopped
1 tablespoon olive oil
1 teaspoon wine vinegar

- Mix all ingredients together.
- Chill for 1 hour.

A quick, easy, tasty and versatile dip, it tastes good with garlic bread, may be used like salsa or as a topping for grilled fish or chicken breast and topped with Monterey Jack cheese.

Makes approximately 2¼ cups

Per tablespoon

Calories 8  Protein .135 g  Carbohydrates .713 g  Fat .5 g  Cholesterol 0 mg  Sodium 11.8 mg

# Artichoke and Lemon Basil Dip
Pamela Jones

½ cup non-fat mayonnaise
3 tablespoons water
1 tablespoon lemon juice
1 teaspoon minced shallot or green onion
¼ cup chopped fresh parsley
½ teaspoon Dijon mustard
½ teaspoon dried basil
2 tablespoons canola or olive oil
2 sprigs celery leaves
1 bay leaf
Juice of ½ lemon
Water
2 large or 4 small artichokes

- Combine mayonnaise, 3 tablespoons water, lemon juice, shallot, parsley, mustard and basil. Chill until ready to serve as dip for artichokes.
- To steam artichokes, add oil, celery leaves, bay leaf and lemon juice to water in bottom of steamer.
- Steam artichokes for 45 to 50 minutes.
- Remove and chill before serving.

Serves 4

Per serving

Calories 67  Protein 4.24 g  Carbohydrates 15.0 g  Fat .2 g  Cholesterol 6.31 mg  Sodium 201.2 mg

# Curry Mayonnaise
Pamela Jones

*Wonderful with freshly steamed artichokes*

1 cup reduced calorie
mayonnaise
1 to 2 tablespoons minced onion
1 teaspoon tarragon vinegar
1½ teaspoons dry mustard
1 teaspoon curry powder

- Combine all ingredients, mixing until well blended.
- Chill until ready to serve.
- Serve as dip for freshly steamed artichokes, other fresh vegetables or boiled shrimp; or as a spicy sandwich spread.

Makes approximately 1 cup

Per tablespoon

Calories 38  Protein .154 g  Carbohydrates 2.74 g  Fat 3 g  Cholesterol 3.74 g  Sodium 77.6 mg

# Italian Artichoke Hearts
Jane Miller Sanders

*Artichoke hearts must marinate for 8 hours*

2 (16 ounce) cans artichoke
hearts, drained and quartered
1 cup Italian salad dressing
¼ cup (1 ounce) grated Romano
cheese
½ cup Italian-seasoned
breadcrumbs

- Marinate artichoke hearts in salad dressing for 8 hours.
- Combine cheese and breadcrumbs in bag.
- Drain artichoke hearts. Place in bag and shake to coat thoroughly with cheese and breadcrumb mixture. Place on baking sheet.
- Bake at 375° for 12 to 15 minutes.

Makes approximately 56

Per piece

Calories 35  Protein .83 g  Carbohydrates 3.52 g  Fat 2 g  Cholesterol .505 mg  Sodium 101 mg

# Swiss Artichoke Puffs
*Shermette Naumann*

18 slices dark rye bread
⅓ pound thinly-sliced Swiss cheese
¾ cup mayonnaise
⅓ cup (1½ ounces) grated Parmesan cheese
1 teaspoon parsley flakes
¼ teaspoon onion powder
¼ teaspoon Worcestershire sauce
1 (16 ounce) can artichoke hearts, drained and cut in half

- Using biscuit or cookie cutter, cut bread slices into bite-sized rounds. Discard trimmings or save for other uses. Toast bread rounds.
- Cut Swiss cheese to fit top of bread rounds. Set aside.
- Combine mayonnaise and Parmesan cheese. Stir in parsley flakes, onion powder and Worcestershire sauce.
- Place artichoke heart half on each toast round. Spread cheese mixture on artichoke and top with Swiss cheese. Place on baking sheet.
- Broil until cheese is melted and lightly browned.

Makes 18

Per piece _____

Calories 157  Protein 4.58 g  Carbohydrates 9.1 g  Fat 11.5 g  Cholesterol 15.5 mg  Sodium 347 mg

★

Steaming fresh artichokes helps them to maintain their fresh, green color. They will turn grayish if cooked in aluminum or iron. For extra flavor, add lemon to the boiling water, or try steaming them over boiling vegetable or chicken broth.

# Easy Black Olive Dip
Linda Cook Uhl

*Chill for several hours*

1 (8 ounce) package cream cheese, softened
3 tablespoons lemon juice
½ teaspoon garlic salt or more to taste
¼ to ⅓ cup milk
1 (4 ounce) can black olives, drained and chopped

- Combine cream cheese, lemon juice and garlic salt, beating until smooth.
- Add milk, a tablespoon at a time, until dip is desired consistency. Fold olives into dip; do not blend or puree.
- Chill for several hours or overnight.
- Serve with chips or crackers.

Makes approximately 2 cups

Per tablespoon _____

Calories 30, Protein .64 g  Carbohydrates .655 g  Fat 3 g  Cholesterol 8.05 mg  Sodium 44.8 mg

# Frijoles Borrachos
Pamela Jones

1 small onion, chopped
2 tablespoons vegetable oil
2 cups cooked pinto beans or 1 (16 ounce) can refried beans
1 cup (4 ounces) grated Cheddar cheese
¼ to ½ cup chopped, seeded, canned jalapeño peppers
½ cup beer
Salt to taste

- Sauté onion in oil in large skillet over medium-high heat until tender.
- Add beans to onion and heat thoroughly, mashing until mixture is almost smooth. Reduce heat to low.
- Add cheese, jalapeño peppers, beer and salt. Cook until cheese is melted.
- Serve warm with tortilla chips.

*Use ½ cup jalapeño peppers for "fire" lovers only—it's very hot!*

Makes approximately 4 cups

Per tablespoon _____

Calories 20  Protein .914 g  Carbohydrates 1.67 g  Fat 1 g  Cholesterol 1.86 mg  Sodium 15.4 mg

# Appetizer Cheesecakes
Linda Cook Uhl

4 *plain biscotti, crushed*
2 *tablespoons butter or margarine, melted*
¾ *cup (6 ounces) herbed cream cheese, softened*
1 *(4½ ounce) package Brie cheese*
1 *egg*
1 *tablespoon dry sherry*
⅛ *teaspoon salt*
⅛ *teaspoon black pepper*
⅛ *teaspoon garlic powder*
6 *cherry tomatoes, quartered*
*Small basil leaves for garnish*

- Combine biscotti crumbs and melted butter or margarine. Press crumbs into bottoms of 1¾-inch muffin pans prepared with vegetable cooking spray.
- Using electric mixer, combine cream cheese, Brie, egg, sherry, salt, black pepper and garlic powder, beating until combined; mixture will not be smooth.
- Spoon cheese mixture into prepared muffin pans, filling cups ⅔ full.
- Bake at 350° for 10 to 12 minutes or until firm. Cool in pans on wire rack.
- Remove cheesecakes from muffin pans. Top each with tomato wedge and basil leaves. Chill until ready to serve.

Makes 2 dozen

Per cheesecake

Calories 73  Protein 2.46 g  Carbohydrates 3.7 g  Fat 5.5 g  Cholesterol 19.9 mg  Sodium 87 mg

★

When entertaining, vary your menu serving both hot and cold hors d'oeuvres. The cold nibbles can be made ahead and refrigerated, allowing you to spend less time in the kitchen just before and during your party.

## Aunt Sophia's Almond Cheese Spread
*Cheryl Briggs Patton*

¼ cup unblanched almonds, toasted and finely chopped
2 slices bacon, crisply cooked and crumbled
1 cup (4 ounces) grated American cheese
1 tablespoon chopped green onion (optional)
½ cup mayonnaise or mayonnaise-type salad dressing

• Combine almonds, bacon, cheese, onion and mayonnaise or salad dressing.
• Serve immediately or refrigerate and use as a sandwich spread or on crackers or vegetables.

*This spread makes a great grilled cheese sandwich.*

Makes approximately 1¾ cups

Per tablespoon _____

Calories 69  Protein 2.24 g  Carbohydrates .496 g  Fat 6.5 g  Cholesterol 10.3 mg  Sodium 145 mg

## Cheese Dip Olé
*Caryn Cluiss*

1 (10 ounce) can tomatoes with green chilies
2 (8 ounce) packages low fat cream cheese, softened
1 (2 ounce) jar pimiento-stuffed green olives, drained
½ teaspoon lemon juice
¼ teaspoon Worcestershire sauce
Salt and black pepper to taste

• Combine all ingredients in blender container. Blend until smooth.
• Chill until ready to serve.
• Serve with tortilla chips.

*Dip is quick to fix and works great with any Mexican dish.*

Makes approximately 2¾ cups

Per tablespoon _____

Calories 26  Protein 1.16 g  Carbohydrates .993 g  Fat 2 g  Cholesterol 5.77 mg  Sodium 95.4 mg

# Baked Brie en Croûte
Cheryl Briggs Patton

1 package puff pastry (2 sheets)
1 (10 to 12 inch) round Brie cheese
1 (6 to 8 ounce) jar apricot preserves, pureed
1 egg white, slightly beaten

- Place 1 sheet of pastry on baking sheet.
- Center cheese round on pastry. Shave white coating from top of cheese. Spread preserves on top of cheese.
- Gently fold pastry edges over cheese, overlapping top approximately ½ inch. Lightly brush edges of pastry with egg white to seal.
- Place second pastry sheet on top of cheese. Trim to fit the top of cheese and press lightly to seal. Lightly brush edges with egg white to seal.
- Using excess pastry pieces, decorate the "Brie cake" with cutout hearts, bells or other designs, attaching with egg white to seal.
- Freeze, covered, on baking sheet overnight or until ready to use.
- Without thawing, bake at 425° for 20 to 30 minutes or until golden and puffed.

If pastry-covered cheese is not frozen when placed in oven, the cheese will be very runny when served.

Serves 24

Per serving _____

Calories 115  Protein 4.45 g  Carbohydrates 8.35 g  Fat 7.5 g  Cholesterol 27.7 mg  Sodium 134 mg

# Chili Cheese Skinny Dip
Vicki Ashley Atkins

1 cup low fat cottage cheese
¼ cup (1 ounce) shredded low-fat Cheddar cheese
¼ cup chopped onion
¼ cup plain non-fat yogurt
¼ cup ketchup
1 tablespoon chopped fresh parsley
¾ teaspoon chili powder
¼ teaspoon garlic powder
⅛ teaspoon ground cumin

- Place cottage cheese in food processor bowl. Using knife blade, process until smooth, scraping sides of bowl once.
- Add remaining ingredients. Process until smooth, scraping sides of bowl once.
- Serve with fresh raw vegetables.

Makes approximately 2 cups

Per tablespoon _____

Calories 10  Protein 1.26 g  Carbohydrates 1.05 g  Fat .1 g  Cholesterol .53 mg  Sodium 53.7 mg

# Easy Swiss Cheese Spread
Barbara Bannister

2 cups (8 ounces) grated Swiss cheese
½ cup mayonnaise
¼ cup chopped chives or green onion tops

- Combine cheese and mayonnaise, mixing lightly but thoroughly. Stir in chives or onion.
- Chill, covered, to blend flavors.
- Serve with crackers.

*Men love this spread and it will keep for several days. A dish of olives provides a good flavor contrast.*

Makes approximately 2¾ cups

Per tablespoon _____

Calories 36  Protein 1.43 g  Carbohydrates .265 g  Fat 3.5 g  Cholesterol 5.97 mg  Sodium 27.1 mg

# Queso Pesos

Ann Bommarito Armstrong

1 (32 ounce) package
pasteurized process cheese spread
2 (8 ounce) packages cream
cheese, softened
2 teaspoons cayenne pepper
powder
1 teaspoon garlic powder
1 jalapeño pepper, finely chopped
2 cups chopped pecans
Chili powder

- Combine cheese spread and cream cheese, mixing until blended.
- Add cayenne, garlic powder, jalapeño pepper and pecans to cheese mixture, blending well.
- Shape cheese mixture into 1x10-inch logs. Roll in chili powder, coating completely. Wrap logs in wax paper.
- Store in refrigerator or freezer.
- Serve by cutting log into ¼ to ½-inch slices and serve on crackers.

*To make a cheese ball, reserve ½ cup pecans, form a portion of the mixture into a ball and roll in pecans. Cheese logs may be stored in the refrigerator for several weeks or in the freezer for a longer period.*

Makes approximately 8 cups

Per tablespoon

Calories 57  Protein 1.99 g  Carbohydrates .613 g  Fat 4.5 g  Cholesterol 10.6 mg  Sodium 112 mg

★

Try substituting lower fat, or no fat, products like reduced calorie cheeses and spreads, and non-fat cream cheese substitutes in your favorite recipes. After adding seasonings you probably won't notice a difference and you and your family will be eating healthier.

# Quiche Strata
*Ann Bommarito Armstrong*

*Chill at least 1 hour before baking*

8 slices whole wheat bread, crusts trimmed
1 (6 ounce) package natural Swiss cheese slices
8 slices bacon, crisply cooked and crumbled
1 (4 ounce) can chopped mushrooms, drained
¼ cup chopped green onion
4 eggs, beaten
2 cups milk
½ teaspoon salt
Dash of black pepper

- Place 4 slices bread in bottom of greased 8x8x2-inch baking dish. Place half of cheese slices on bread.
- Combine bacon, mushrooms and green onion. Sprinkle evenly on cheese layer.
- Top with remaining cheese slices and cover with remaining bread.
- Combine eggs, milk, salt and black pepper. Pour over bread layer.
- Chill, covered, for at least 1 hour or overnight.
- Bake at 325° for 1 hour. Let stand for 10 minutes before cutting into small squares.

*Garnish with additional sliced mushrooms, chopped green onion or crumbled bacon for a company brunch dish.*

Serves 16

Per serving _____
Calories 135  Protein 7.72 g  Carbohydrates 10.6 g  Fat 7 g  Cholesterol 68.6 mg  Sodium 435 mg

──────★──────

Always keep a bag in your freezer for bread trimmings. When a recipe calls for bread crumbs, just remove the desired amount, thaw, and crumble.

# Raspberry Cheese Ball
*Donna Earle Crain*

1 (8 ounce) package cream cheese, softened
2 tablespoons sherry
¼ cup chopped walnuts
¼ cup seedless raspberry preserves

- Combine cream cheese, sherry and walnuts, mixing until well blended.
- Chill mixture for 30 minutes.
- At serving time, shape into a ball. Make a hollow on the top of the ball. Spoon preserves into hollow and around sides of ball.
- Serve with club crackers.

*This is the Cookbook Committee's favorite cheese ball.*

Serves 24

Per tablespoon

Calories 51  Protein .918 g  Carbohydrates 2.73 g  Fat 4 g  Cholesterol 10.4 mg  Sodium 29.4 mg

# Roquefort Grapes with Pistachios
*Donna Earle Crain*

10 ounces shelled pistachios
1 (8 ounce) package cream cheese, softened
1 (2 ounce) package Roquefort cheese
2 tablespoons cream
1 pound seedless grapes, washed and blotted dry

- Toast nuts at 275° for 10 to 20 minutes on a cookie sheet. Allow to cool and chop finely.
- Blend cream cheese, cheese and cream in blender or processor until smooth.
- Dip each grape into cheese mixture then roll in nuts. Place on wax paper lined baking sheet and chill until ready to serve.

*Serve with Sauvignon Blanc.*

Makes approximately 50 grapes

Per serving

Calories 60  Protein 1.82 g  Carbohydrates 3.19 g  Fat 5 g  Cholesterol 6.23 mg  Sodium 34.6 mg

# Mock Guac
Debi A. Leavitt

1 (8 ounce) package frozen asparagus, cooked and drained, or 1 (15 ounce) can asparagus spears
½ cup picanté sauce
1 tablespoon fresh lemon juice
⅛ teaspoon garlic powder or 1 clove garlic, minced
¾ teaspoon cumin
½ teaspoon oregano
2 tablespoons non-fat yogurt
2 tablespoons non-fat reduced calorie mayonnaise

• Combine all ingredients in food processor bowl or blender container. Process until smooth and consistency of guacamole.
• Chill before serving.

Serves 32

Per serving _____

Calories 8  Protein .417 g  Carbohydrates .986 g  Fat .5 g  Cholesterol .293 mg  Sodium 80.9 mg

# Marinated Mushrooms
Cheryl Briggs Patton

Must prepare in advance

3 pounds mushrooms, cleaned and stems removed
2⅔ cups vegetable oil
2 cups garlic wine vinegar
¼ cup chopped fresh parsley
4 teaspoons sugar
4 teaspoons salt or to taste
1 tablespoon freshly ground black pepper
4 cloves garlic, coarsely chopped

• Combine mushrooms, oil, vinegar, parsley, sugar, salt, black pepper and garlic in large jar.
• Marinate the mushrooms in dressing for 2 days (but not more than 2 days).
• Drain mushrooms before serving.

Serves 12

Per serving _____

Calories 249  Protein 2.45 g  Carbohydrates 7.53 g  Fat 25 g  Cholesterol 0 mg  Sodium 361 mg

# Spicy Nuts
*Donna Earle Crain*

2 tablespoons vegetable oil
1½ teaspoons chili powder
¼ teaspoon cayenne pepper
½ teaspoon garlic salt
2 teaspoons Worcestershire sauce
1½ cups dry-roasted cashews
1½ cups dry-roasted peanuts

- In large bowl combine oil and seasonings.
- Add nuts, toss to coat.
- Spread evenly in a 13x9x2-inch baking pan and bake at 300° for 20 minutes, stirring once or twice.

Makes approximately 3 cups

Per ¼ cup serving _____

Calories 227  Protein 7.01 g  Carbohydrates 9.96 g  Fat 19.5 g  Cholesterol 0 mg  Sodium 123 mg

# B.J.'s Salsa Almost Fresca
*Cheryl Briggs Patton*

4 cups coarsely chopped peeled tomatoes
1 cup chopped onion
1 cup chopped jalapeño peppers
1 cup chopped sweet cherry peppers
1 (15 ounce) can tomato sauce
1 (16 ounce) jar mild picanté sauce
1 cup cider vinegar

- Bring all ingredients to a boil in a glass non-aluminum pan. Stir with a wooden spoon.
- Simmer for about 1½ hours.
- Pour hot vegetable mixture into hot sterilized jars. Process and seal according to jar manufacturer's directions.

*This sauce is fabulous when prepared with homegrown tomatoes and jalapeños. For a milder sauce, remove seeds from half the jalapeño peppers. To peel tomatoes easily, blanch in boiling water for 10 to 15 seconds or until skin pops, then plunge into chilled water.*

Serves 16

Per serving _____

Calories 44  Protein 1.46 g  Carbohydrates 9.97 g  Fat .5 g  Cholesterol .334 mg  Sodium 475 mg

# Bryan's Fresh Salsa

Bryan Rumble Norton

2 cups chopped tomatoes
¼ cup chopped green onion
2 tablespoons diced onion
1 teaspoon diced fresh jalapeño
pepper
2 tablespoons chopped fresh
cilantro
2 cloves garlic, chopped
1 teaspoon fresh lime juice
¼ teaspoon salt

- Combine all ingredients in medium bowl.
- Mix thoroughly.

Serves 8

Per serving _____

Calories 15.3  Protein .629 g  Carbohydrates 3.41 g  Fat .2 g  Cholesterol 0 mg  Sodium 77.7 mg

# City Girls' Hot Salsa

Amy Beattie

10 cups chopped cherry tomatoes
3 cups chopped onion
1 to 2 cups chopped garlic
½ to 1 bunch fresh cilantro,
chopped
16 small jalapeño peppers,
chopped
1 cup cider vinegar
3½ teaspoons salt

- Chop cherry tomatoes in food
  processor. Add onions, cloves,
  cilantro and jalapeño peppers and
  pulse to mix well.
- Put processed vegetables in a
  large kettle and add cider vinegar
  and salt. Bring ingredients to a
  full boil. Simmer for additional 15
  minutes.
- Pour cooked ingredients into hot
  sterilized jars. Fill within ¼ inch of
  top. Put in a hot water bath for 15
  minutes.

To vary intensity of flavor, remove all seeds
from jalapeño peppers for a mild sauce or
remove half the seeds for a medium hot
sauce. Cherry tomatoes offer a sweeter flavor
but regular tomatoes may be used.

Makes 7 or 8 pints

Per tablespoon _____

Calories 29  Protein 1.17 g  Carbohydrates 6.57 g  Fat .2 g  Sodium 255 mg

# Betty's Sweet Potato Chips
Donna Earle Crain

*¼ pound sweet potatoes*
*Ice water*
*Vegetable oil for deep frying*
*Powdered sugar or salt*

- Peel sweet potatoes. Cut cross-wise in very thin slices. Soak in ice water for a few hours or chill in cold water overnight.
- Drain sweet potato slices and blot with paper towel to dry.
- Deep fry in vegetable oil at 375° until crisp.
- Drain on paper towel. Sprinkle with powdered sugar or salt to taste.

*Sweet potato chips are excellent with salad.*

Serves 1

Per serving _____

Calories 172  Protein 1.87 g  Carbohydrates 30.7  Fat 5 g  Cholesterol 0 mg  Sodium 14.8 mg

# Creamy Vegetable Rollups
Dee Williamson

*¼ cup (2 ounces) low fat cream cheese, softened*
*¼ cup low fat cottage cheese*
*¼ cup coarsely shredded carrot*
*2 tablespoons minced celery*
*1 tablespoon minced green onion*
*1 tablespoon minced green bell pepper*
*1 tablespoon chopped parsley*
*2 teaspoons diced pimiento*
*¼ teaspoon dried dillweed*
*⅛ teaspoon garlic powder*
*4 (6 inch) flour tortillas*

- Combine all ingredients except tortillas in bowl. Mix well. Chill, covered, for at least 2 hours.
- Spoon 3 tablespoons cheese mixture on each tortilla, spreading to edges. Roll up, jelly roll fashion.
- Cut into bite-sized slices and place on serving plate.

Serves 8

Per serving _____

Calories 77  Protein 4.59 g  Carbohydrates 11.2 g  Fat 1 g  Cholesterol 2.81 mg  Sodium 199 mg

# Sausage Stuffed Mushrooms
*Kathy Sweigard*

2 pounds fresh mushrooms
1 (16 ounce) package sage-
flavored bulk pork sausage
1 (8 ounce) package cream
cheese, softened

- Remove stems and finely chop; reserve caps for stuffing.
- Cook sausage until browned, stirring to crumble. Remove from heat, mix with finely chopped mushroom stems and cool.
- Combine sausage mixture and cream cheese, blending well. Spoon about 1 teaspoon sausage mixture into each mushroom cap. Place on rimmed baking sheet.
- Bake at 350° for 15 to 20 minutes.

Makes approximately 4 dozen

Per piece

Calories 61  Protein 1.86 g  Carbohydrates 1.1 g  Fat 5.5 g  Cholesterol 11.6 mg  Sodium 77.7 mg

# Teriyaki Meat Strips
*Barbara Bittner*

2 pounds sirloin tip steak
½ cup soy sauce
1 clove garlic, minced
3 tablespoons sugar
1 tablespoon sherry
⅛ teaspoon ground ginger

- Slice steak diagonally (across grain) into 2x1x¼-inch strips.
- Combine remaining ingredients.
- Marinate meat strips in soy sauce mixture for 30 minutes.
- Remove meat from marinade, reserving liquid. Thread strips on bamboo skewers. Grill or broil until done, basting several times while cooking.

*While meat is marinating, soak bamboo skewers in water to prevent burning when cooking.*

Makes approximately 4 dozen

Per piece

Calories 43  Protein 5.9 g  Carbohydrates 1.06 g  Fat 1.5 g  Cholesterol 16.8 mg  Sodium 184 mg

# Hazel's Swedish Meatballs
*Cheryl Briggs Patton*

3 pounds ground beef
3 cups white breadcrumbs
3 tablespoons chopped onion
2 teaspoons salt
¾ teaspoon nutmeg
6 tablespoons butter, melted
3½ cups ketchup
3½ cups sherry
½ teaspoon oregano
½ teaspoon hot pepper sauce

- Combine ground beef, breadcrumbs, onion, salt, nutmeg and butter, mixing well. Shape mixture into small balls and place on rimmed baking sheet.
- Brown in oven at 350° for 15 to 20 minutes.
- Combine ketchup, sherry, oregano and hot pepper sauce in large saucepan. Simmer for 30 minutes.
- Add meatballs to sauce and heat thoroughly.
- Serve in chafing dish.

*Meatballs and sauce may be frozen. Thaw before reheating to serve.*

Makes approximately 100 meatballs.

Per piece _____

Calories 77.3  Protein 4.55 g  Carbohydrates 5.02 g  Fat 3.5 g  Cholesterol 15.3 mg  Sodium 180 mg

# Cocktail Reubens
*Rosemary Bennett Douglass*

½ pound cooked corned beef, chopped
¾ cup Thousand Island salad dressing
25 slices cocktail rye bread
1 cup sauerkraut, well drained
1½ cups (6 ounces) shredded Swiss cheese
4 dill pickles, sliced, for garnish

- Combine corned beef and salad dressing, mixing well.
- Spread corned beef mixture on bread slices. Top each with sauerkraut, cheese and pickle slice.
- Broil 5 inches from heat source for 4 minutes or until cheese is melted.

Makes 25

Per slice _____

Calories 97  Protein 4.3 g  Carbohydrates 5.62 g  Fat 6.44 g  Cholesterol 16.8 mg  Sodium 414 mg

# Tuna Pâté

Kari J. Tobias

1 (8 ounce) package low fat
cream cheese, softened
1 tablespoon grated onion
1 tablespoon chili sauce
1 teaspoon Worcestershire sauce
2 tablespoons snipped parsley
2 (7 ounce) cans water-pack
tuna, drained and flaked
2 tablespoons dry sherry
Salt to taste

- Combine cream cheese, onion, chili sauce, Worcestershire sauce and parsley, mixing until well blended.
- Add tuna and sherry and mix well. Season with salt.
- Shape tuna mixture into mound in serving bowl or press into 3-cup mold lined with plastic wrap. Invert on serving plate.
- Serve with raw vegetables or crackers.

Makes approximately 3 cups

Per tablespoon _____

Calories 27.1  Protein 2.48 g  Carbohydrates .27 g  Fat 1.5 g  Cholesterol 7.68 mg  Sodium 48 mg

# Crab Dip Gourmet

Mary Lauderman Tavcar

1 (8 ounce) package cream
cheese, softened
½ cup mayonnaise
¼ cup sherry
1 teaspoon Worcestershire sauce
Juice of 1 lemon
Salt and black pepper to taste
1 pound crab meat
Parsley sprigs for garnish
Paprika for garnish

- Combine all ingredients except crab meat in chafing dish. Heat over low flame, stirring constantly, until well blended.
- Add crab meat to sauce, stirring gently to mix.
- Garnish with parsley and sprinkle with paprika. Serve with French bread cubes.

This recipe is guaranteed to please.

Makes approximately 4 cups

Per tablespoon _____

Calories 33  Protein 1.72 g  Carbohydrates .313 g  Fat 3 g  Cholesterol 12 mg  Sodium 45.1 mg

# Creamy Clam Bake
*Barbara Stromberg Boyd*

1 (6½ *ounce*) *can minced clams,*
*drained and liquid reserved*
2 (8 *ounce*) *packages cream*
*cheese, softened*
2 *tablespoons lemon juice*
*Water*
1 *teaspoon salt*
5 *or* 6 *green onions, chopped*
2 *tablespoons parsley flakes*
1 *round loaf sourdough bread*

• Combine clams, cream cheese and lemon juice, mixing thoroughly.

• Add water to reserved clam liquid to measure ½ cup. Stir into clam mixture.

• Add salt, green onion and parsley flakes to clam mixture, blending thoroughly.

• Cut top third from loaf of bread, reserving top. Hollow out to form a bowl. Spoon clam mixture into bowl. Place top on loaf.

• Place on baking sheet. Bake at 250° for 3 hours.

• Serve with chips and assorted crackers.

*The bowl can be eaten. This recipe always gets compliments.*

Makes approximately 3 cups

Dip, per tablespoon

Calories 37  Protein 1.26 g  Carbohydrates .48 g  Fat 3.5 g  Cholesterol 11.8 mg  Sodium 78.6 mg

———— ★ ————

Texas' long, beautiful gulf coast provides a multitude of fresh seafood, a bounty Texans put to good use in appetizers, soups, salads, and entrees.

# Oriental Crab Dip
Kathy Gordon

1 (3 ounce) package reduced calorie cream cheese, softened
1 tablespoon reduced sodium soy sauce
1 (6 ounce) can crab meat, drained
1 (8 ounce) can water chestnuts, drained and chopped
Green bell pepper, chopped (optional)
Green onion, chopped (optional)

- Combine all ingredients in a bowl. Mix well.
- Chill until ready to serve.
- Serve with your favorite crackers.

Makes approximately 1¼ cups

Per tablespoon ──────────────────────────

Calories 25  Protein 2.34 g  Carbohydrates 1.78 g  Fat 1 g  Cholesterol 9.94 mg  Sodium 93.2 mg

# Quick and Easy Crab Dip
Barbara Stromberg Boyd

1 (8 ounce) package cream cheese, softened
¼ cup margarine, melted
1 tablespoon lemon juice
2 tablespoons milk
3 green onions, chopped
1 (6 ounce) can crab meat, drained
¾ teaspoon garlic salt or to taste

- Cream together all ingredients in a medium bowl.
- Cover and chill for several hours to blend flavors.
- Remove from refrigerator 30 to 45 minutes before serving. Serve with chips or assorted crackers.

Decorate with parsley or a decorative vegetable to add pizzazz.

Makes approximately 2¼ cups

Per tablespoon ──────────────────────────

Calories 37  Protein 1.43 g  Carbohydrates .321 g  Fat 3.5 g  Cholesterol 10.6 mg  Sodium 47.1 mg

# Andy's Creole Shrimp
Pam Posey Brown

5 pounds unpeeled shrimp
1 (24 ounce) bottle Italian salad
dressing
½ cup lemon juice
2 sticks butter or margarine, cut
in bits
¼ cup Worcestershire sauce
1 tablespoon hot pepper sauce or
to taste
2 cloves garlic, pressed
½ teaspoon cayenne pepper or to
taste

- Place shrimp in oven-proof Dutch oven. Pour salad dressing and lemon juice over shrimp. Add Worcestershire sauce, hot pepper sauce, garlic and cayenne pepper and top with bits of butter.

- Bake at 300° for about 1 hour, stirring frequently. Liquid should nearly cover shrimp.

- Drain and serve in "peel and eat" style. May be served warm or chilled.

*Great hors d'oeuvre for an outdoor supper. Have plenty of napkins available!*

Serves 20

Per ¼ pound shrimp with 1 tablespoon liquid

Calories 191  Protein 23.1 g  Carbohydrates 2.35 g  Fat 9.5 g  Cholesterol 182.2 mg  Sodium 283 mg

# Green Chili Shrimp Dip
Nanci Norin Jordt

1 (8 ounce) package cream
cheese, softened
½ cup butter, softened
1 (4½ ounce) can deveined
medium shrimp, drained and
liquid reserved
½ pound shrimp, cooked, peeled,
deveined and cut in bite-sized
pieces
1 (4 ounce) can green chilies,
drained and chopped
1½ tablespoons chopped chives

- Combine cream cheese, butter and reserved liquid from canned shrimp, mixing until smooth.

- Add canned shrimp, fresh shrimp, green chilies and chives to cheese mixture.

- Chill; serve with crackers or raw vegetables.

Makes approximately 3½ cups

Per tablespoon

Calories 74  Protein 2.31 g  Carbohydrates 5.47 g  Fat 5 g  Cholesterol 22.5 mg  Sodium 136 mg

# Shrimp Con Queso Dip

Donna Earle Crain

1 (32 ounce) package pasteurized process cheese spread
1 (8 ounce) package cream cheese
1 (10¾ ounce) can cream of shrimp soup, undiluted
2 (10 ounce) cans tomatoes with green chilies
2 tablespoons dried onion flakes
½ teaspoon dried minced garlic
2 tablespoons cumin seed
1 teaspoon basil
½ teaspoon hot pepper sauce
½ teaspoon sugar
2 tablespoons Worcestershire sauce
1 pound cooked shrimp (about 2 cups), cut in bite-sized pieces

- Combine all ingredients except shrimp in top of large double boiler. Heat, stirring frequently, until cheese is melted and mixture is well blended.
- Add shrimp to cheese mixture.
- Pour into chafing dish. Serve with large corn chips.

Dip may be frozen for up to 6 weeks.

Makes approximately 11 cups

Per tablespoon

Calories 29  Protein 1.85 g  Carbohydrates .462 g  Fat 2 g  Cholesterol 11.5 mg  Sodium 112 mg

# Shrimp Mold

Julie M. Kirk

½ (10½ ounce) can tomato soup, undiluted
1 envelope unflavored gelatin
½ cup mayonnaise
1 (8 ounce) package cream cheese, softened
½ cup chopped celery
½ cup chopped onion
1 (7½ ounce) can small shrimp, chopped

- Combine soup and gelatin in saucepan. Cook over low heat until gelatin is melted.
- Cream mayonnaise and cream cheese together until smooth.
- Mix all ingredients together. Pour into 4-cup mold and chill.
- Invert mold on serving platter. Serve with crackers.

Makes approximately 4 cups

Per tablespoon

Calories 32  Protein 1.49 g  Carbohydrates .632 g  Fat 2.5 g  Cholesterol 10.6 mg  Sodium 44.1 mg

# Spicy Shrimp Spread
Beverly Woldhagen James

½ *pound unpeeled medium shrimp*
1 ½ *cups boiling water*
½ *cup margarine*
1 *teaspoon horseradish*
¼ *teaspoon salt*
¼ *teaspoon garlic powder*
*Dash of hot pepper sauce*
*Dash of paprika*

- Add shrimp to boiling water and cook for 3 to 5 minutes. Drain and rinse with cold water. Chill.

- Peel and devein shrimp. Using food processor, finely chop shrimp.

- Add margarine, horseradish, salt, garlic powder and hot pepper sauce to shrimp in food processor bowl. Process until smooth.

- Spoon spread into serving dish and sprinkle with paprika.

Makes approximately 1 cup

Per tablespoon

Calories 66  Protein 2.95 g  Carbohydrates .266 g  Fat 6 g  Cholesterol 21.6 mg  Sodium 123 mg

# Shrimp with Rémoulade Sauce
Pamela Jones

½ *cup tarragon vinegar*
¼ *cup Creole mustard*
2 *tablespoons ketchup*
1 *clove garlic, pressed*
1 *teaspoon salt*
½ *teaspoon cayenne pepper*
1 *tablespoon paprika*
1 *cup vegetable oil*
½ *cup finely minced green onion with tops*
½ *cup finely minced celery*
4 *cups (about 2 pounds) peeled cooked shrimp, chilled*

- In blender container, combine vinegar, mustard, ketchup, garlic, salt, cayenne pepper and paprika. Blend until mixed.

- Add oil and blend thoroughly. Add green onion and celery, blending just until mixed.

- Place sauce in a serving dish surrounded by chilled shrimp for dipping.

Serves 8

Per serving

Calories 160  Protein 23.6 g  Carbohydrates .706 g  Fat 6.5 g  Cholesterol 221 mg  Sodium 317.8 mg

# Marinated Shrimp with Tarragon Mayonnaise

Cheryl Briggs Patton

*Should be marinated overnight*

Juice of 1 orange
Juice of 2 lemons
Juice of 3 limes
¾ cup olive oil
Salt and black pepper to taste
1 onion, thinly sliced
2 pounds large shrimp, peeled
and deveined

**Tarragon Mayonnaise**
1 cup low-fat mayonnaise
2 tablespoons prepared mustard
2 tablespoons minced tarragon

• Combine orange, lemon and lime juice with olive oil in large mixing bowl. Season with salt and black pepper. Add onion and set aside.

• Boil shrimp in large pot of salted water, until just cooked through. Drain and place immediately in marinade mixture, stirring to coat thoroughly. Cover and refrigerate overnight.

• Blend mayonnaise, mustard and tarragon. Chill, covered, until ready to serve.

• Remove shrimp from marinade and serve with tarragon mayonnaise.

*Sourdough bread makes a great accompaniment.*

Serves 6

Per serving of shrimp _____

Calories 195  Protein 31.6 g  Carbohydrates 1.34 g  Fat 6 g  Cholesterol 295 mg  Sodium 338 mg

Per tablespoon of mayonnaise _____

Calories 37.2  Protein .608 g  Carbohydrates 8.26 g  Fat .5 g  Cholesterol 0 mg  Sodium 517 mg

# Citrus Apple Cider

*Mary Ellen Schmidt*

8 cups apple cider
½ cup sugar
½ cup firmly-packed brown sugar
1 cinnamon stick
1 teaspoon whole allspice
6 whole cloves
½ cup orange juice
⅓ cup lemon juice

- Pour cider into stock pot. Add sugar, brown sugar, cinnamon, allspice and cloves, stirring to dissolve sugar. Simmer for 30 minutes.

- Add orange and lemon juices to cider. Simmer briefly or serve immediately.

Makes approximately 10 cups

Per ½ cup serving

Calories 80  Protein .131 g  Carbohydrates 20.3 g  Fat .1 g  Cholesterol 0 mg  Sodium 4.77 mg

# Hot Fruit Cider

*Carla Fisher*

5 cups apple cider
4 cups cranberry juice
9 cups pineapple juice
4 cups water
½ cup firmly-packed brown sugar
4 cinnamon sticks
1 tablespoon whole cloves
Pinch of salt

- Combine all ingredients in stock pot.

- Simmer until thoroughly heated and sugar is dissolved.

*Cider mixture can be heated in a large capacity coffee pot.*

Makes approximately 22 cups

Per 1 cup serving

Calories 123  Protein .383 g  Carbohydrates 30.8 g  Fat .5 g  Cholesterol 0 mg  Sodium 19.1 mg

# Rosy Glow Cranberry Cider
Lee Ann Lamb

4 cups cranberry juice cocktail
2½ cups water
½ cup lemon juice
⅓ cup sugar
¼ teaspoon salt
¼ teaspoon cinnamon
¼ teaspoon nutmeg
⅛ teaspoon whole cloves
Cinnamon sticks

- Combine all ingredients, except cinnamon sticks, in large saucepan and mix well.
- Simmer for 10 minutes.
- Serve hot in mugs with cinnamon sticks for stirring.

Makes approximately 7 cups

Per ½ cup serving _____

Calories 62  Protein .038  Carbohydrates 16 g  Fat .1 g  Cholesterol 0 mg  Sodium 41 mg

# Barbara's Big Bunch Punch
Barbara Bump

2 (40 ounce) bottles cranberry juice cocktail
1 (6 ounce) can frozen orange juice concentrate, thawed, undiluted
1 (6 ounce) can frozen grapefruit juice concentrate, thawed, undiluted
1 (6 ounce) can frozen lemonade concentrate, thawed, undiluted
2 quarts club soda
2 quarts ginger ale

- Combine cranberry, orange and grapefruit juices and lemonade in large jug or container.
- Gently add club soda and ginger ale to fruit juices just before serving. Serve over ice.

Makes approximately 28 cups

Per ½ cup serving _____

Calories 37  Protein .142 g  Carbohydrates 9.37 g  Fat .1 g  Cholesterol 0 mg  Sodium 9.78 mg

# Café Vienna Punch
*Pamela Jones*

*Must be brewed the day before serving*

1 gallon strongly-brewed coffee
6 cinnamon sticks
⅔ cup sugar
1 quart whipping cream, whipped
½ gallon vanilla ice cream

- Brew coffee. While coffee is still hot, add cinnamon sticks and sugar, stirring to dissolve sugar. Let stand overnight to cool.
- Just before serving, add whipped cream and ice cream.

Makes approximately 28 cups

Per ½ cup serving _____

Calories 86  Protein 1.02 g  Carbohydrates 9.76 g  Fat 5.5 g  Cholesterol 19.9 mg  Sodium 20.5 mg

# Christmas Cranberry Punch
*Sue Kidwell*

6 cups chilled cranberry juice
3 cups chilled orange juice
1 cup chilled pineapple juice
1 cup chilled lemonade
1 quart chilled lemon-lime carbonated drink

**Wreath Float**
(optional, not included in nutritional analysis)
2 cups sugar
2 cups water
1 (12 ounce) package fresh cranberries
1 cup orange juice
Cranberry juice

- If using wreath, prepare a day in advance. Combine sugar, water and cranberries in large saucepan. Bring to a boil and cook until berries "pop". Let stand until cool.
- Add orange juice to cranberry sauce. Pour into ring mold. Add cranberry juice, if needed, to fill mold.
- Freeze wreath mold until firm and ready to serve punch.
- Prepare punch by combining cranberry, orange and pineapple juices and lemonade in large punch bowl. Add lemon-lime drink.
- Float frozen wreath in punch.

Makes approximately 15 cups

Per ½ cup serving _____

Calories 61  Protein .209 g  Carbohydrates 15 g  Fat .1 g  Cholesterol 0 mg  Sodium 2.41 mg

# Zippy Cranberry Cooler
Kathy Marsh

6 cups cranberry juice
6 cups cold water
3 (6 ounce) cans frozen lemonade concentrate, undiluted
5¼ cups ginger ale

- Combine cranberry juice, water and lemonade, mixing well.
- Just before serving, stir in ginger ale and add ice cubes.

Makes approximately 20 cups

Per 1 cup serving _____

Calories 105  Protein .077 g  Carbohydrates 27 g  Fat .1 g  Cholesterol 0 mg  Sodium 8.68 mg

# Christmas Punch
Rosemary Bennett Douglass

1 quart peppermint ice cream
4 cups milk
1½ quarts chilled lemon-lime carbonated drink

- Cut ice cream into 1-inch cubes. Place in punch bowl.
- Pour milk over ice cream chunks. Stir until well blended.
- Stir in lemon-lime drink just before serving.

Makes approximately 14 cups

Per ½ cup serving _____

Calories 92  Protein 1.89 g  Carbohydrates 11.4 g  Fat 4.5 g  Cholesterol 17.6 mg  Sodium 30.1 mg

# Piña Colada Punch
Judy Fincannon

1 (15 ounce) can cream of coconut
1 (46 ounce) can pineapple juice
1 (2 liter) bottle club soda
½ gallon pineapple sherbet, softened

- Combine cream of coconut and pineapple juice, blending well. Add club soda and sherbet.
- Serve immediately.

Makes approximately 23½ cups

Per ½ cup serving _____

Calories 78  Protein .633 g  Carbohydrates 14 g  Fat 2.5 g  Cholesterol 1.63 mg  Sodium 25.4 mg

# Sparkling Eggnog

Linda Uchiyama Kelley

4 eggs
⅓ cup sugar
1½ teaspoons nutmeg
4 cups chilled half and half
1 teaspoon vanilla
3½ cups chilled lemon-lime
carbonated drink
½ gallon vanilla ice cream,
softened
½ cup quartered maraschino
cherries

- Combine eggs, sugar and nutmeg. Beat until light and lemon colored.

- Stir in half and half and vanilla to egg mixture. Pour into punch bowl.

- Slowly add lemon-lime drink to half and half mixture.

- Add ice cream, by the spoonful, to punch. Sprinkle cherries on top.

Add 2 cups rum if desired.

Makes approximately 16½ cups

Per ½ cup serving

Calories 133  Protein 2.79 g  Carbohydrates 14.3 g  Fat 7.5 g  Cholesterol 50.6 mg  Sodium 48.1 mg

# Spiced Pineapple Punch

Kari J. Tobias

4 cups unsweetened pineapple
juice
1 cup orange juice
2 cups apple cider
1 (12 ounce) can apricot nectar
2 cinnamon sticks, broken in
half
1 teaspoon whole cloves
1 teaspoon cardamom

- Combine all ingredients in large saucepan.

- Bring to a boil, then reduce heat and simmer, uncovered, for 15 minutes.

- Strain punch and discard spices.

Makes approximately 8 cups

Per 1 cup serving

Calories 139  Protein .851 g  Carbohydrates 34.5 g  Fat .5 g  Cholesterol 0 g  Sodium 5.51 mg

# Strawberry Punch

Gwen Walden Irwin

3 (3 ounce) package strawberry-
flavored gelatin
3 cups hot water
3 (12 ounce) cans frozen pink
lemonade concentrate, undiluted
3 (10 ounce) packages frozen
sliced strawberries
½ cup plus 1 tablespoon sugar
(optional if strawberries are
sweetened)
10½ cups ginger ale

- Dissolve gelatin in hot water. Pour gelatin into punch bowl.
- Add lemonade and strawberries to gelatin, stirring well. Sweeten with sugar, if needed, stirring to dissolve.
- Just before serving, add ginger ale.

Makes approximately 22 cups

Per ½ cup serving _____

Calories 99  Protein .605 g  Carbohydrates 25.2 g  Fat .1 g  Cholesterol 0 mg  Sodium 20.3 mg

# Citrus Mint Tea

Beverly Woldhagen James

7 regular tea bags
7 sprigs mint
1 cup sugar
4 cups boiling water
3¾ cups water
2¼ cups pineapple juice
1 (6 ounce) can frozen lemonade
concentrate, thawed, undiluted
Mint sprigs for garnish

- Place tea bags, mint and sugar in large container. Pour boiling water over tea mixture and steep for 30 to 45 minutes.
- Remove tea bags and mint sprigs. Add 3¾ cups water, pineapple juice and lemonade.
- Garnish individual servings with mint sprigs.

Makes approximately 10 cups

Per 1 cup serving _____

Calories 141  Protein .231 g  Carbohydrates 36.2 g  Fat .1 g  Cholesterol 0 mg  Sodium 12 mg

# Cranberry Tea
Pamela Jones

1 (16 ounce) package fresh
cranberries
10 cups water, divided
1½ cups sugar
2 cinnamon sticks
2 cups orange juice
3 tablespoons lemon juice

- Rinse cranberries.
- Combine cranberries and 8 cups water in large saucepan. Cook until berries "pop." Remove from heat and let stand for 5 minutes.
- Strain juice from cranberries, pressing pulp to release the juice. Return juice to saucepan; discard the pulp.
- Add sugar, 2 cups water and cinnamon sticks. Bring to a boil and boil for 1 minute. Stir in orange and lemon juices.
- Serve immediately.

*Tea may be prepared in advance and stored in refrigerator. Remove cinnamon sticks before chilling. To reheat tea, bring to a simmer and serve.*

Makes approximately 12 cups

Per 1 cup serving _____

Calories 138  Protein .496 g  Carbohydrates 35.2 g  Fat .1 g  Cholesterol 0 mg  Sodium 6.12 mg

---
★
---

For a beautiful, decorative ice ring, freeze about one inch of water in a bundt pan or mold until almost solid. Arrange berries (or fruit slices) and mint leaves over ice. Add water just to cover and return to freezer. When almost solid, add another layer of water about one inch thick and return to freezer until frozen solid. Add the ring to your punch bowl just before serving.

# Grapefruit Tea Cooler

Colleen Cannon

*Tastes best when chilled at least one hour before serving*

2 cups boiling water
6 regular tea bags
¼ cup chopped mint leaves
1⅓ cups sugar
1⅓ cups fresh grapefruit juice
1 cup fresh lemon juice
4 cups water

- Pour boiling water over tea bags and mint. Cover and steep for 5 minutes.
- Strain tea. Discard tea bags and mint leaves.
- Stir in sugar, grapefruit and lemon juices and 4 cups water to tea.

*Frozen grapefruit juice may be substituted for fresh juice. For more mint flavor, mint tea bags may be used.*

Makes approximately 8 cups

Per 1 cup serving
Calories 150  Protein .317 g  Carbohydrates 38.8 g  Fat .1 g  Cholesterol 0 mg  Sodium 6.39 mg

# Raspberry Cooler

Vicki Ashley Atkins

1 (10 ounce) package frozen raspberries in light syrup, thawed
3 cups chilled sparkling apple cider
½ cup chilled club soda

- Place raspberries with syrup in blender or food process and process until smooth. Strain and discard solids.
- Combine raspberry puree, cider and club soda in a large pitcher and stir gently. Serve immediately over crushed ice.

Makes approximately 4 cups

Per 1 cup serving
Calories 160  Protein .608 g  Carbohydrates 40.3 g  Fat .5 g  Cholesterol 0 mg  Sodium 12.5 mg

# Banana-Orange Freeze
Mary Lou Cindrich

2 ripe bananas, sliced
1 teaspoon lemon juice
½ cup orange juice
½ cup milk
2 cups orange sherbet

- Combine all ingredients in blender container. Blend until smooth.
- Pour into glasses and serve with straws.

*Very refreshing on a summer day.*

Makes approximately 4 cups

Per 1 cup serving
Calories 217  Protein 2.87 g  Carbohydrates 47.3 g  Fat 3.5 g  Cholesterol 8.95 mg  Sodium 60 mg

# Island Breeze
Nanci Norin Jordt

4 cups orange juice
½ cup fresh strawberries
½ cup fresh raspberries
2 large bananas
6 ice cubes
Whole strawberries and/or raspberries for garnish

- Combine half of each ingredient, except whole berries, in blender. Process until frothy.
- Pour into stemmed glasses and garnish each serving with a whole berry.
- Repeat procedure with remaining ingredients.

Makes approximately 8 cups

Per ½ cup serving
Calories 42  Protein .607 g  Carbohydrates 10 g  Fat .5 g  Cholesterol 0 mg  Sodium .755 mg

# Mock Champagne

Mary Francis

1 (6 ounce) can frozen lemonade concentrate, undiluted
¾ cup pineapple juice
1 (6 ounce) can frozen white grape juice, undiluted
2 cups cold water
1¾ cups ginger ale
1¾ cups sparkling water

- Combine all ingredients in 2-quart pitcher.

Makes approximately 8 cups

Per ½ cup serving

Calories 64  Protein .25 g  Carbohydrates 16.2 g  Fat .1 g  Cholesterol 0 mg  Sodium 4.78 mg

# Texas Sunrise

Sally Guyton Joyner

4 cups cran-raspberry juice
2 cups pineapple juice
2 cups orange juice
2 cups club soda
1 lime
1 cup whole strawberries

- Combine cran-raspberry, pine-apple and orange juices in punch bowl or large pitcher. Add club soda.
- Cut lime into thin round slices, discarding ends. Float some or all of slices in punch. Stir in straw-berries.
- Add ice, if desired, and serve.

Makes approximately 10 cups

Per ½ cup serving

Calories 62  Protein .361 g  Carbohydrates 15.5 g  Fat .1 g  Cholesterol 0 mg  Sodium 6.58 mg

# Breakfast Shake

*Sherrie Smith*

1 (8 ounce) container low-fat
vanilla yogurt
1 banana
2 cups fresh strawberries
½ cup orange juice
Sweetener (optional)

- Combine all ingredients in blender container. Blend until smooth.

*Good as an afternoon pick-me-up, too.*

Makes approximately 4 cups

Per 1 cup serving _____

Calories 97  Protein 3.91 g  Carbohydrates 19 g  Fat 1.5 g  Cholesterol 3.45 mg  Sodium 41.1 mg

# Mexican Hot Chocolate

*Nanci Norin Jordt*

1½ cups water
3 (1 ounce) squares unsweetened
chocolate
½ cup sugar
3 tablespoons instant coffee
granules
1 teaspoon cinnamon
½ teaspoon nutmeg
¼ teaspoon salt
4 cups milk
Whipped cream for garnish

- Combine all ingredients, except milk and whipped cream.
- Bring to a boil over medium heat, stirring occasionally. Reduce heat and simmer for 4 minutes, stirring constantly.
- Stir in milk and heat thoroughly.
- Beat hot chocolate with rotary beater for about 1 minute or until frothy.
- Garnish individual servings with dollop of whipped cream.

Makes approximately 6 cups

Per 1 cup serving _____

Calories 244  Protein 7.06 g  Carbohydrates 29.3 g  Fat 13.5 g  Cholesterol 22.1 mg  Sodium 173 mg

# Old Fashioned Chocolate Soda   Nanci Norin Jordt

2 to 3 tablespoons chocolate
syrup
Chilled club soda, ginger ale or
lemon-lime carbonated drink
2 scoops (approximately 1 cup)
vanilla ice cream
1 large marshmallow (optional)
1 red maraschino cherry
(optional)

- Pour chocolate syrup into tall glass. Fill glass half full with soda.
- Add ice cream and stir well.
- Garnish soda with large marshmallow and cherry. Serve with straw.

*For a chocolate-peppermint soda, substitute peppermint ice cream for vanilla ice cream.*

Serves 1

Per serving _____

Calories 389  Protein 5.69 g  Carbohydrates 64.2 g  Fat 15 g  Cholesterol 58 mg  Sodium 207 mg

# Strawberry Smoothie   Nancy Norin Jordt

1 cup skim or 2% milk
1 cup plain non-fat or regular
yogurt
2 tablespoons sugar
2 teaspoons vanilla extract
2 cups fresh or frozen
strawberries

- Combine milk, yogurt, sugar and vanilla in blender container. Process until smooth.
- Gradually add strawberries, blending until smooth and thickened.

Makes approximately 4 cups

Per 1 cup serving _____

Calories 117  Protein 5.65 g  Carbohydrates 19.3 g  Fat 2 g  Cholesterol 6.17 mg  Sodium 74.5 mg

# Wassail

*Nanci Norin Jordt*

Orange slices
Whole cloves
6 cups apple cider or juice
1 cinnamon stick
¼ teaspoon nutmeg
¼ cup honey
1 teaspoon grated lemon peel
1 (18 ounce) can unsweetened pineapple juice
Cinnamon sticks

- Prepare Orange Stars or Cloved Oranges to float in wassail. For Orange Stars, cut orange in ¼-inch slices. Insert 5 whole cloves at equal intervals in edge of each slice. Between cloves, cut and remove wedge of peel and pulp.

- For Cloved Oranges, insert whole cloves at ½ inch intervals in 3 oranges. Place in 8x8x2-inch baking pan and add just enough water to cover bottom of pan. Bake at 325° for 30 minutes. Oranges may be prepared and baked a day in advance. Store, covered in refrigerator, until ready to serve.

- Combine cider and 1 cinnamon stick in large saucepan. Bring to a boil, then reduce heat and simmer, covered, for 5 minutes.

- Add nutmeg, honey, lemon peel and pineapple to cider. Simmer uncovered for 5 minutes longer.

- Pour wassail into punch bowl. Float Orange Stars or Cloved Oranges in wassail and serve with cinnamon sticks for stirring individual servings.

Makes approximately 9 cups

Per ½ cup serving _____

Calories 73  Protein .219 g  Carbohydrates 18.7 g  Fat .1 g  Cholesterol 0 mg  Sodium 3.38 mg

## Apricot Sours

Sandy Wyatt Niederstadt

1 (6 ounce) can frozen lemonade concentrate, undiluted
1 (6 ounce) can frozen orange juice concentrate, undiluted
1 cup apricot brandy
1¾ cups water

- Mix all ingredients in a blender container until well blended.
- Serve over ice.

Makes approximately 4 cups

Per ½ cup serving

Calories 138  Protein .572 g  Carbohydrates 18.1 g  Fat .1 g  Cholesterol 0 mg  Sodium 3.05 mg

## Bloody Mary Mix

Martha Rife

1 quart tomato juice
¼ cup beef broth
¼ cup Worcestershire sauce
Juice of 1 lemon
7 dashes hot pepper sauce
1 tablespoon horseradish
1 tablespoon black pepper
1½ teaspoons celery salt

- In blender container, combine all ingredients. Blend well.
- Store mix in refrigerator.

Makes approximately 4 cups

Per 1 cup serving

Calories 60  Protein 2.49 g  Carbohydrates 14.4 g  Fat .1 g  Cholesterol 0 mg  Sodium 1076 mg

# Champagne Punch
*Martha Rife*

¼ *cup sugar*
*Juice of 2 lemons*
*1 (10 ounce) package frozen sliced strawberries*
½ *cup orange juice*
½ *cup Cointreau or Triple Sec liqueur*
*1 bottle champagne*
*1½ cups carbonated water*
*Orange slices for garnish*

- Combine all ingredients except orange slices in punch bowl or pitcher.
- Float orange slices in punch and serve chilled.

Makes approximately 7 cups

Per ½ cup serving

Calories 95  Protein .264 g  Carbohydrates 11.7 g  Fat .1 g  Cholesterol 0 mg  Sodium 9.37 mg

# Election Day Punch
*Sandy Wyatt Niederstadt*

*8 cups cranberry juice*
*1 (6 ounce) can frozen orange juice concentrate, thawed, undiluted*
¼ *cup sugar*
*2 cups vodka*
*Large block of ice*
*1¾ cups club soda*
*Orange and lemon slices*

- Combine cranberry juice, orange juice and sugar in a punch bowl and stir until sugar is dissolved.
- Stir in vodka and add large block of ice.
- Carefully pour club soda over punch.
- Garnish with orange and lemon slices.

Makes approximately 12 cups

Per ½ cup serving

Calories 110  Protein .169 g  Carbohydrates 15.7 g  Fat .1 g  Cholesterol 0 mg  Sodium 5.41 mg

# Lemon Sangría
Pamela Jones

3½ cups white wine
½ cups cognac or brandy
¼ cup sugar
3 lemons, sliced
1 orange, sliced
1¼ cups club soda
8 to 10 small clusters green
grapes for garnish (optional)

- Combine all ingredients except club soda and grapes. Chill overnight.
- Just before serving, add club soda. Pour over crushed ice.
- Garnish with grapes.

Makes approximately 5½ cups

Per ½ cup serving _____

Calories 145  Protein .436 g  Carbohydrates 10.5 g  Fat .1 g  Cholesterol 0 mg  Sodium 12.6 mg


# Sparkling Rosé Punch
Barbara Bittner

2 (10 ounce) packages frozen
strawberries
½ cup sugar
2 quarts rosé wine
2 (6 ounce) cans frozen
lemonade concentrate, undiluted
3½ cups sparkling water

- Combine strawberries, sugar and 1 bottle wine. Let stand, covered, for about 1 hour or until strawberries are thawed.
- Strain punch into punch bowl (if desired).
- Add lemonade, remaining wine and sparkling water.
- Add ice and serve.

Makes approximately 13½ cups.

Per ½ cup serving _____

Calories 97  Protein .221 g  Carbohydrates 17.3 g  Fat .1 g  Cholesterol 0 mg  Sodium 5.64 mg

## Lake Austin Iced Tea
Sandy Wyatt Niederstadt

2 (6 ounce) cans frozen
lemonade concentrate, undiluted
1 (6 ounce) can frozen orange
juice concentrate, undiluted
1 cup sugar or to taste
6 cups water
2 cups strongly-brewed tea
1½ cups bourbon

- Combine all ingredients in 1-gallon container. Blend well.
- Serve in tall glasses over crushed ice.

Makes approximately 13 cups

Per 1 cup serving

Calories 193  Protein .391 g  Carbohydrates 32.8 g  Fat .1 g  Cholesterol 0 mg  Sodium 6.24 mg

## Texas Tickle
Nanci Norin Jordt

1 (6 ounce) can frozen lemonade
concentrate, undiluted
¾ cup vodka
½ cup apricot brandy
2 medium peaches, unpeeled and
sliced
Cracked ice

- Combine all ingredients except ice in the container of an electric blender, process until smooth.
- Gradually add ice, processing until mixture reaches desired consistency.

Makes approximately 2½ cups

Per ½ cup serving

Calories 212  Protein .346 g  Carbohydrates 19.9 g  Fat .1 g  Cholesterol 0 mg  Sodium 1.92 mg

# Holiday Wassail Bowl

Kathy Marsh

4 cups cranberry juice cocktail
2 (6 ounce) cans frozen orange
juice concentrate, undiluted
4 cups water
2 tablespoons sugar
2 cups Triple Sec or Grand
Marnier liqueur
½ teaspoon allspice
18 whole cloves
2 bottles white wine
Cranberries for garnish
(optional)

- Bring all ingredients except wine to a simmer.
- Add wine and heat through, but do not boil.
- Chill for several hours.
- Serve in a punch bowl with a decorative ice ring, whole fresh cranberries and holly sprig.

Makes approximately 17½ cups

Per ½ cup serving _____

Calories 121  Protein .309 g  Carbohydrates 15.7 g  Fat .1 g  Cholesterol 0 mg  Sodium 5.62 mg

# Brandy Cream

Mary Lou Cindrich

Wonderful frozen and served as a dessert

½ gallon vanilla ice cream,
softened
⅓ cup apricot brandy
⅓ cup Kahlúa liqueur
⅓ cup Cointreau liqueur

- Using electric mixer at low speed, blend ice cream with apricot brandy, Kahlúa and Cointreau.
- Serve immediately or store in covered container and place in freezer until ready to serve.

Makes approximately 9 cups

Per ½ cup serving _____

Calories 167  Protein 2.06 g  Carbohydrates 18.8 g  Fat 6.5 g  Cholesterol 25.8 mg  Sodium 47.7 mg

# Salads

Texans often hold even the most elegant of luncheons outdoors. Here, the rush of downtown Austin fades into the background when dishes as tempting as chilled **Shrimp and Rice Salad** drizzled with French dressing, **Strawberry Spinach Salad** (an updated old favorite), **Corn and Black Bean Salad**, and creamy **Apricot Mango Mousse** are served. For added flair, **Marbelized Tea Eggs** complete the menu.

*Thank you to the Hyatt Regency Hotel, on the banks of Town Lake in Austin, Texas, for use of their lovely deck for this photo setting.*

## Broccoli Sunflower Salad
Jane Miller Sanders

2 bunches broccoli, chopped
1 cup sunflower seeds
½ cup raisins
6 slices bacon, cooked and crumbled

**Dressing**
1 cup mayonnaise
2 tablespoons sugar
2 tablespoons cider vinegar

- Prepare dressing by blending mayonnaise, sugar and vinegar.
- Combine dressing and broccoli, mixing well.
- Add sunflower seeds, raisins and bacon to broccoli, tossing to mix.

*Great to serve with pork or chicken.*

Makes approximately 6 cups

Per ½ cup serving
Calories 260  Protein 5.44 g  Carbohydrates 12.7 g  Fat 22.5 g  Cholesterol 13.6 mg  Sodium 168 mg

## Betsy's Vegetable Salad
Donna Earle Crain

*Prepare a day in advance*

1 head cauliflower, cut in bite-sized pieces
1 bunch broccoli, flowerets only
2 yellow squash, sliced
¼ cup sliced black olives
1½ cups (6 ounces) grated Cheddar cheese

**Dressing**
1 (12 ounce) carton cottage cheese
1 cup mayonnaise
1 envelope ranch style dressing mix

- Combine cauliflower, broccoli, squash and olives.
- Prepare dressing by blending cottage cheese, mayonnaise and dressing mix in a food processor until smooth.
- Add enough dressing to vegetables to coat thoroughly.
- Chill, covered, overnight.
- Just before serving, sprinkle cheese on salad. Serve with remaining dressing, if desired.

Makes approximately 8 cups

Per ½ cup serving
Calories 177  Protein 6.43 g  Carbohydrates 3.41 g  Fat 16 g  Cholesterol 22.5 mg  Sodium 387 mg

# Green and White Salad

Nanci Norin Jordt

*Chill overnight*

1 small bunch broccoli, cut in flowerets
1 small head cauliflower, cut in flowerets
¼ cup chopped onion
1½ cups sliced celery
1 (2 ounce) jar pimiento-stuffed green olives, drained and sliced
3 hard-cooked eggs, chopped
Salt and black pepper to taste
Cayenne pepper to taste

**Dressing**

1 cup mayonnaise
1 teaspoon fresh lemon juice
1 teaspoon dill weed

- Steam broccoli and cauliflower, using small amount of water, until crisp tender. Drain and chill.
- Prepare dressing by blending mayonnaise, lemon juice and dill weed in large bowl.
- Add broccoli, cauliflower, onion, celery, olives and eggs to dressing, tossing gently to coat all ingredients.
- Season with salt, black pepper and cayenne pepper. Chill overnight.

Makes approximately 8 cups

Per ½ cup serving ───────────────

Calories 128  Protein 2.21 g  Carbohydrates 2.79 g  Fat 12.5 g  Cholesterol 47.9 mg  Sodium 215 mg

# Corn Bread Salad

Donna Earle Crain

8 cups crumbled corn bread
1 medium-sized onion, chopped
1 green bell pepper, chopped
2 tomatoes, chopped
1 (16 ounce) package bacon, cooked and crumbled
1½ cups low-fat mayonnaise-type salad dressing

- About 15 to 20 minutes before serving, combine crumbled corn bread, onion, bell pepper, tomatoes, bacon and salad dressing, tossing lightly but thoroughly. If mixed too far in advance, cornbread will become soggy.

*I love to take this to luncheons and have people guess what is in it. They guess potatoes and seafood but never cornbread.*

Makes approximately 13 cups

Per ½ cup serving ───────────────

Calories 143  Protein 3.83 g  Carbohydrates 15.8 g  Fat 7.5 g  Cholesterol 19.5 mg  Sodium 357 mg

# *Ensalada de España*

Pat Patton

*Improves if marinated overnight*

10 *bell peppers (equal amounts of yellow, red and green)*
¼ *cup plus 1 tablespoon coarsely chopped garlic*
¼ *cup red wine vinegar*
1 *cup olive oil*
*Lettuce leaves*

- Grill peppers on outdoor grill until blackened or place on lightly greased broiler pan and broil until blackened, turning occasionally.
- Place peppers in paper bag, close tightly and let peppers cool for 20 minutes.
- Combine garlic, wine vinegar and olive oil. Set aside.
- Peel peppers and remove stems and seeds. Cut in halves or in small strips. Place in container.
- Add dressing to peppers, mixing well to coat peppers thoroughly.
- Marinate, covered, in refrigerator for at least 1 hour before serving. Flavor improves if marinated overnight.
- Serve at room temperature on lettuce.

*This delightful salad, a nice change of pace from the usual lettuce and tomato salad, is served in Spain where fresh pimiento is used instead of bell peppers. The garlic is very subtle and great for digestion.*

Serves 10

Per serving _____

Calories 218  Protein .929 g  Carbohydrates 6.53 g  Fat 22 g  Cholesterol 0  Sodium 2.27 mg

# Corn-Black Bean Salad
Jeanne Cassidy

*Chill for several hours to capture the full flavor*

4 cups cooked black beans
2 cups canned or frozen corn
1 large red bell pepper, diced
1 large purple onion, chopped
½ cup minced cilantro or parsley
Chopped fresh jalapeño pepper to taste (optional)
Salt and black pepper to taste
Chopped avocados and tomatoes (optional)

**Dressing**
2 cloves garlic, minced
½ to ¾ cup vinaigrette dressing
Juice of 1 small lime

• Combine beans, corn, bell pepper, onion, cilantro and jalapeño pepper. If canned beans are used, rinse and drain.

• Prepare dressing by mixing garlic, vinaigrette and lime juice.

• Add dressing to vegetables. Chill for several hours before serving.

• Just before serving, add avocado and tomato.

*This salad is great served with grilled meat, fish or quesadillas.*

Makes approximately 8 cups

Per ½ cup serving _____

Calories 115  Protein 4.65 g  Carbohydrates 16.3  Fat 4 g  Cholesterol 0  Sodium 159 mg

# Cilantro Corn Salad
Pamela Jones

3 (10 ounce) packages frozen corn, thawed
¾ cup chopped red bell pepper
½ cup chopped fresh cilantro
¼ cup chopped green onion
Salt to taste

**Dressing**
⅓ cup vegetable oil
⅓ cup white wine vinegar
2 tablespoons Dijon mustard
½ teaspoon black pepper
1 tablespoon minced jalapeño pepper

• Combine corn, bell pepper, cilantro and green onion.

• Prepare dressing by combining oil, wine vinegar, mustard, black pepper and jalapeño pepper, whisking until well blended.

• Add dressing to vegetable mixture, stirring to coat thoroughly. Season with salt.

• Chill, covered, before serving.

Makes approximately 5 cups

Per ½ cup serving _____

Calories 140  Protein 2.53 g  Carbohydrates 17.2 g  Fat 8.5 g  Cholesterol 0  Sodium 380 mg

# Corn Salad del Rancho
Jennie Hentges

1 cucumber, seeds removed and diced
2 (16 ounce) cans corn, drained
3 tomatoes, diced
1 onion, diced
1 envelope ranch style dressing mix
1 tablespoon sugar
3 tablespoons mayonnaise

- Combine cucumber, corn, tomatoes and onion.
- Sprinkle dressing mix on vegetable mixture and stir to combine.
- Blend sugar and mayonnaise. Add to vegetable mixture, mixing well.
- Chill before serving.

Makes approximately 7 cups

Per ½ cup serving

Calories 88 Protein 2.2 g Carbohydrates 15.5 g Fat 3 g Cholesterol 1.74 mg Sodium 381 mg

# Corn Salad with Salsa Dressing
Linda Cook Uhl

1 (16 ounce) package frozen corn, thawed
Juice of 1 lemon
¼ cup coarsely chopped cilantro
¾ cup (3 or 4 ounces) cubed Monterey Jack cheese
1 firm ripe avocado
Lemon juice

**Dressing**
2 ripe tomatoes, peeled
½ small onion, minced
½ to 1 fresh jalapeño pepper, seeds removed and minced
½ to 1 teaspoon salt
1 teaspoon fresh lime juice
½ teaspoon vegetable oil
½ teaspoon vinegar

- Combine corn, juice of 1 lemon and cilantro in serving dish.
- Prepare dressing by combining tomatoes, onion, jalapeño pepper, salt, lime juice, oil and vinegar in food processor. Pulse to salsa consistency; do not puree. Set aside.
- One-half hour before serving, add cheese to corn mixture. Peel, pit and cube avocado, tossing with lemon juice to prevent darkening. Add to corn mixture.
- Serve salad chilled or at room temperature with salsa dressing on the side.

To peel tomatoes easily, blanch in boiling water for 10 to 15 seconds or until skin pops and plunge into chilled water.

Makes 4 cups

Per ½ cup serving

Calories 144 Protein 5.4 g Carbohydrates 15.7 g Fat 8 g Cholesterol 9.5 mg Sodium 205 mg

# Eggplant Salad

Pamela Jones

1 *large eggplant*
2 *cloves garlic, crushed*
¼ *cup olive oil*
¼ *cup vinegar*
1 *or 2 plum or rosa tomatoes,*
*chopped*
*Salt to taste*
*Cucumber, parsley and black*
*olives for garnish*

- Place eggplant on grill over very low heat or on broiler pan. Grill or broil for about 20 minutes or until soft. Let stand to cool. Remove peel, if desired, and dice eggplant pulp.
- Add garlic, olive oil, vinegar, tomatoes and salt to eggplant, mixing gently.
- Place salad on platter and garnish with cucumber, parsley and black olives.
- Chill before serving.

*This versatile Turkish dish is wonderful served chilled or at room temperature, with French bread, as an appetizer.*

Serves 4

Per serving ────────────────────────────

Calories 168  Protein 1.48 g  Carbohydrates 11.7 g  Fat 14 g  Cholesterol 0  Sodium 140 mg

───────★───────

Never rinse mushrooms - they will absorb the water. They should simply be wiped clean with a damp cloth prior to using.

# Greek Mushroom Salad
Vicki Ashley Atkins

½ bunch parsley, stems removed and sprigs chopped
4 green onion tops, chopped
1 cup (4 ounces) Swiss cheese, cubed
1 pound fresh mushrooms, sliced

**Dressing**
¼ cup red wine vinegar
½ cup vegetable oil
1 tablespoon Greek seasoning

- Combine parsley, green onion, cheese and mushrooms, tossing to mix. Chill.
- Prepare dressing by blending wine vinegar, oil and Greek seasoning.
- Add dressing to salad 15 to 20 minutes before serving, tossing to coat thoroughly.
- Chill until ready to serve, then toss again.

*A great salad to serve with steak.*

Serves 6

Per serving _____

Calories 259  Protein 7.38 g  Carbohydrates 6.03 g  Fat 24 g  Cholesterol 17.3 mg  Sodium 521 mg

# Chilled Dilled Peas
Jeanne Cassidy

1 cup sour cream
1 small bunch fresh chives, snipped, or 4 green onions with tops, minced
2 tablespoons fresh snipped dill or 1 tablespoon dried dill weed
1 teaspoon curry powder
Salt and freshly ground black pepper to taste
1 (16 ounce) package frozen petite green peas, thawed

- Combine sour cream, chives or green onion, dill, curry powder, salt and black pepper.
- Add peas and gently mix.
- Chill thoroughly or overnight. Serve chilled.

Makes approximately 3 cups

Per ½ cup serving _____

Calories 147  Protein 5.52 g  Carbohydrates 13.5 g  Fat 8.5 g  Cholesterol 17 mg  Sodium 197 mg

# German Potato Salad

Mary Lou Cindrich

¼ cup vinegar
½ cup sugar
2 to 2½ cups water
10 medium unpeeled potatoes
¼ small onion, minced
6 to 8 slices bacon, chopped
3 tablespoons all-purpose flour
Salt and black pepper to taste

- Combine vinegar, sugar and water. Set aside.
- Cook potatoes in water to cover until just tender. Drain and let stand until warm. Cut in ⅛-inch slices.
- Add onion to potatoes.
- Fry bacon in large skillet until crisp and browned.
- Add flour to bacon, stirring to mix. Gradually stir in vinegar mixture and bring to a boil. Sauce should be consistency of thin gravy; add additional water if too thick.
- Pour sauce over vegetables. Season with salt and black pepper. Pour warm salad into 2-quart serving dish. Serve warm.

*Prepare salad 3 to 4 hours in advance. Reheat in microwave just before serving instead of maintaining warmth for long period of time.*

Serves 10

Per serving _____

Calories 192  Protein 3.72 g  Carbohydrates 34.9 g  Fat 4.5 g  Cholesterol 5.67 mg  Sodium 123 mg

# Pesto Potato Salad
*Pamela Jones*

3 pounds new potatoes, cooked and cubed
1½ cups coarsely chopped cucumber
¾ cup sliced green onion

**Pesto Dressing**
⅔ cup olive oil
⅓ cup white wine vinegar
2 cloves garlic, minced
½ cup chopped fresh basil
½ cup (2 ounces) grated Parmesan cheese
½ teaspoon salt

- Combine potatoes, cucumber and green onion. Set aside.
- Prepare dressing by combining all ingredients in food processor or blender. Process until smooth.
- Add enough Pesto Dressing to vegetables to coat well, tossing to mix.
- Chill, covered, for several hours.
- Stir in remaining Pesto Dressing just before serving.

Serves 8

Per serving _____

Calories 346  Protein 6.32 g  Carbohydrates 37.1 g  Fat 20 g  Cholesterol 4.92 mg  Sodium 259 mg

# Grandma's Sauerkraut Salad
*Mary Lauderman Tavcar*

Must chill overnight

1 (21 ounce) can sauerkraut
1 large onion, minced
2 cups diced celery
1 (2 ounce) jar diced pimiento, drained
1 carrot, grated (optional)

**Dressing**
½ cup vegetable oil
½ cup vinegar
¾ cup sugar
1 teaspoon celery seed

- Combine sauerkraut, onion, celery, pimiento and carrot.
- Blend together all dressing ingredients.
- Add dressing to vegetables, mixing well.
- Chill, covered, overnight.

A German tradition served with pork as a New Year's Day kickoff in hopes of bringing prosperity and good fortune all year long.

Makes approximately 6 cups

Per ½ cup serving _____

Calories 150  Protein .852 g  Carbohydrates 17.4 g  Fat 9 g  Cholesterol 0  Sodium 347 mg

# Beautiful Vegetable Salad

Martha Rife

*Chill at least 24 hours before serving*

¾ *cup white vine vinegar*
¼ *cup water*
½ *cup vegetable oil*
2 *tablespoons sugar*
½ *teaspoon black pepper*
½ *teaspoon oregano*
1 *head cauliflower, cut in bite-sized pieces*
5 *carrots, sliced*
5 *stalks celery, cut into sticks*
1 *green bell pepper, sliced*
1 *purple onion, sliced*
1 *(3¼ ounce) can green olives, drained*
2 *or 3 jalapeño peppers*
1 *(15 ounce) can baby corn, drained*

- Combine vinegar, water, oil, sugar, black pepper and oregano in large saucepan. Bring to a boil.

- Add cauliflower, carrots, celery sticks, bell pepper, onion, olives, jalapeño peppers and corn to vinegar mixture. Bring to a boil and cook for 5 minutes.

- Let stand until cool. Store in glass jars. Chill at least 24 hours before serving. Drain before serving.

*Nice to serve at a buffet or as a change from a tossed salad.*

Makes approximately 12 cups

Per ½ cup serving _____

Calories 78  Protein 1.09 g  Carbohydrates 8.25 g  Fat 5 g  Cholesterol 0  Sodium 154 mg

★

Nothing conveys friendship and goodwill more fully than gifts from the kitchen. Seal jars of "Beautiful Vegetable Salad" according to the jar manufacturer's directions, then decorate the tops and add a handwritten label for a lovely gift with a personal touch.

# Watercress Cucumber Salad
*Jane Miller Sanders*

1 cup coarsely chopped
watercress
½ cup sliced purple onion
1 medium cucumber, cut
lengthwise in quarters and sliced
1 small head Boston bib lettuce,
torn in bite-sized pieces

**Dressing**
½ cup low-fat sour cream
2 tablespoons lemon juice
2 tablespoons skim milk
2 teaspoons dill weed
1 teaspoon sugar
¼ teaspoon salt
¼ teaspoon black pepper

- Combine watercress, onion, cucumber and lettuce in large bowl, tossing gently. Chill until ready to serve.
- Combine all dressing ingredients, blending thoroughly. Chill until ready to serve.
- Just before serving, drizzle 2 to 3 tablespoons dressing over salad. Toss to mix. Serve remaining dressing with salad.

Serves 8

Per serving of salad _____

Calories 11  Protein .738 g  Carbohydrates 2.3 g  Fat .1 g  Cholesterol 0  Sodium 3.71 mg

Per tablespoon of dressing _____

Calories 14  Protein .369 g  Carbohydrates 1.02 g  Fat 1 g  Cholesterol 3.34 mg  Sodium 43.4 mg

# Apricot Mango Mousse
*Cookbook Committee*

1 (6 ounce) package apricot
gelatin
1 envelope unflavored gelatin
2 cups boiling water
1 (15 ounce) can mangos,
undrained
1 (16 ounce) can apricots,
undrained
1 (8 ounce) package cream
cheese, softened
Kiwi slices for garnish

- Dissolve apricot and unflavored gelatin in boiling water.
- Using food processor, blend mangos, apricots and cream cheese thoroughly. Add gelatin and mix well.
- Pour gelatin mixture into individual parfait dishes or 8-cup mold. Chill until firm.
- Garnish with kiwi slices.

Serves 14

Per ½ cup serving _____

Calories 140  Protein 2.96 g  Carbohydrates 20.6 g  Fat 6 g  17.8 mg  Sodium 82.5 mg

# Blueberry Salad

Wanda Rich

1 (6 ounce) package raspberry gelatin
2 cups boiling water
1 (15 ounce) can blueberries, undrained
1 (6 ounce) can crushed pineapple, undrained

**Topping**
1 (8 ounce) package cream cheese, softened
1 cup sour cream
½ cup sugar
1 teaspoon vanilla
½ to 1 cup chopped pecans

- Dissolve gelatin in boiling water.
- Add blueberries and pineapple to gelatin. Pour into 13x9x2-inch baking dish. Chill until firm.
- Prepare topping by blending cream cheese, sour cream, sugar and vanilla together until smooth. Spread topping on congealed salad and sprinkle with pecans.

Is also great as a dessert.

Makes 12 3-inch squares.

Per serving _____

Calories 267  Protein 3.8 g  Carbohydrates 33.5 g  Fat 14 g  Cholesterol 29.2 mg  Sodium 104 mg

# Kari's Sunday Salad

Kari J. Tobias

1 cup sour cream (light or low-fat)
1 (3 ounce) package low-fat cream cheese, softened
½ cup sugar
2 (16 ounce) cans whole cranberry sauce
1 (8 ounce) can crushed pineapple, drained
1 cup chopped pecans
1 (8 ounce) carton low-calorie frozen whipped topping, thawed

- Using electric mixer, mix sour cream, cream cheese and sugar until smooth and well blended.
- Stir cranberry sauce, pineapple and pecans into creamed mixture. Fold in whipped topping.
- Pour into 6-cup mold prepared with vegetable cooking spray. Freeze until firm.
- To serve, dip mold in warm water until salad separates from sides of mold and invert on platter. Salad should be only slightly thawed.

Serves 12

Per ½ cup serving _____

Calories 277  Protein 2.51 g  Carbohydrates 45.6 g  Fat 11.5 g  Cholesterol 11.7 mg  Sodium 71.4 mg

# Holiday Cherry Salad
*Rosemary Bennett Douglass*

1 (3 ounce) package raspberry gelatin
1 cup boiling water
1 (22 ounce) can cherry pie filling
1 (3 ounce) package lemon gelatin
1 cup boiling water
1 (3 ounce) package cream cheese, softened
⅓ cup mayonnaise
1 (8 ounce) can crushed pineapple, undrained
1 cup whipping cream, whipped
1½ cups miniature marshmallows
Chopped pecans for garnish (optional)

- Dissolve raspberry gelatin in 1 cup boiling water.
- Stir pie filling into dissolved gelatin liquid. Pour into 2-quart baking dish. Chill until partially firm.
- Dissolve lemon gelatin in 1 cup boiling water.
- Combine cream cheese and mayonnaise, beating until smooth. Gradually add lemon gelatin to cream cheese mixture, mixing well.
- Stir pineapple into cream cheese mixture. Fold in whipped cream, then marshmallows.
- Spread pineapple mixture on raspberry gelatin layer. Chill until firm.
- Sprinkle pecans on salad.

*This has become a favorite at our house for Christmas and Easter.*

Serves 12

Per serving _____

Calories 245  Protein 2.39 g  Carbohydrates 35.1 g  Fat 11.5 g  Cholesterol 25 mg  Sodium 126 mg

## Margaret's Beet Jelly Mold
Bryan Rumble Norton

2 envelopes unflavored gelatin
½ cup cold water
1 (16 ounce) can beets
1½ cups sugar
¾ teaspoon salt
½ cup vinegar
1 cup finely chopped celery
1 tablespoon horseradish

- Soften gelatin in cold water.
- Drain beets, reserving liquid. Finely chop beets and set aside. Add water to reserved beet liquid to measure 2 cups and pour into saucepan.
- Add softened gelatin to beet liquid. Heat, stirring until gelatin is dissolved. Add sugar, salt and vinegar, blending well. Cool until thickened to consistency of egg white.
- Add beets, celery and horseradish to partially thickened gelatin. Pour into 6-cup mold. Chill until firm.

*Chop beets and celery in food processor for ideal consistency.*

Serves 12

Per serving _____
Calories 115  Protein 1.4 g  Carbohydrates 28.5 g  Fat .1 g  Cholesterol 0  Sodium 245 mg

★

Unmolding a gelled or frozen creation needn't be a nightmare. Simply set the mold in a pan of very hot water for a few seconds. Remove and invert onto a serving platter. If it doesn't loosen immediately, let it sit for a while, covered by a hot, damp towel.

# Fresh Peaches and Gorgonzola

LaNyce Whittemore

Juice of 1 small orange
Juice of 2 limes
¼ cup hazelnut oil
½ teaspoon salt
⅛ teaspoon white pepper
4 medium-sized fresh peaches, peeled and cut in ¼-inch thick slices
1 bunch red leaf lettuce, separated into leaves
¾ cup (3 ounces) crumbled Gorgonzola cheese
¼ cup sliced or chopped hazelnuts or pecans, toasted

- Combine orange and lime juice. Gradually add hazelnut oil, whisking to incorporate. Stir in salt and white pepper.
- Add sliced peaches. Marinate for 10 minutes.
- Arrange lettuce leaves on individual salad plates. Arrange peach slices in spoke or flower design on leaves.
- Drizzle remaining marinade over peaches and lettuce. Sprinkle with cheese and nuts.
- Serve immediately.

*To ease peeling of peaches, immerse in boiling water for approximately 20 seconds, remove immediately and peel.*

Serves 6

Per ½ cup serving

Calories 226  Protein 5.38 g  Carbohydrates 16 g  Fat 17 g  Cholesterol 12.5 mg  Sodium 435 mg

★

To simplify the peeling of peaches, drop them into boiling water for 60 seconds, remove quickly with a slotted spoon and immerse them in cool water for several seconds. The skins will slip off easily.

# Avocado, Corn and Rice Salad
*Laurie Shaw Davis*

3 cups cooked brown rice
1 avocado, peeled and mashed
1 cup canned corn or 2 ears
corn, cooked and cut from cob
½ cup roasted cashews
1 onion, minced

**Dressing**

1 teaspoon lemon juice
1 teaspoon olive oil
1 teaspoon brown rice vinegar
1 teaspoon soy sauce
Garlic salt to taste
Black pepper to taste
Lettuce leaves

- Combine rice, avocado, corn, cashews and onion, mixing well.
- Prepare dressing by blending lemon juice, olive oil, rice vinegar and soy sauce.
- Add dressing to rice mixture, stirring to mix. Season with garlic salt and black pepper.
- Chill until ready to serve. Serve individual portions on lettuce.

Makes approximately 5½ cups

Per ½ cup serving _____

Calories 160  Protein 3.47 g  Carbohydrates 22.8 g  Fat 7 g  Cholesterol 0  Sodium 69.8 mg

# Pecan Rice and Feta Cheese Salad
*Linda Cook Uhl*

*May be prepared up to 24 hours in advance*

1 (7 ounce) package wild pecan
long grain rice
1 cup (4 ounces) crumbled feta
cheese
½ cup chopped green bell pepper
½ cup chopped yellow bell pepper
½ cup chopped onion
⅓ cup toasted chopped pecans
1 (2 ounce) jar diced pimiento,
drained

**Dressing**

¼ cup olive oil
2 tablespoons tarragon white
wine vinegar
⅛ teaspoon black pepper
Lettuce leaves (optional)

- Prepare rice according to package directions, using 1 teaspoon salt. Let stand to cool slightly.
- Combine cheese, bell peppers, onion, pecans, pimiento and rice in medium bowl.
- Prepare dressing by blending olive oil, wine vinegar and black pepper.
- Add dressing to rice mixture and toss thoroughly. Chill for up to 24 hours.
- Serve individual portions on lettuce leaves or from salad bowl.

Makes approximately 5 cups

Per ½ cup serving _____

Calories 161  Protein 4.12 g  Carbohydrates 13.5 g  Fat 10.5 g  Cholesterol 10.1 mg  Sodium 342 mg

# Wild Rice Salad with Ham and Avocado
Ann Bommarito Armstrong

3 cups cooked wild rice (not seasoned wild rice mix)
1½ cups cubed cooked ham
1 avocado, peeled and cubed
1 teaspoon lemon juice
1 large tomato, seeds removed and cubed

**Dressing**
¾ cup mayonnaise
¼ cup honey mustard sauce

- Combine wild rice and ham. Toss avocado with lemon juice. Add with tomato to rice mixture.
- Prepare dressing by blending mayonnaise and honey mustard sauce.
- Fold dressing into rice mixture.
- Chill several hours before serving.

Makes approximately 7 cups

Per ½ cup serving _____

Calories 165  Protein 3.9 g  Carbohydrates 10 g  Fat 12.5 g  Cholesterol 11.7 mg  Sodium 248 mg

# Cat's Spaghetti Salad
Mary Francis

1 (8 ounce) package spaghetti, cooked
1 large squash, diced
1 large zucchini squash, diced
½ cup sliced cherry tomatoes
1 medium cucumber, sliced
½ cup chopped mushrooms
⅓ cup minced parsley

**Dressing**
½ cup low-fat Catalina salad dressing
½ cup low-fat French salad dressing
3 tablespoons low-fat Italian salad dressing
1 teaspoon garlic powder
½ teaspoon lemon pepper or black pepper

- Prepare dressing by blending salad dressings, garlic powder and pepper.
- Add dressing to spaghetti, tossing to coat thoroughly. Add squash, tomatoes, cucumber, mushrooms and parsley, tossing gently.
- Chill before serving.

Makes approximately 8 cups

Per ½ cup serving _____

Calories 95  Protein 2.34 g  Carbohydrates 17.4 g  Fat 2 g  Cholesterol 1.46 mg  Sodium 217 mg

# Fettuccine Salad

Barbara Bump

1 (16 ounce) can corn, drained and liquid reserved
4 quarts water
1 tablespoon salt
1 (16 ounce) package fettuccine pasta
2 chicken bouillon cubes, crushed
1 cup (4 ounces) grated Parmesan cheese
2 cups fat-free mayonnaise
½ bunch green onions, minced
1 red bell pepper, diced
1 tablespoons black pepper
1 teaspoon garlic or more to taste

- Combine corn liquid, water and salt in stock pot. Bring to a boil.
- Break fettuccine strands and drop into boiling water. Reduce heat and simmer for 5 to 7 minutes, stirring constantly. Pour into colander and rinse fettuccine with cool water. Chill until ready to use.
- Combine bouillon cubes, corn, cheese, mayonnaise, onion, bell pepper, black pepper and garlic in microwave-safe container. Cook at 100 percent power briefly, just until warm. Stir to blend.
- Pour sauce over cold fettuccine in large bowl and mix thoroughly.
- Chill before serving.

For a complete meal, top salad portions with sliced grilled chicken.

Makes approximately 12 cups

Per ½ cup serving _____

Calories 74  Protein 3.17 g  Carbohydrates 12.5 g  Fat 1.5 g  Cholesterol 3.33 mg  Sodium 714 mg

# Greek Pasta Salad

*Linda Cook Uhl*

1 (12 ounce) package rotelle
pasta
1 *small green bell pepper, cut
crosswise in thin strips*
1 *small yellow bell pepper, cut
crosswise in thin strips*
1 *small red bell pepper, cut
crosswise in thin strips*
1 *medium tomato, cut in thin
wedges*
¼ *cup toasted pine nuts*
¼ *cup sliced black olives*
1 *(8 ounce) package feta cheese,
cubed*
2 *tablespoons chopped basil*
¼ *teaspoon crushed dried
oregano*

### Dressing

⅔ *cup olive oil*
3 *tablespoons red wine vinegar*
2 *tablespoons chopped basil*
2 *tablespoons chopped green
onion*
2 *tablespoons grated Parmesan
cheese*
1¼ *teaspoons salt*
¼ *teaspoon black pepper*

- Prepare pasta according to package directions. Drain and set aside to cool.

- Prepare dressing by combining oil, vinegar, basil, green onion, cheese, salt and black pepper in food processor. Process until smooth.

- Combine pasta, bell peppers, tomato, nuts and olives in large bowl.

- Add dressing to salad, tossing to coat thoroughly.

- Roll cubed cheese in basil, add to salad and toss to mix. Sprinkle oregano on salad surface.

- Serve at room temperature.

Makes approximately 8 cups

Per ½ cup serving _____

Calories 176  Protein 4.4 g  Carbohydrates 8.54 g  Fat 14.5 g  Cholesterol 13.2 mg  Sodium 354 mg

# Italian Festival Salad

Linda Stockton

1 (12 ounce) package garden style rotini pasta
½ pound hard salami, cubed
1 (8 ounce) package Provolone cheese, cubed
1½ cups cherry tomatoes, cut in halves
¾ cup black olives, sliced
¾ cup chopped green bell pepper
1 (2 ounce) jar diced pimiento, drained
1 (8 ounce) bottle Italian salad dressing

- Prepare pasta according to package directions. Drain and set aside to cool.
- Combine pasta, salami, cheese, tomatoes, olives, bell pepper and pimiento in large bowl.
- Add dressing to salad, tossing to coat thoroughly.
- Chill, stirring occasionally.

Makes approximately 12 cups

Per ½ cup serving

Calories 144  Protein 5.47  Carbohydrates 6.37 g  Fat 11 g  Cholesterol 14 mg  Sodium 399 mg

# West Lynn Pasta Salad

West Lynn Café

1 (16 ounce) package rotini pasta
1 cup diced red bell pepper
1 cup thinly sliced green onion
1 cup sliced black olives
1 cup toasted pecan pieces
1 cup coarsely chopped artichoke hearts

**Dressing**

½ cup olive oil
¼ cup red wine vinegar
¼ cup tamari (naturally brewed soy sauce)
3 cloves garlic
1 (½ ounce) bunch fresh basil

- Prepare pasta according to package directions. Drain, rinse to cool and let drain again for 5 minutes.
- Combine pasta, bell pepper, green onion, olives, pecans and artichoke hearts, mixing well.
- Combine all dressing ingredients in blender container. Blend until garlic is pureed.
- Add dressing to pasta mixture and toss until thoroughly coated.

Makes approximately 13 cups

Per ½ cup serving

Calories 145  Protein 3.14 g  Carbohydrates 15.7 g  Fat 8 g  Cholesterol 0  Sodium 165 mg

# Tortellini Salad

Linda Cook Uhl

1½ cups cooked cheese tortellini
pasta
1½ cups broccoli flowerets,
blanched
1½ cups sliced carrots, blanched
½ cup (2 ounces) diced
mozzarella cheese
3 tablespoons finely diced green
bell pepper
3 tablespoons minced purple
onion
2 tablespoons chopped fresh basil
or Italian parsley
Salt to taste

**Dressing**
1 tablespoon water
1 tablespoon olive oil
1 tablespoon red wine vinegar
1 tablespoon Dijon mustard

- Prepare dressing, using wire whisk to blend water, oil, vinegar and mustard until smooth.

- Combine tortellini, broccoli and carrots. Add dressing and mix well. Stir in cheese, bell pepper, onion and basil, tossing to coat thoroughly, Season with salt.

- Serve at room temperature or chilled.

Makes approximately 5 cups

Per ½ cup serving

Calories 97  Protein 5.89 g  Carbohydrates 6.82 g  Fat 5 g  Cholesterol 30.9 mg  Sodium 239 mg

★

Blanching is accomplished by submerging vegetables in boiling water for two to three minutes. This process will preserve the nutrients in the vegetables, as well as the bright color and flavor. It will also destroy any harmful bacteria. When the cooking time is complete, plunge the vegetables into cold water for about two or three minutes, then drain and pat dry.

When collecting recipes from our members and their friends and family, we received over 30 different recipes for chicken salads. We chose only the best of the bunch for publication. We think the 12 chicken salad recipes that follow exemplify the variety and imagination of Texas cooks. We hope you will try them all!

# Chicken, Broccoli and Pasta Salad    Linda Cook Uhl

4 skinless, boneless chicken breast halves, cooked
1 (8 ounce) package rotelle pasta, cooked and drained
3 cups broccoli flowerets, steamed and chilled

**Dressing**
½ cup toasted coarsely chopped walnuts
1 cup mayonnaise
½ cup basil leaves
½ cup (2 ounces) freshly grated Parmesan cheese
1 tablespoon lemon juice
2 teaspoons coarsely chopped garlic

- Tear chicken into narrow strips. Combine chicken, pasta and broccoli in large bowl.
- Prepare dressing by blending walnuts, mayonnaise, basil, cheese, lemon juice and garlic in food processor, processing until smooth.
- Add dressing to chicken mixture, tossing to moisten all ingredients.
- Chill thoroughly before serving.

To toast walnuts, bake at 350° for 5 to 7 minutes.

Makes approximately 8 cups

Per ½ cup serving _____

Calories 278  Protein 20.5 g  Carbohydrates 6.92 g  Fat 19 g  Cholesterol 58.2 mg  Sodium 185 mg

# Thai Chicken and Pasta Salad
Linda Bush

2½ cups cubed cooked chicken breast
1 (8 ounce) package vermicelli, cooked and drained
½ cup sliced green onion
¼ cup chopped red bell pepper
½ cup snow peas, blanched
Lettuce or other salad greens

### Dressing
⅓ cup canola oil
2 tablespoons white wine vinegar
3 tablespoons creamy peanut butter
1 tablespoon soy sauce
¼ to ½ teaspoon crushed red pepper flakes
½ teaspoon freshly-grated ginger root

- Combine chicken, vermicelli, green onion, bell pepper and snow peas in large bowl.
- Prepare dressing by blending oil, wine vinegar, peanut butter, soy sauce, red pepper flakes and ginger.
- Add dressing to salad, tossing gently to mix.
- Serve individual portions on lettuce leaves.

Makes approximately 8 cups

Per ½ cup serving
Calories 113  Protein 8.28 g  Carbohydrates 5.65 g  Fat 6.5 g  Cholesterol 16.4 mg  Sodium 97.9 mg

★

After cooking pasta for use in salads or other chilled dishes, rinse well and drain before adding dressings or other ingredients.

# Chicken and Rice Salad
*Barbara Boyd*

2 cups cooked rice, cooled
2 cups diced cooked chicken
1½ cups cooked peas, drained
and cooled
1½ cups diced celery
2 to 3 tablespoons grated onion
Lettuce (optional)
1 tomato, cut in wedges
(optional)

**Dressing**
1 cup mayonnaise
1 teaspoon salt
¼ teaspoon black or cayenne
pepper
¼ teaspoon paprika

- Combine rice, chicken, peas, celery and onion in large bowl.
- Prepare dressing by blending mayonnaise, salt, black or cayenne pepper and paprika.
- Add dressing to chicken mixture, mixing thoroughly. Adjust seasonings to taste.
- Chill salad for at least 2 hours.
- Serve on lettuce, garnished with tomato wedges.

Makes approximately 8 cups

Per ½ cup serving _____

Calories 185  Protein 7.5 g  Carbohydrates 10.2 g  Fat 12.5 g  Cholesterol 24.1 mg  Sodium 270 mg

# Almond Curry Chicken Salad
*Marilyn Markham*

3 cups cubed cooked chicken
1 tart apple, chopped
2 teaspoons chopped onion
½ cup chopped celery
½ cup grape halves
½ cup slivered almonds, toasted
Fresh lemon juice to taste
1 cup mayonnaise
⅓ teaspoon salt
Dash of black pepper
Dash of seasoned salt
⅓ teaspoon curry powder
Lettuce leaves

- Combine chicken, apple, onion, celery, grapes and almonds.
- Blend lemon juice, mayonnaise, salt, black pepper, seasoned salt and curry powder together. Fold into chicken mixture.
- Serve on lettuce leaves.

Makes approximately 6½ cups

Per ½ cup serving _____

Calories 228  Protein 10.9 g  Carbohydrates 4.52 g  Fat 19 g  Cholesterol 36.2 mg  Sodium 187 mg

# Chinese Chicken Salad
*Julie Strait*

20 *green onions, divided*
4 *quarter-size slices ginger root*
4 *cups water*
¼ *cup rice wine*
4 *skinless, boneless chicken breast halves*
2 *cucumbers, peeled and cubed*
1 *cup bean sprouts*
3 *carrots, peeled and cut in thin sticks*
1 *cup snow peas, blanched*

**Dressing**
6 *green onions*
6 *quarter-size slices ginger root*
2 *tablespoons sesame oil*
6 *small dried red chilies, seeded and cut in halves*
¼ *cup plus 2 tablespoons soy sauce*
2 *tablespoons plus 1½ teaspoons Chinese rice vinegar*
2 *tablespoons rice wine*

- Chop 4 green onions. Combine with ginger, water and wine in saucepan. Simmer for 5 minutes.
- Add chicken and bring to a boil, reduce heat and simmer for 20 minutes. Drain chicken and set aside to cool.
- Prepare dressing by lightly crushing green onions and ginger.
- Heat oil in wok or heavy skillet over high heat until smoking. Add chilies, green onion and ginger. Stir, cover and remove from heat. Let stand until room temperature.
- Strain oil, discarding vegetables and seasonings. Add soy sauce, rice vinegar and wine, stirring to blend.
- Shred chicken and 16 green onions. Combine chicken, onion, cucumber, bean sprouts, carrots and snow peas.
- Pour dressing over chicken mixture and toss lightly.

Serves 8

Per serving _____

Calories 290  Protein 43.5 g  Carbohydrates 14.1 g  Fat 6 g  Cholesterol 98.6 mg  Sodium 765 mg

# Chutney Chicken Salad

*Cookbook Committee*

2 cups diced cooked chicken
1 cup diagonally sliced celery
¼ cup salted peanuts
1 (13 ounce) can pineapple
tidbits, drained
½ cup sliced green onion

**Dressing**

⅔ cup mayonnaise
2 tablespoons fresh lime juice
½ teaspoon grated lime peel
¼ teaspoon salt
2 tablespoons chutney
½ teaspoon curry powder

- Combine chicken, celery, peanuts, pineapple and green onion, tossing to mix.
- Prepare dressing by blending mayonnaise, lime juice and peel, salt, chutney and curry powder, mixing well.
- Add dressing to chicken mixture and mix thoroughly.
- Chill before serving.

Makes approximately 6 cups

Per ½ cup serving _____

Calories 201  Protein 11.6 g  Carbohydrates 7.74 g  Fat 14 g  Cholesterol 35.6 mg  Sodium 167 mg

# Chicken Pecan Salad

*Lee Ann Lamb*

3 medium peaches, peeled and
sliced, or ½ pound seedless
grapes
3 cups cubed cooked chicken
breast
1 cup diced celery
¼ cup toasted whole pecans

**Dressing**

½ cup fat-free mayonnaise
2 tablespoons vegetable oil
1 tablespoon vinegar
½ teaspoon salt
1 tablespoon celery seeds

- Combine peaches, chicken and celery.
- Prepare dressing by blending mayonnaise, oil, vinegar, salt and celery seed.
- Add dressing to chicken mixture and mix thoroughly.
- Chill until ready to serve. Fold in pecans just before serving.

*Use large chunks of fruit, chicken and celery for a more attractive salad.*

Makes approximately 6 cups

Per ½ cup serving _____

Calories 125  Protein 10.8 g  Carbohydrates 5.25 g  Fat 7 g  Cholesterol 28.4 mg  Sodium 234 mg

# Lemon Chicken Salad

*Laurie Shaw Davis*

4 *skinless, boneless chicken breast halves*
2 *tablespoons lemon curd*
2 *teaspoons lemon pepper*
1 *teaspoon garlic powder*
1 *cup frozen French-cut green beans*
1 *tablespoon fat-free mayonnaise*
1 *tablespoon toasted slivered almonds*
2 *green onions, chopped*

- Place chicken in shallow baking dish. Spread lemon curd, lemon pepper and garlic powder evenly on chicken.

- Bake at 350° for 45 minutes or until cooked and tender.

- While chicken is baking, prepare green beans according to package directions; do not overcook. They should be crisp.

- Chop chicken into small pieces. Add mayonnaise, almonds, green onion and green beans.

- Chill until ready to serve.

*Chicken may be served hot as a main dish with green beans on the side.*

Serves 4

Per serving _____

Calories 218  Protein 15.8 g  Carbohydrates 19.4 g  Fat 9 g  Cholesterol 77.2 mg  Sodium 132 mg

★

Frozen vegetables are the next-best-thing to fresh. They retain more of their nutrients, color, and flavor than do canned vegetables, and are crisper and more fresh tasting.

## Picnic Chicken Salad

Donna Earle Crain

4 cups cubed cooked chicken
2 cups chopped celery
½ cup toasted slivered almonds
5 slices bacon, cooked and crumbled
Sliced mushrooms (optional)

**Dressing**
1 cup fat-free mayonnaise
1 cup fat-free sour cream
2 tablespoons lemon juice
1 teaspoon salt

- Combine chicken, celery, almonds, bacon and mushrooms.
- Prepare dressing by blending mayonnaise, sour cream, lemon juice and salt.
- Add dressing to chicken mixture, tossing thoroughly.
- Chill until ready to serve.

Makes approximately 8 cups

Per ½ cup serving _____

Calories 145  Protein 11.6 g  Carbohydrates 5.2 g  Fat 8.5 g  Cholesterol 28.3 mg  Sodium 384 mg


## Southwestern Chicken Salad

Barbara Bump

3 cups chopped cooked chicken
1 cup chopped celery
4 slices bacon, cooked and crumbled
1 (4 ounce) can chopped green chilies, drained
1 cup peanuts, chopped
½ cup fat-free mayonnaise
Salt and black pepper to taste
½ head lettuce, chopped
Tortilla chips or melon slices (optional)

- Combine chicken, celery, bacon, chilies, peanuts and mayonnaise, tossing to mix well. Season with salt and black pepper.
- Chill until ready to serve.
- Arrange lettuce on individual salad plates. Place ½ cup chicken mixture on lettuce. Serve with chips or melon.

Makes approximately 6 cups

Per ½ cup serving _____

Calories 165  Protein 14.5 g  Carbohydrates 5.49 g  Fat 10 g  Cholesterol 30.2 mg  Sodium 343 mg

# Summer Salad with Raspberry Mayonnaise

Nanci Norin Jordt

6 skinless, boneless chicken breast halves, cooked and cut in ½-inch strips
¼ cup plus 2 tablespoons white wine
2 cups cooked fresh peas
2 cups thinly sliced celery
½ pound fresh snow peas, cooked crisp tender
3 medium tomatoes, peeled and each cut in 8 wedges
¼ cup minced shallots
¼ cup minced parsley
4 hard-cooked eggs, cut in wedges
Large green olives
Large ripe olives
Lettuce leaves

**Raspberry Mayonnaise**
1 egg
½ teaspoon salt
¼ teaspoon dry mustard
2 tablespoons raspberry vinegar
1¼ to 1⅓ cups vegetable oil

• Marinate chicken in wine for 1 hour in refrigerator.

• Prepare mayonnaise by blending egg, salt and mustard in food processor. With processor running, add vinegar and slowly drizzle oil in steady stream until consistency of mayonnaise. Set aside.

• Combine peas, celery, snow peas, ½ of tomatoes, shallots and parsley. Fold enough Raspberry Mayonnaise into vegetables to moisten. Chill.

• Arrange lettuce leaves on large platter. Mound vegetables in center and arrange chicken around vegetables. Decorate platter with egg wedges, olives and remaining tomato wedges.

• Serve with remaining Raspberry Mayonnaise.

*For a quick alternative to mayonnaise, combine ½ cup low-fat raspberry yogurt and 1 cup fat-free mayonnaise.*

Serves 12

Per serving _____

Calories 338  Protein 12.7 g  Carbohydrates 8.85 g  Fat 28 g  Cholesterol 109 mg  Sodium 281 mg

# Chicken Waldorf Salad

Vicki Ashley Atkins

2 cups cubed cooked chicken breast
1½ cups seedless red grapes
1 cup cubed unpeeled red apple
⅔ cup sliced celery
¼ cup raisins (optional)
2 tablespoons diced purple onion

**Dressing**
⅓ cup plain non-fat yogurt
2 tablespoons reduced-calorie mayonnaise
1½ tablespoons lemon juice
⅛ to ¼ teaspoon celery salt

- Combine chicken, grapes, apple, celery, raisins and onion, tossing gently to mix.
- Prepare dressing by blending yogurt, mayonnaise, lemon juice and celery salt.
- Add dressing to chicken mixture and toss gently to coat thoroughly.
- Chill, covered, until ready to serve.

Makes approximately 6 cups

Per ½ cup serving

Calories 89  Protein 8.37 g  Carbohydrates 7.65 g  Fat 3 g  Cholesterol 22.3 mg  Sodium 86.8 mg

# Turkey Fruit Salad

Kari J. Tobias

1 (8 ounce) carton low-fat lemon yogurt
1 teaspoon minced mint
2 cups cubed cooked turkey
2 cups shredded lettuce
2 fresh pears, cut in ½-inch pieces
1 (11 ounce) can mandarin oranges, drained
½ cup chopped pecans

- Blend yogurt and mint together. Chill for 1 hour.
- Combine turkey, lettuce, pears, oranges and pecans.
- Pour yogurt over salad and toss.
- Serve immediately.

Use leftover turkey from Thanksgiving for a light dinner after the big feast.

Serves 6

Per cup serving

Calories 216  Protein 17 g  Carbohydrates 16.8 g  Fat 9.5 g  Cholesterol 37.2 mg  Sodium 61.9 mg

# Tuna Parmesan Salad
*Barbara Bump*

1 (12 *ounce*) *package medium shell macaroni*
2 (6⅛ *ounce*) *cans water-packed tuna*
1 (10 *ounce*) *package frozen chopped broccoli, thawed*
½ *cup chopped green onion*
½ *cup chopped red bell pepper*
*Lettuce leaves*
*Fruit slices for garnish*

## Dressing

1 *cup mayonnaise*
2 *tablespoons low-fat milk*
⅓ *cup grated Parmesan cheese*
1 *teaspoon hot pepper sauce*
1 *teaspoon lemon pepper*
½ *teaspoon garlic powder*

- Prepare macaroni according to package directions. Drain, rinse with cold water and set aside to cool.
- Prepare dressing by blending mayonnaise, milk, cheese, hot pepper sauce, lemon pepper and garlic powder, mixing well.
- Combine macaroni, tuna, broccoli, onion and bell pepper, tossing to mix. Add dressing and blend thoroughly.
- Chill, covered, stirring occasionally.
- Serve individual portions on lettuce leaves and garnish with fruit slices.

Makes approximately 12 cups

Per ½ cup serving _____

Calories 115  Protein 5.76 g  Carbohydrates 5.42 g  Fat 8 g  Cholesterol 11.2 mg  Sodium 134 mg

# Italian Tuna Walnut Salad
*Kari J. Tobias*

*To enhance flavor, chill at least 4 hours*

2 *cups broccoli flowerets*
1 *cup 1-inch carrot strips*
1 *cup cauliflowerets*
1 *cup sliced cucumber*
1 *cup pitted ripe olives*
¾ *cup chopped walnuts*
1 *cup cherry tomatoes*
¾ *cup reduced-calorie Italian salad dressing*
2 (6⅛ *ounce*) *cans water-packed tuna, drained*

- Combine broccoli, carrots, cauliflowerets, cucumber, olives, walnuts, tomatoes and salad dressing, tossing to mix thoroughly.
- Fold tuna into salad.
- Chill, covered, for at least 4 hours before serving.

Makes approximately 10 cups

Per ½ cup serving _____

Calories 74  Protein 5.73 g  Carbohydrates 3.37 g  Fat 4.5 g  Cholesterol 5.32 mg  Sodium 182 mg

# Tuna Salad Unique

*Cheryl Briggs Patton*

1 (6 ounce) package wild and long grain rice mix
1 tablespoon prepared mustard
½ cup low-fat mayonnaise type salad dressing
1 cup non-fat sour cream
¾ cup finely chopped celery
¾ cup minced white or purple onion
2 (6⅛ ounce) cans water-packed white tuna, drained
Salt and black pepper to taste
Lettuce leaves
Tomato wedges
Pickled okra or peppers for garnish

- Prepare rice according to package directions. Chill until ready to use.

- Combine mustard, salad dressing, sour cream, celery, onion and tuna. Add rice and stir. Chill for at least 1 hour.

- Serve individual portions of salad on lettuce with tomato wedges. Garnish with okra or peppers.

Makes approximately 7 cups

Per ½ cup serving

Calories 102  Protein 9.54 g  Carbohydrates 12.1 g  Fat 2 g  Cholesterol 9.99 mg  Sodium 216 mg

# Cool Crab Salad

Rosemary Bennett Douglass

1 (7½ ounce) can crab meat,
drained and cartilage removed
1 cup (4 ounces) diced Swiss
cheese
2 hard-cooked eggs, chopped
⅓ cup chopped sweet pickle
¼ cup chopped celery
2 tablespoons chopped green bell
pepper

**Dressing**
½ cup sour cream
1½ tablespoons lemon juice
2 tablespoons chopped onion
¼ teaspoon sugar
¼ teaspoon salt
Dash of black pepper
½ teaspoon dill weed

- Combine crab meat, cheese, eggs, pickle, celery and bell pepper in large bowl.
- Prepare dressing by blending sour cream, lemon juice, onion, sugar, salt, black pepper and dill weed.
- Add dressing to salad, gently tossing to mix.
- Chill until ready to serve.

Makes approximately 3 cups

Per ½ cup serving

Calories 209  Protein 16.4 g  Carbohydrates 8.43 g  Fat, 12.5 g  Cholesterol 131 mg  Sodium 464 mg

## Hot Crab Meat Avocado Salad

Nanci Norin Jordt

1 (7½ ounce) can crab meat, drained and cartilage removed
⅓ cup chopped celery
3 hard-cooked eggs, chopped
2 tablespoons chopped pimiento
1 tablespoon chopped onion
½ teaspoon salt
½ cup mayonnaise or salad dressing
3 large ripe avocados, unpeeled
Lemon juice
Salt
3 tablespoons dry breadcrumbs
1 teaspoon butter, melted
2 tablespoons slivered almonds

- Combine crab meat, celery, eggs, pimiento, onion, salt and mayonnaise, mixing lightly.

- Cut avocados in halves lengthwise and remove pits. Brush cut surfaces with lemon juice and sprinkle lightly with salt.

- Spoon crab meat mixture into avocado halves.

- Toss breadcrumbs with butter. Sprinkle on crab meat.

- Place stuffed avocados in ungreased shallow baking dish.

- Bake, uncovered, at 400° for 10 minutes. Sprinkle almonds on crumb topping and bake for additional 5 minutes or until bubbly.

Serves 6

Per serving

Calories 405  Protein 13.7 g  Carbohydrates 11.7 g  Fat 35.5 g  Cholesterol 150 mg  Sodium 571 mg

──────── ★ ────────

No kitchen should ever be without fresh lemons. Their juice enhances the flavor of most meats and vegetables, and stops freshly cut fruits from darkening. Even the skin may be used to add zest to everything from pies and cakes to sauces and beverages.

# Shrimp Avocado Salad
Ann Bommarito Armstrong

*May be prepared 1 day in advance*

1 (10 ounce) package frozen cooked shrimp, thawed and drained
2 cups cooked rice
2 avocados, peeled and chopped
Lemon juice
¾ cup chopped onion
2 tablespoons chopped pimiento
1 large tomato, seeds removed and diced
½ cup chopped black olives
½ cup chopped green olives
Salt to taste
1 tablespoon plus 1 teaspoon fat-free mayonnaise

- Combine shrimp and rice. Chill.
- Sprinkle avocado with lemon juice, tossing to coat avocado.
- Combine avocado, onion, pimiento, tomato and olives. Add vegetables to shrimp and rice mixture. Season with salt.
- Add mayonnaise to salad, stirring lightly.
- Chill until ready to serve. Salad may be prepared a day in advance.

Makes approximately 6 cups

Per ½ cup serving

Calories 139  Protein 6.84 g  Carbohydrates 14.2 g  Fat 6.5 g  Cholesterol 46.1 mg  Sodium 222 mg

# Greek Salad
LaNyce Whittemore

*May be prepared several hours in advance*

½ medium-sized purple onion, thinly sliced
1 pound fresh spinach, rinsed, stems removed and torn
½ cup (4 ounces) crumbled feta cheese
½ cup coarsely chopped walnuts
½ cup Greek olives, pitted and cut in halves

- Layer, in order listed, onion, spinach, cheese, walnuts and olives in salad bowl. Cover and chill until ready to serve.
- Just before serving, toss with favorite dressing.

*Basil Vinaigrette, page 93, is especially good on this salad.*

Serves 8

Per serving

Calories 92  Protein 4.61 g  Carbohydrates 4.21 g  Fat 7.1 g  Cholesterol 12.6 mg  Sodium 203 mg

# Shrimp and Rice Salad
Nanci Norin Jordt

1 cup cooked shrimp
3 cups cooked rice
¼ cup sliced celery
¼ cup sliced pimiento-stuffed
green olives
¼ cup chopped green bell pepper
¼ cup chopped pimiento
¼ cup minced onion
Crisp lettuce leaves
2 tomatoes, cut in wedges, for
garnish, or melon slices
French salad dressing
Lemon wedges

**Dressing**
3 tablespoons mayonnaise or
salad dressing
½ teaspoon salt
¼ teaspoon black pepper

- Cut each shrimp lengthwise. Add rice, celery, olives, bell pepper, pimiento and onion, mixing well. Chill, covered.
- Just before serving, prepare dressing by blending mayonnaise, salt and black pepper.
- Add dressing to shrimp mixture, tossing to coat thoroughly.
- Serve individual portions of shrimp salad on lettuce leaves. Garnish with tomato or melon. Serve with French dressing and lemon wedges.

Makes approximately 5 cups

Per ½ cup serving _____

Calories 194  Protein 5.26 g  Carbohydrates 22.5 g  Fat 9.5 g  Cholesterol 31.8 mg  Sodium 412 mg

# Green Olive Salad
Sue Atkins Loyd

1 clove garlic, cut in halves
1 head lettuce, chopped
4 medium tomatoes, chopped
1 (3 ounce) jar pimiento-stuffed
green olives, drained and liquid
reserved, sliced
½ cup vegetable oil
Salt and black pepper to taste
¼ cup lemon juice

- Rub wooden salad bowl with cut side of garlic. Discard garlic.
- Combine lettuce, tomatoes and olives in bowl.
- Drizzle oil on vegetables. Toss until well coated.
- Combine lemon juice and re-served olive liquid, pour over vegetables and mix well.
- Season with salt and black pepper.

Serves 8

Per serving _____

Calories 149  Protein .987 g  Carbohydrates 4.17 g  Fat 15 g  Cholesterol 0  Sodium 261 mg

# Marinated Artichoke Salad
Linda Stockton

*½ pound spinach, rinsed, stems removed*
*1 large head iceberg lettuce, chilled and washed*
*3 (6 ounce) jars marinated artichoke hearts, undrained*
*3 (12 ounce) cans pitted ripe olives, drained*
*⅓ cup herb salad dressing*

- Tear spinach and lettuce into bite-sized pieces (about 12 cups).
- Chill until ready to assemble salad.
- Combine artichoke hearts, olives and salad dressing.
- Just before serving, add artichoke mixture to greens, tossing to coat thoroughly.

*To toss easily, place all ingredients except salad dressing in plastic bag. Pour in dressing and shake until ingredients are well coated with dressing.*

Serves 12

Per serving _____

Calories 113  Protein 2.28 g  Carbohydrates 7.19 g  Fat 9.5 g  Cholesterol 0  Sodium 465 mg

# Santa Fe Citrus Salad
Pamela Jones

*5 cups loosely-packed torn romaine lettuce*
*1 cup sliced purple onion*
*1 cup thinly sliced peeled jícama*
*¼ cup chopped cilantro*
*1 cup pink grapefruit sections*
*1½ cups fresh orange sections (about 4 medium-sized oranges)*

- Combine lettuce, onion, jícama and cilantro in large bowl.
- Prepare dressing by blending orange juice, oil, sugar and cumin.
- Drizzle dressing over salad. Add grapefruit and orange sections and toss gently.
- Serve immediately.

**Dressing**
*¼ cup fresh orange juice*
*1½ tablespoons vegetable oil*
*1 teaspoon sugar*
*½ teaspoon ground cumin*

Per serving _____

Calories 72  Protein 1.59 g  Carbohydrates 11.3 g  Fat 3 g  Cholesterol 0  Sodium 4.53 mg

## Sesame Romano Salad

Donna Earle Crain

1 head iceberg lettuce, torn in bite-sized pieces
½ cup (2 ounces) shredded Romano cheese
⅓ cup toasted sesame seeds
½ cup Italian salad dressing
⅓ cup sliced almonds

- Place lettuce in salad bowl.
- Sprinkle cheese and sesame seeds on lettuce.
- Add salad dressing and almonds, tossing to mix thoroughly.

Amounts of ingredients may be adjusted to suit individual tastes.

Serves 8

Per serving _____

Calories 158  Protein 4.6 g  Carbohydrates 5.33 g  Fat 14 g  Cholesterol 6.5 mg  Sodium 198 mg

## Sweet and Sour Lettuce

Karen Strong Ball

½ cup half and half
3 tablespoons vinegar
1 tablespoon sugar
¼ teaspoon salt
2 bunches green leaf lettuce, torn in bite-sized pieces
3 hard-cooked eggs, sliced
½ cup crumbled cooked bacon
¼ cup (1 ounce) grated Parmesan cheese

- Blend half and half, vinegar, sugar and salt in large bowl.
- Add lettuce to dressing, stirring to coat leaves thoroughly.
- Place egg slices on lettuce and sprinkle with bacon and cheese.
- Toss salad just before serving.

Serves 8

Per serving _____

Calories 111  Protein 6.57 g  Carbohydrates 3.85 g  Fat 8 g  Cholesterol 92.9 mg  Sodium 257 mg

# Shanghai Spinach Salad
*Sandy Wyatt Neiderstadt*

1 pound fresh spinach, rinsed, stems removed and torn
½ cup bean sprouts
1 (8 ounce) can water chestnuts, drained and rinsed
4 slices bacon, cooked and crumbled
½ purple onion, thinly sliced in rings
½ cup sliced mushrooms
3 hard-cooked eggs, sliced
Croutons (optional)

**Dressing**

½ cup vegetable oil
¼ cup red wine vinegar
¼ cup plus 2 tablespoons sugar
2 tablespoons ketchup
1 teaspoon salt

- Combine spinach, sprouts, water chestnuts, bacon, onion and mushrooms, tossing gently to mix.

- Prepare dressing by mixing oil, vinegar, sugar, ketchup and salt in dressing shaker jar. Chill until ready to serve.

- Add croutons and dressing to salad, tossing to mix thoroughly.

Serves 8

Per serving _____

Calories 243  Protein 5.78 g  Carbohydrates 17.9 g  Fat 17.5 g  Cholesterol 82.2 mg  Sodium 444 mg

★

Make your own fat free croutons in the microwave. Simply spread a very thin layer of Dijon mustard on both sides of two slices of day old bread. Cut into cubes and arrange in a single layer on waxed paper. Microwave on high for 1½ minutes on each side, or until dry.

# Strawberry Spinach Salad

Donna Earle Crain

1 *pound fresh spinach, rinsed,*
*stems removed and torn*
1 *cup diagonally sliced celery*
1 *pint fresh strawberries, hulled*
*and cut in halves*
1 *cup sugar*
1 *cup chopped pecans*

### Poppy Seed Dressing

¼ *cup sugar*
1 *teaspoon salt*
1 *teaspoon dry mustard*
⅓ *cup vinegar*
2 *scallions, chopped*
1 *cup vegetable oil*
1½ *tablespoons poppy seed*

- Combine spinach, celery and strawberries.
- Prepare caramelized pecans by slowly cooking sugar and pecans in skillet over low heat until all sugar has melted onto pecans and they are browned; DO NOT OVERCOOK. Immediately place pecans on wax paper and let stand until cool.
- Prepare dressing by blending sugar, salt, mustard, vinegar and scallions in food processor. Gradually add oil, processing to mix well. Stir in poppy seeds. Chill until ready to use.
- Add pecans and Poppy Seed Dressing to salad, tossing gently to mix.

Serves 10

Per serving of salad _____

Calories 177  Protein 2.48 g  Carbohydrates 26.1 g  Fat 8.5 g  Cholesterol 0  Sodium 46.8 mg

Per 1 tablespoon dressing _____

Calories 186  Protein .313 g  Carbohydrates 5.06 g  Fat 19 g  Cholesterol 0  Sodium 178 mg

★

Always thoroughly rinse fresh spinach to remove any grit that may be clinging to the leaves. Pat the leaves dry and remove their stems before adding to your salads.

# Sweet and Sour Slaw

*Vicki Ashley Atkins*

*Must be chilled for at least 6 hours*

1 *head cabbage, shredded*
½ *small onion, thinly sliced*
¼ *cup sugar*

**Dressing**

½ *cup vinegar*
½ *teaspoon sugar*
½ *teaspoon celery seeds*
½ *teaspoon salt*
½ *teaspoon prepared mustard*
¼ *cup plus 2 tablespoons canola oil*

- Alternate layers of cabbage and onion in 3-quart casserole. Sprinkle with sugar.
- Prepare dressing by combining vinegar, sugar, celery seeds, salt and mustard in saucepan. Stirring often, bring to a boil. Add oil and bring back to a boil.
- Pour hot dressing over cabbage and onion.
- Chill, covered, for at least 6 hours, stirring well after 1 hour. Slaw may be stored in refrigerator for several weeks.

Makes approximately 6 cups

Per ½ cup serving

Calories 102  Protein 1.24 g  Carbohydrates 10.1 g  Fat 7 g  Cholesterol 0  Sodium 108 mg

# Marbleized Tea Eggs

Donna Earle Crain

*Attractive addition to your favorite salad*

12 hard-cooked eggs
2 tablespoons soy sauce
2 tablespoons salt
6 regular tea bags or 3 family-size tea bags
Water

- Allow eggs to cool slightly. Gently crack shells all over without removing any part of shells. Place in single layer in large saucepan.
- Add soy sauce, salt, tea bags and enough water to cover eggs. Bring to a boil, then reduce heat and simmer for about 30 minutes.
- Remove pan from heat and let stand until cool. Drain.
- Peel eggs. They will look as though they have been carved from marble.

*For variety, omit the soy sauce and tea bags and cover the eggs with beet juice instead of water. You will achieve the same effect but with a beautiful rose color.*

Serves 12

Per serving _____

Calories 80  Protein 6.46 g  Carbohydrates 1.06 g  Fat 5.5 g  Cholesterol 212 mg  Sodium 371 mg

# Dijon Salad Dressing

Pamela Jones

3 tablespoons Dijon mustard
¾ cup low-fat plain yogurt
½ teaspoon salt
Pinch of black pepper
3 tablespoons lemon juice
1 teaspoon sugar
1 clove garlic, minced
1 tablespoon capers, drained

- Combine mustard, yogurt, salt and black pepper.
- Add lemon juice, sugar, garlic and capers to yogurt mixture, whisking to blend.
- Serve on green salads.

Makes 1¼ cups

Per tablespoon _____

Calories 9  Protein .615 g  Carbohydrates 1.26 g  Fat .5 g  Cholesterol .559 mg  Sodium 90.1 mg

# Basil Vinaigrette

LaNyce Whittemore

2 large cloves garlic, minced
1 tablespoon dried basil or 3 tablespoons chopped fresh basil
2 teaspoons sugar
½ teaspoon salt
½ teaspoon freshly ground black pepper
¼ cup sherry wine vinegar
½ cup olive oil

- Combine garlic and basil in food processor. Add sugar, salt, black pepper and wine vinegar.
- With chopping blade running, gradually add oil in steady stream.
- May be prepared at least 1 day in advance. Dressing may be stored in refrigerator for up to 1 week.

*Fantastic served on fresh tomatoes from the garden or with a mixture of favorite salad greens, mushrooms and herbs. For a clear vinaigrette, place garlic and basil in a bowl, add other ingredients and whisk to blend. Flavored oils and vinegars may be substituted.*

Makes 1 cup

Per tablespoon

Calories 64  Protein .072 g  Carbohydrates 1.08 g  Fat 7 g  Cholesterol 0  Sodium 66.8 mg

# Parmesan Dressing

Mary Lauderman Tavcar

1 garlic clove, cut in halves
¾ cup vegetable oil
¼ cup lemon juice
2 tablespoons grated Parmesan cheese
¼ teaspoon sugar
¾ teaspoon salt

- Combine garlic, oil, lemon juice, cheese, sugar and salt in jar. Shake to blend thoroughly.
- Store in refrigerator until ready to use. Before serving, discard garlic and shake again.

Makes 1 cup

Per tablespoon

Calories 95  Protein .351 g  Carbohydrates .403 g  Fat 10.5 g  Cholesterol .615 mg  Sodium 115 mg

# Mom's French Dressing with Variations

Mary Francis

¾ cup vegetable or olive oil
¼ cup lemon juice or cider vinegar
1 tablespoon sugar
¾ teaspoon salt
¼ teaspoon paprika
¼ teaspoon dry mustard
¼ teaspoon black pepper

- Combine oil, lemon juice, sugar and salt in blender container. Add paprika, dry mustard and black pepper. Blend until smooth.
- Add 1 of variations listed and mix well.
- Store in refrigerator. Serve on green salads.

Makes approximately 1 cup basic dressing

## Variations

¼ cup sour cream for creamy French dressing
¼ teaspoon curry powder
¾ teaspoon prepared horseradish
¾ cup (3 ounces) crumbled Roquefort cheese plus 2 teaspoons water
1 cup lemon juice (omit oil), ½ cup honey, ¼ teaspoon grated lemon peel and ½ teaspoon celery seed

Per 1 tablespoon basic dressing _____

Calories 94  Protein .028 g  Carbohydrates 1.07 g  Fat 10 g  Cholesterol 0  Sodium 102 mg

★

When making homemade salad dressing, remember the wonderful flavored vinegars that are now commercially available. They can add unexpected zest to any salad.

# Green Herb Mayonnaise
Pamela Jones

¼ cup watercress leaves
¼ cup parsley sprigs
¼ cup fresh dill
¼ cup fresh cilantro leaves
¼ cup snipped chives
1 egg yolk, at room temperature
3 to 4 tablespoons fresh lemon juice
½ teaspoon salt
¼ teaspoon freshly-ground black pepper
½ cup canola oil
¼ cup water, divided
½ cup olive oil

- Combine watercress, parsley, dill, cilantro and chives in food processor. Grind to fine consistency.
- Add egg yolk, lemon juice, salt and black pepper.
- With blade running, slowly stream in, one at a time, canola oil, 2 tablespoons water, olive oil and 2 tablespoons water.
- Store, covered, in refrigerator. May be prepared a day in advance.

*Especially good with smoked meats and fish.*

Makes 1½ cups

Per tablespoon

Calories 83  Protein .177 mg  Carbohydrates .228 g  Fat 9.5 g  Cholesterol 8.83 mg  Sodium 45.8 mg

# Parsley Dressing
Rosemary Bennett Douglass

1 egg
1 teaspoon sugar
1 teaspoon salt
1 green onion top
3 dashes hot pepper sauce
3 tablespoons vinegar
1 clove garlic
1 cup parsley sprigs
¾ cup vegetable oil

- Combine egg, sugar, salt, green onion top, hot pepper sauce, vinegar, garlic and parsley in blender or food processor, chopping well.
- Gradually add oil, blending thoroughly.
- Chill before serving and store in refrigerator.

*Excellent dressing on tossed green salads or mandarin orange and avocado salad or as dip for boiled shrimp.*

Makes 1 cup

Per tablespoon

Calories 98  Protein .528 g  Carbohydrates .808 g  Fat 10.5 g  Cholesterol 13.3 mg  Sodium 170 mg

# Poppy Seed Dressing

Pamela Jones

¾ cup sugar
⅓ cup cider vinegar
1 teaspoon salt
1 teaspoon dry mustard
1 teaspoon finely grated onion
1 cup vegetable oil
1 tablespoon poppy seed

- Combine sugar, vinegar, salt, mustard and onion. Using electric mixer, beat until sugar is dissolved.
- Gradually beat in oil. Stir in poppy seed.
- Store in refrigerator. Shake or stir before serving.
- Serve on fruit salad or spinach salad.

Makes 1½ cups

Per tablespoon

Calories 108  Protein .106 g  Carbohydrates 6.57 g  Fat 9.5 g  Cholesterol 0  Sodium 89 mg

# Sweet and Sour Salad Dressing

Mary Lauderman Tavcar

1 small onion
1 teaspoon prepared mustard
1 teaspoon salt
1 teaspoon celery seed
⅓ cup vinegar
1 cup vegetable oil
⅔ cup sugar

- Combine onion, mustard, salt and celery seed in food processor.
- Add vinegar, oil and sugar, processing until well blended.
- Store in refrigerator until ready to use.
- Serve on green salad, shaking before using.

Makes 2½ cups

Per tablespoon

Calories 62  Protein .047 g  Carbohydrates 3.7 g  Fat 5.5 g  Cholesterol 0  Sodium 55.1 mg

★

Serve your dressings on the side in pretty, cut glass cruets. Your salad will stay fresh and crisp, and individual preferences will be accommodated.

# Vegetables

We have come a long way since grandmother's day, when fresh vegetables meant harvesting the fields. Today, Austin cooks simply line up at the Travis County Farmer's Market eager to take home fresh produce. And, oh, how preparation has changed! Instead of simmering vegetables for hours and losing the nutrients, grilling, steaming and baking are popular now. **Grilled Corn on the Cob** seasoned with lemon pepper; **Asparagus Mornay** with cheesy sauce on the side; baked **Zucchini Gondolas** stuffed with tomato, green pepper, green onion and part-skim mozzarella, and **Tomato Toppers** are a few healthy choices.

*Thank you to the local growers at the Travis County Farmer's Market for the photo setting. Serving pieces shown are courtesy of Clarksville Pottery and Gallery and hold special meaning for Texans. They were created by local ceramic artist Teri Vance Hubbeling, who was commissioned by President George Bush to design dinnerware for use at the 1991 Houston Economic Summit.*

# Artichoke Casserole

Betty M. Williams

1 (14 ounce) can artichoke hearts, drained and quartered
3 hard-cooked eggs, sliced
½ cup pimiento-stuffed green olives, sliced
¼ cup water chestnuts, sliced
1 (10¾ ounce) can cream of mushroom soup, undiluted
¼ cup milk
½ cup buttered breadcrumbs
½ cup (2 ounces) grated Cheddar cheese

- Layer artichoke hearts, eggs, olives and water chestnuts in greased 9x9x2-inch baking dish.

- Blend soup and milk together. Pour over ingredients in casserole dish.

- Top with breadcrumbs and cheese.

- Bake, uncovered, at 350° for 25 to 30 minutes or until bubbly and browned.

*This dish is a tradition in our family with all holiday meals. The only disagreement is who gets to bring it! We rarely have leftovers and, when we do, they don't last long.*

Serves 8

Per ½ cup serving

Calories 144  Protein 6.55 g  Carbohydrates 10.8 g  Fat 9 g  Cholesterol 88.4 mg  Sodium 646 mg

★

An egg slicer is an indispensable kitchen tool. In addition to providing perfectly sliced eggs, it can also be used to quickly slice mushrooms, olives, peeled avocados, banana pieces, and other soft fruits and vegetables.

# Asparagus Mornay

Mary Lou Cindrich

2 *pounds fresh asparagus spears*
2 *tablespoons butter*
1 *tablespoon flour*
⅛ *teaspoon salt*
*Dash of white pepper*
1 *cup milk*
½ *cup (2 ounces) shredded sharp
process American cheese*
¼ *cup slivered blanched
almonds, toasted*

- Cook asparagus in small amount of water until just tender. Drain and place in warm serving dish. Keep warm.
- Melt butter in small saucepan over low heat. Combine flour, salt and white pepper. Blend into melted butter.
- Add milk. Cook, stirring constantly, until mixture is thickened and bubbly. Reduce heat and cook for 2 minutes, stirring constantly.
- Add cheese and stir until melted. Pour cheese sauce over asparagus. Sprinkle with almonds.
- Serve immediately.

Serves 8

Per ¼ pound asparagus with 2½ tablespoons sauce _____

Calories 119  Protein 5.98 g  Carbohydrates 8.09 g  Fat 8 g  Cholesterol 18.6 mg  Sodium 248 mg

─────── ★ ───────

Before steaming fresh vegetables, squeeze half a lemon into the water, drop in the shell and steam as usual. Your vegetables will have a delicious flavor without adding fat!

# Black Beans

LaNyce Whittemore

1 *pound black beans*
2 *quarts water*
2 *teaspoons salt, divided*
1 *teaspoon ground cumin*
1 *teaspoon oregano*
¼ *teaspoon dry mustard*
2 *onions, chopped*
2 *cloves garlic*
1 *or 2 green bell peppers,*
*chopped*
2 *tablespoons olive oil*
1 *tablespoon fresh lemon juice*
1 *or 2 jalapeño peppers, chopped*
¼ *cup pureed tomatoes*

- Soak beans in water in Dutch oven overnight. For quick soak method, place beans in water, bring to a boil, cook for 3 minutes, turn off heat and let stand for 2 to 3 hours.

- After soaking, add 1 teaspoon salt to water. Bring to a boil and cook, covered, until beans are almost tender. Black beans require a longer cooking period than other varieties.

- Combine 1 teaspoon salt, cumin, oregano and mustard.

- Chop onion and garlic in food processor. Remove from bowl. Chop bell pepper in food processor.

- Sauté onion and garlic in olive oil in large skillet for 5 minutes. Add bell pepper and sauté until onion is tender.

- Add seasoning mixture and lemon juice to vegetables. Stir in ½ cup hot bean liquid. Simmer, covered, for 10 minutes.

- Add seasoned vegetable mixture to beans. Stir in jalapeño peppers and tomatoes. Cook for about 1 hour or until beans are tender.

- To thicken, remove 1 cup beans with liquid, pour into food processor and pulse to liquefy. Return puree to beans in Dutch oven.

*Serve in bowls with mound of ½ cup hot cooked rice in center, garnished with sliced green onion, lemon slice, cilantro and dollop of sour cream. Beans also make a great soup; omit preparation of 1 cup bean puree.*

Makes approximately 6 cups

Per ½ cup serving

Calories 87  Protein 3.92 g  Carbohydrates 12.9 g  Fat 2.5 g  Cholesterol 0  Sodium 403 mg

# Herbed Green Beans

Pamela Jones

1½ pounds fresh slender green
beans
½ cup sliced green onion
½ cup sliced mushrooms
¼ cup lightly-salted margarine
1 (4 ounce) jar diced pimiento,
drained
¼ teaspoon black pepper
½ teaspoon dried basil
½ teaspoon dried marjoram

- Cook beans in small amount of boiling water for 10 to 15 minutes or until tender. Drain well.
- Sauté green onion and mushrooms in margarine until tender.
- Add green beans, pimiento, black pepper, basil and marjoram to onion and mushrooms. Cook over medium heat, stirring constantly, until thoroughly heated.
- Serve immediately.

Serves 16

Per ½ cup serving _____

Calories 44, Protein 1.03 g, Carbohydrates 4.13 g, Fat 3 g, Cholesterol 0, Sodium 27 mg

# Swiss Beans

Nanci Norin Jordt

2 tablespoons butter
2 tablespoons all-purpose flour
½ teaspoon salt
⅛ teaspoon black pepper
1 teaspoon sugar
½ teaspoon grated onion
1 cup sour cream
2 (16 ounce) cans French-cut
green beans, drained
1⅓ cups (5⅓ ounces) grated
Swiss cheese
Paprika

- Melt butter in saucepan. Stir in flour, salt, black pepper, sugar and onion. Gradually add sour cream, stirring to blend.
- Add green beans to sauce. Pour into 8-inch pie plate.
- Cover with grated cheese.
- Bake at 350° for 20 minutes. Garnish with paprika.

Serves 6

Per ½ cup serving _____

Calories 252  Protein 10.4 g  Carbohydrates 12 g  Fat 19 g  Cholesterol 50.2 mg  Sodium 681 mg

# Pennsylvania Dutch Green Beans

*Mary Lauderman Tavcar*

3 slices bacon
2 small onion, sliced
2 teaspoons cornstarch
¼ teaspoon salt
¼ teaspoon dry or prepared mustard
½ teaspoon vegetable bouillon granules
½ cup hot water
1 tablespoon brown sugar
1 tablespoon vinegar
1 (16 ounce) package frozen green beans, thawed, or 1 pound fresh green beans, steamed until tender
1 hard-cooked egg, sliced

- Fry bacon in 12-inch skillet until crisp. Drain, crumble and set aside. Remove all but 1 tablespoon bacon drippings from skillet.

- Sauté onions in bacon drippings until lightly browned. Stir in cornstarch, salt and mustard.

- Dissolve bouillon in hot water. Add to onion. Bring to a boil, stirring often. Blend in brown sugar and vinegar.

- Add beans to sauce. Heat thoroughly. Pour into serving dish and garnish with egg and crumbled bacon.

Serves 6

Per ½ cup serving _____

Calories 71  Protein 3.44 g  Carbohydrates 9.36 g  Fat 2.5 g  Cholesterol 38.1 mg  Sodium 322 mg

★

Most green beans today are stringless. Just snap off the ends as you wash them.

# Broccoli-Bleu Cheese Casserole
Ginny Ashley

2 (10 ounce) packages frozen chopped broccoli
2 tablespoons butter or margarine
2 tablespoons all-purpose flour
½ cup skim milk
½ cup half and half
¼ teaspoon salt
¼ teaspoon white pepper
1 (3 ounce) package cream cheese, softened and cubed
¼ cup (1 ounce) crumbled mild bleu cheese
½ cup slivered almonds
½ cup seasoned croutons (optional)

- Place broccoli in colander. Rinse with hot tap water until thawed, drain well and set aside.
- Melt butter in heavy saucepan over low heat. Add flour, stirring until smooth, and cook for 1 minute, stirring constantly.
- Gradually add skim milk and half and half. Cook over medium heat, stirring constantly, until sauce is thickened and bubbly.
- Add salt, white pepper, cream cheese and bleu cheese to sauce. Stir until cheese is melted.
- Stir broccoli and almonds into sauce, mixing lightly. Pour broccoli and sauce into buttered 2-quart casserole.
- Bake at 350° for 15 minutes. Sprinkle with croutons and bake for additional 15 minutes or until hot and bubbly.

Serves 6

Per ½ cup serving _____

Calories 242  Protein 9.04 g  Carbohydrates 11.8 g  Fat 19 g  Cholesterol 39.2 mg  Sodium 290 mg

★

Broccoli, cabbage and cauliflower are known as cruciferous vegetables. They are high in vitamin C and beta-carotene, and have shown to be effective in protecting against some types of cancer.

# Sesame Broccoli

Vicki Ashley Atkins

1½ pounds fresh broccoli, cut
into spears
1 tablespoon sesame seeds
1 teaspoon vegetable oil
1 tablespoon lemon juice
1 tablespoon soy sauce
1 tablespoon sugar

- Steam broccoli over boiling water for 7 minutes or until tender. Drain, place in serving bowl and keep warm.

- Sauté sesame seeds in oil in saucepan over medium heat, stirring constantly, until lightly browned.

- Add lemon juice, soy sauce and sugar. Bring to a boil. Immediately drizzle sauce over broccoli and toss lightly to coat.

Serves 4

Per ½ cup serving

Calories 87  Protein 5.93 g  Carbohydrates 12.9 g  Fat 3 g  Cholesterol 0  Sodium 305 mg

# Broccoli with Walnuts

Kathy Gordon

3 (10 ounce) packages frozen
chopped broccoli, cooked and
drained
¼ cup margarine
¼ cup all-purpose flour
1½ tablespoons chicken bouillon
granules
2 cups milk
⅔ cup hot water
6 tablespoons margarine
2 cups herb-seasoned stuffing
mix
⅔ cup chopped walnuts

- Arrange broccoli in buttered 13x9x2-inch baking pan.

- Melt ¼ cup margarine in sauce-pan. Add flour and bouillon, stirring until smooth, and cook for a few minutes, stirring constantly.

- Add milk and stir until sauce is thickened and smooth. Pour sauce over broccoli.

- Melt 6 tablespoons margarine in hot water. Add stuffing mix and toss. Stir in walnuts. Spoon on top of broccoli.

- Bake, uncovered, at 400° for 30 minutes.

Serves 10

Per ½ cup serving

Calories 263  Protein 7.17 g  Carbohydrates 19.5 g  Fat 18.5 g  Cholesterol 6.83 mg  Sodium 471 mg

# Herbed Brussels Sprouts

Vicki Ashley Atkins

2 pounds fresh Brussels sprouts
½ cup chopped chives
½ cup chopped parsley
¾ teaspoon dried whole marjoram
¾ teaspoon dried whole thyme
½ teaspoon salt
1 tablespoon plus 1 teaspoon olive oil

- Clean and trim Brussels sprouts.
- Steam over boiling water for 10 minutes or until tender. Drain and set aside.
- Sauté chives, parsley, marjoram, thyme and salt in olive oil in non-stick skillet over medium heat for 3 minutes.
- Add Brussels sprouts and sauté for additional 2 minutes, stirring to coat well with herbs.

Serves 8

Per ½ cup serving ————

Calories 71  Protein 4.06 g  Carbohydrates 10.6 g  Fat 2.5 g  Cholesterol 0  Sodium 164 mg

# Sweet-Sour Red Cabbage

Sandy Wyatt Niederstadt

Salt
4 tablespoons vinegar, divided
1 medium-sized head purple cabbage, shredded
4 slices bacon, diced
¼ cup firmly-packed brown sugar
2 tablespoons all-purpose flour
½ cup water
1 teaspoon salt
⅛ teaspoon black pepper
1 small onion, sliced
Bacon bits for garnish

- Cook cabbage 5 minutes in ½ inch boiling water with salt and 2 tablespoons vinegar. Set aside.
- Fry bacon until browned, remove from skillet and set aside.
- Retain 1 tablespoon bacon drippings in skillet. Stir in brown sugar and flour. Add 2 table-spoons vinegar, ½ cup water, 1 teaspoon salt, black pepper and onion. Cook over medium heat for 5 minutes, stirring constantly.
- Add sauce mixture and bacon to cabbage. Heat thoroughly.
- Garnish with extra bacon.

Serves 8

Per ½ cup serving ————

Calories 59  Protein 1.9 g  Carbohydrates 9.92 g  Fat 1.5 g  Cholesterol 2.7 mg  Sodium 324 mg

# Apricot Glazed Carrots

*Nanci Norin Jordt*

1½ pounds baby carrots
1¼ cups water
1 tablespoon sugar
¼ cup butter, divided
¾ teaspoon salt, divided
⅓ cup apricot preserves
¼ teaspoon freshly grated nutmeg
Dash of white pepper
¼ teaspoon grated orange peel (optional)
Fresh lemon juice to taste
Minced parsley

- Combine carrots, water, sugar, 1 tablespoon butter and ½ teaspoon salt in saucepan. Cook until crisp tender. Drain and set aside.
- Heat preserves until liquid and reserve juices; discard solids.
- Melt 3 tablespoons butter in skillet. Stir in preserve liquid, nutmeg, ¼ teaspoon salt, white pepper, orange peel and lemon juice. Add carrots and stir to glaze.
- Garnish carrots with parsley.

Serves 8

Per ½ cup serving _____
Calories 122  Protein .876 g  Carbohydrates 17.1 g  Fat 6.5 g  Cholesterol 15.5 mg  Sodium 295 mg


# Carrots in Cranberry Sauce

*Kathy Gordon*

4 cups sliced carrots
¼ cup water
¼ cup margarine
¼ cup jellied cranberry sauce
2 tablespoons brown sugar

- Combine carrots and water in microwave-safe casserole. Cook until tender and drain.
- Combine margarine, cranberry sauce and brown sugar in skillet. Cook over low heat until cranberry sauce is melted.
- Add carrots to sauce and stir to coat thoroughly.

*This dish is great served with turkey.*

Serves 8

Per ½ cup serving _____
Calories 108  Protein .931 g  Carbohydrates 13.8 g  Fat 6 g  Cholesterol 0  Sodium 103 mg

# Carrot Fritters

Linda Uchiyama Kelley

1 pound peeled carrots, cut in
small pieces
Salt
1 cup all-purpose flour
1 teaspoon baking powder
½ cup sugar
1 teaspoon vanilla
2 teaspoons margarine, melted
1 egg, beaten
½ cup olive oil

- Cook carrots in small amount of salted water for 15 to 20 minutes or until tender. Drain and let stand until cool.

- Puree carrots in blender. Combine carrot puree, flour, baking powder, sugar, vanilla, margarine and egg, mixing well.

- Drop carrot mixture by table-spoonful into oil heated to 375° in skillet. Cook, turning once, until golden brown. Drain on paper towel.

Makes 18

Per fritter _____

Calories 120  Protein 1.34 g  Carbohydrates 13.7 g  Fat 7 g  Cholesterol 11.8 mg  Sodium 24.1 mg


# Marmalade Carrots

Donna Earle Crain

2 pounds carrots, cut julienne
¼ cup plus 2 tablespoons orange
juice
¼ cup maple syrup
2 tablespoons orange marmalade

- Steam carrots over boiling water just until tender. Drain and set aside.

- Combine orange juice, maple syrup and marmalade in sauce-pan. Bring to a boil, stirring constantly.

- Add carrots and stir to coat thoroughly. Reduce heat and simmer for 3 minutes.

Serves 8

Per ½ cup serving _____

Calories 93  Protein 1.27 g  Carbohydrates 22.7 g  Fat .5 g  Cholesterol 0  Sodium 43.6 mg

# Cauliflower-Carrot Pie

Nanci Norin Jordt

2 cups herb-seasoned stuffing
mix
¼ cup butter or margarine,
melted
1 medium head cauliflower
¼ cup butter or margarine
1 cup minced onion
1 clove garlic, minced
½ cup thinly sliced carrots
¼ teaspoon salt
¼ teaspoon ground oregano
1 cup (4 ounces) shredded
Cheddar cheese
2 eggs
¼ cup milk

• Combine stuffing mix and melted butter, mixing well. Press stuffing in bottom and along sides of 9-inch pie plate. Bake at 375° for 8 minutes. Set aside.

• Separate cauliflower into flowerets, then quarter flowerets.

• Melt ¼ cup butter in large skillet. Add cauliflower, onion, garlic, carrots, salt and oregano. Cook over medium heat for 10 minutes, stirring often.

• Sprinkle ½ cup cheese on stuffing shell. Spoon cooked vegetables into shell and top with remaining cheese.

• Combine eggs and milk, beating well. Pour over vegetables and cheese.

• Bake at 375° for 35 minutes.

Serves 8

Per serving

Calories 274  Protein 9.34 g  Carbohydrates 19.6 g  Fat 18.5 g  Cholesterol 100 mg  Sodium 553 mg

★

Always use fresh carrots. They are available year-round, and there really is no comparison. Frozen and canned varieties lose their texture.

# Italian Cauliflower

Vicki Ashley Atkins

1 cup cauliflowerets
Salt
¼ cup diced onion
1 small clove garlic, minced
1 teaspoon margarine
1 teaspoon olive oil
1 cup cooked elbow macaroni
1 tablespoon chopped parsley, divided
½ cup low-fat ricotta cheese, at room temperature
Dash of freshly ground black pepper
1 tablespoon plus 1 teaspoon dry breadcrumbs, lightly toasted
2 teaspoons grated Parmesan cheese
½ ounce toasted almonds, finely ground
Parsley sprigs for garnish (optional)

- Cook cauliflower in salted boiling water for 10 minutes or until tender. Drain, reserving ¾ cup cooking liquid. Keep cauliflower warm.

- Heat margarine and olive oil over medium heat until bubbly.

- Sauté onion and garlic in margarine and olive oil for 1 minute; do not brown.

- Add ¾ cup cauliflower to onion and garlic. Mash with fork tines. Stir in macaroni, remaining cauliflower, reserved cooking liquid and 2 teaspoons parsley.

- Spoon macaroni mixture into serving bowl. Top with ricotta cheese and sprinkle with 1 teaspoon parsley, black pepper, breadcrumbs, Parmesan cheese and almonds.

- Garnish with parsley sprigs.

Serves 4

Per ½ cup serving _____

Calories 156  Protein 7.34 g  Carbohydrates 16.5 g  Fat 7 g  Cholesterol 10.3 mg  Sodium 360 mg

# Bacon Fried Corn
Wanda Rich

4 slices bacon, diced
1 small onion, chopped
2 cups fresh corn, cut from 4 ears
½ cup diced red bell pepper
2 tablespoons minced parsley
2 tablespoons milk
Salt and freshly ground black pepper to taste

- Fry bacon in heavy skillet until crisp. Remove bacon and set aside.
- Retain 2 tablespoons bacon drippings in skillet. Cook onion in drippings for about 5 minutes or until softened.
- Add corn and bell pepper to onion. Cook for 3 to 4 minutes or until just softened.
- Add parsley, milk, salt and black pepper to vegetables, mixing well.
- Sprinkle bacon bits on vegetables.

Serves 4

Per ½ cup serving

Calories 177  Protein 5.07 g  Carbohydrates 17.7 g  Fat 11 g  Cholesterol 12.5 mg  Sodium 185 mg

# Creamy Corn Mushroom Casserole
Jennie Hentges

1 (8 ounce) package cream cheese, softened
¼ cup all-purpose flour
1 teaspoon salt
1 (17 ounce) can cream style corn
½ pound fresh mushrooms, sliced, or 1 (4 ounce) can mushrooms, drained
½ cup chopped onion
2 tablespoons margarine
1 (16 ounce) can whole kernel corn, drained
½ cup (2 ounces) shredded Swiss cheese
½ cup breadcrumbs

- Combine cream cheese, flour and salt, blending well. Add cream corn and mix thoroughly.
- Sauté mushrooms and onion in margarine until vegetables are softened. Stir into cream cheese mixture.
- Add whole kernel corn and Swiss cheese to cream cheese mixture. Spread mixture in greased 1½-quart casserole. Sprinkle with breadcrumbs.
- Bake at 350° for 35 to 40 minutes.

Serves 10

Per ½ cup serving

Calories 231  Protein 6.84 g  Carbohydrates 25.7 g  Fat 13 g  Cholesterol 29.9 mg  Sodium 642 mg

# Corn and Rice Con Queso

Rhonda Copeland Gracely

1 cup uncooked regular rice
½ cup chopped onion
1 cup chopped green bell pepper
1 cup chopped celery
½ cup butter or margarine
1 or 2 large jalapeño peppers, minced
2 (17 ounce) cans cream style corn
1 cup (4 ounces) shredded Cheddar cheese
Green bell pepper rings (optional)
Cherry tomato halves (optional)
Parsley sprigs (optional)

- Prepare rice according to package directions. Set aside.
- Sauté onion, bell pepper and celery in butter until vegetables are tender.
- Combine rice, sautéed vegetables, jalapeño peppers, corn and cheese, mixing well. Pour mixture into lightly greased 13x9x2-inch baking dish.
- Bake at 350° for 40 to 45 minutes.
- Garnish with bell pepper, tomatoes and parsley.

Serves 16

Per ½ cup serving _____

Calories 170  Protein 3.83 g  Carbohydrates 21.6 g  Fat 8.5 g  Cholesterol 23 mg  Sodium 289 mg

# Triple Corn Bake

Jennie Hentges

1 (16 ounce) can cream style corn
1 (16 ounce) can whole kernel corn, undrained
1 (8 ounce) package cornbread mix
1 cup low-fat sour cream
¾ cup butter, melted

- Combine cream style and whole kernel corn, cornbread mix, sour cream and butter, mixing lightly but thoroughly. Pour batter into greased 13x9x2-inch baking dish.
- Bake, uncovered, at 350° for 30 to 35 minutes.

Serves 12

Per ½ cup serving _____

Calories 250  Protein 4.42 g  Carbohydrates 29 g  Fat 14.5 g  Cholesterol 31.3 mg  Sodium 570 mg

──────── ★ ────────

For maximum flavor and freshness, always buy corn on the cob, with its husk still intact. Shuck and clean just prior to cooking for an almost fresh from the garden treat.

# Eggplant Italian Style

*Pamela Jones*

1 cup thinly sliced onion
1 clove garlic, minced
¼ cup olive oil
1 eggplant, cubed
1 green bell pepper, cut in thin strips
1 cup diced tomatoes
½ teaspoon salt
½ teaspoon black pepper
½ teaspoon oregano
Grated Parmesan cheese (optional)

- Sauté onion and garlic in olive oil in large skillet for 5 minutes.
- Add eggplant and bell pepper. Sauté for 5 minutes, stirring frequently.
- Add tomatoes, salt, black pepper and oregano. Simmer, covered, for 15 to 20 minutes, stirring occasionally.
- Sprinkle with Parmesan cheese.

*Zucchini squash may be substituted for eggplant. Canned tomatoes may be used instead of fresh tomatoes.*

Serves 6

Per ½ cup serving _____

Calories 132  Protein 2.04 g  Carbohydrates 12.2 g  Fat 9.5 g  Cholesterol 0  Sodium 186 mg

★

Eggplant has a great capacity for absorbing oil. But, if salted and allowed to drain for about half an hour, then rinsed and patted dry, they will absorb much less oil when prepared.

# Mushroom Curry

Vicki Ashley Atkins

⅓ cup sliced onion
1 teaspoon minced ginger root
2 teaspoons low-fat margarine
¼ teaspoon crushed basil leaves
¼ teaspoon crushed thyme leaves
¼ teaspoon crushed marjoram leaves
¼ teaspoon dill seed
¼ teaspoon minced parsley
⅛ teaspoon ground turmeric
1½ cups small mushrooms
⅔ cup small cauliflowerets
1 medium tomato, seeds removed and diced
1 teaspoon lemon juice
½ bay leaf
½ teaspoon curry powder

• Sauté onion and ginger in margarine until onion is softened.
• Add basil, thyme, marjoram, dill, parsley and turmeric, mixing well.
• Stir mushrooms, cauliflower, tomato, lemon juice, bay leaf and curry powder into seasoned onion mixture. Reduce heat and simmer, covered, for about 10 minutes or until vegetables are tender, stirring frequently.
• Discard bay leaf. Serve vegetables immediately.

*This dish is wonderful served with steamed Jasmine rice.*

Serves 4

Per ½ cup serving _____

Calories 40  Protein 1.81 g  Carbohydrates 6.69 g  Fat 1.5 g  Cholesterol 0  Sodium 22.8 mg

# Mushrooms in Sake

Linda Uchiyama Kelley

1 pound fresh mushrooms
2 tablespoons olive oil
1 cup beef bouillon
½ cup sake

• Sauté mushrooms in olive oil until tender.
• Add bouillon to mushrooms. Cook until liquid is reduced by ½. Stir in sake.

*This makes an excellent side dish or topping for steak.*

Serves 4

Per ½ cup serving _____

Calories 135  Protein 2.76 g  Carbohydrates 8.15 g  Fat 7.5 g  Cholesterol 0  Sodium 347 mg

# Mushrooms Florentine

Pamela Jones

1 pound fresh mushrooms
1 tablespoon margarine
2 (10 ounce) packages frozen chopped spinach, thawed
1 teaspoon salt
¼ cup chopped onion
¼ cup margarine, melted
1 cup (4 ounces) grated Cheddar cheese
⅛ teaspoon garlic salt

- Cut stems from mushrooms. Sauté stems and caps in 1 tablespoon margarine until browned. Drain and set aside.
- Remove excess liquid from spinach by pressing between paper towels. Combine spinach, salt, onion and melted margarine. Spread mixture in 13x9x2-inch baking dish.
- Sprinkle ½ cup cheese on spinach, layer mushrooms on cheese, season with garlic salt and top with remaining cheese.
- Bake at 350° for 20 minutes or until cheese is melted.

Serves 12

Per ½ cup serving

Calories 104  Protein 4.7 g  Carbohydrates 4.73 g  Fat 8 g  Cholesterol 9.92 mg  Sodium 341 mg

★

"Sake" is a Japanese alcoholic beverage made from fermented rice. When called for in recipes, dry vermouth may be substituted.

# Rivertown Mushrooms and Red Wine

Barbara Bittner

1 pound fresh mushrooms
2 tablespoons minced onion
1 clove garlic, minced
2 tablespoons chopped green bell
pepper
3 tablespoons butter
¼ cup red wine
¼ teaspoon salt
⅛ teaspoon black pepper
½ teaspoon Worcestershire sauce
½ teaspoon parsley flakes

- Cut large mushrooms in halves or quarters. Sauté mushrooms, onion, garlic and bell pepper in butter for 5 minutes.

- Add wine, salt, black pepper, Worcestershire sauce and parsley to vegetables. Cook until liquid is reduced and sauce is thickened.

*Mushrooms are good accompaniment to steak or chops.*

Serves 4

Per ½ cup serving

Calories 120 Protein 2.64 g Carbohydrates 6.61 g Fat 9 g Cholesterol 23.3 mg Sodium 234 mg

# Creole Okra

Pamela Jones

½ cup chopped onion
½ cup chopped green bell pepper
2 tablespoons margarine
2½ cups cooked tomatoes
2 cups diced celery
2 cups chopped fresh or frozen
okra
2 teaspoons salt
¼ teaspoon black pepper
½ teaspoon basil
½ teaspoon oregano
¼ to ½ teaspoon cayenne pepper

- Sauté onion and bell pepper in margarine until softened.

- Add tomatoes, celery, okra, salt, black pepper, basil, oregano and cayenne pepper to onion and bell pepper. Cook for 15 to 20 minutes or until celery is crisp tender.

Serves 10

Per ½ cup serving

Calories 61 Protein 1.79 g Carbohydrates 9.49 g Fat 2.5 g Cholesterol 0 Sodium 636 mg

# Polenta with Marinara Sauce
*Jeanne Cassidy*

2½ cups water, divided
¾ cup yellow cornmeal
¾ cup (3 ounces) freshly grated
Parmesan cheese, divided
2 tablespoons minced parsley
½ teaspoon salt
1 teaspoon Italian seasoning
1 egg, beaten
1 tablespoon vegetable oil
2 cups marinara sauce
(homemade preferred)
Parsley sprigs for garnish

- Bring 1¼ cups water to boil in medium saucepan.

- Combine 1 cup water, cornmeal, ½ cup cheese, parsley, salt and Italian seasoning.

- Gradually add batter to boiling water, stirring constantly. Cook, stirring frequently, until bubbly and thickened; reduce heat to low and cook for 5 minutes, stirring often.

- Stir ¼ cup polenta into beaten egg. Return to saucepan; stir to combine.

- Pour polenta into greased 13x9x2-inch baking pan. Chill, covered for 1 hour or until firm.

- Cut polenta into 24 portions. Shape into smooth balls. Sauté in small amount of oil in non-stick skillet until lightly browned.

- To serve, spoon ¼ cup marinara sauce on serving plate, add 3 polenta balls, sprinkle with pinch of cheese and garnish with parsley.

*After chilling, polenta can be cut into squares, then triangles, and lightly browned for serving as an attractive side dish for grilled meats or seafood.*

Serves 8

Per serving _____

Calories 150  Protein 6.54  Carbohydrates 15.7 g  Fat 7.5 g  Cholesterol 30.8 mg  Sodium 714 mg

## Mal's Easy Potatoes

*Pamela Jones*

4 to 6 brown, white or red
potatoes (about 2 pounds),
thinly sliced
2 cups light cream
Salt and black pepper to taste

- Layer potatoes in 11x7x1½-inch baking dish.
- Pour cream over potatoes. Season with salt and black pepper.
- Bake at 350° for 1 hour for scalloped potatoes or 1½ hours for crispy top and drier potatoes.

Serves 8

Per ½ cup serving _____

Calories 185  Protein 2.59 g  Carbohydrates 23.6 g  Fat 9.5 g  Cholesterol 33.1 mg  Sodium 49.2 mg

## Party Potatoes

*Linda Cook Uhl*

8 to 10 medium potatoes, peeled
1 cup sour cream
1 (8 ounce) package cream
cheese, softened
¼ cup butter
⅓ cup chopped chives
Salt and black pepper to taste
Butter
Paprika for garnish

- Cook potatoes in water until tender. Drain and keep warm.
- Combine sour cream and cream cheese, beating well. Add warm potatoes and beat until smooth. Add butter, chives, salt and black pepper.
- Spread mixture in well greased 2½-quart casserole. Dot potatoes with butter and sprinkle lightly with paprika.
- Bake at 350° for 25 minutes.

*This dish can be prepared a day in advance and stored in refrigerator.*

Makes approximately 10 cups

Per ½ cup serving _____

Calories 138  Protein 2.33 g  Carbohydrates 13.3 g  Fat 9 g  Cholesterol 23.7 mg  Sodium 79.4 mg

# Potato Casserole

*Linda Moore*

6 medium potatoes, peeled
1 (12 ounce) carton small-curd cottage cheese
⅓ cup sour cream
2 tablespoons minced onion
1 teaspoon salt
1 tablespoon butter, melted
¼ cup toasted slivered almonds

- Cook potatoes in water until tender. Drain. Mash until smooth.
- Combine potatoes, cottage cheese, sour cream, onion and salt. Spread mixture in lightly greased 2-quart casserole.
- Drizzle with butter and sprinkle with almonds.
- Bake, uncovered, at 350° for 30 minutes or until thoroughly heated.

Makes approximately 8 cups

Per ½ cup serving

Calories 97  Protein 4.25 g  Carbohydrates 13 g  Fat 3.5 g  Cholesterol 5.92 mg  Sodium 228 mg

# Scalloped Potatoes

*Debbie Harris*

1 (10¾ ounce) can cream of mushroom soup, undiluted
½ cup milk
¼ cup chopped parsley
Dash of black pepper
4 cups thinly sliced potatoes
1 small onion, thinly sliced
1 tablespoon butter or margarine
3 slices bacon, cooked and crumbled
½ to 1 cup (2 to 4 ounces) shredded Cheddar cheese

- Combine soup, milk, parsley and black pepper.
- In 2-quart casserole, arranged alternate layers of potatoes, onion and soup mixture, ending with soup. Dot with butter.
- Bake, covered, at 375° for 1 hour. Remove cover and bake additional 15 minutes or until potatoes are tender.
- Sprinkle with bacon and cheese. Return to oven just until cheese is melted.

Makes approximately 6 cups

Per ½ cup serving

Calories 111  Protein 3.56 g  Carbohydrates 12.1 g  Fat 5.5 g  Cholesterol 10.5 mg  Sodium 279 mg

# Spinach-Stuffed Baked Potatoes

Linda Simmons

2 small baking potatoes
2 tablespoons low-fat margarine
3 tablespoons low-fat (2 percent) milk
½ (10 ounce) package frozen chopped spinach, thawed and drained
4 tablespoons grated Parmesan cheese, divided
2 tablespoons low-fat sour cream
1 tablespoon chopped green onion
1 clove garlic, crushed
Salt to taste
Dash of ground red pepper

- Bake potatoes until done. Cut in halves lengthwise, carefully scoop out pulp and set shells aside.
- Combine pulp, margarine and milk. Mash until smooth.
- Add spinach, 3 tablespoons cheese, sour cream, green onion, garlic, salt and red pepper. Mix well.
- Spoon spinach mixture into potato shells. Sprinkle with 1 tablespoon cheese. Place potatoes in ungreased 9x9x2-inch baking dish.
- Bake at 350° for 30 minutes or until thoroughly heated.

Serves 4

Per serving _____
Calories 190  Protein 6.75 g  Carbohydrates 28.8 g  Fat 6 g  Cholesterol 8.67 mg  Sodium 256 mg

★

For microwave "baked" potatoes, be careful not to overcook or the pulp will lose its fluffy consistency. Microwave until just soft to the touch, wrap in foil and allow to stand for 5 to 10 minutes.

# Praline Sweet Potatoes
Barbara Hoover McEachern

5 cups mashed cooked sweet
potatoes
1 cup sugar
2 eggs
1 teaspoon vanilla
⅓ cup milk
½ cup plus ⅓ cup butter or
margarine, divided
1 cup firmly-packed brown sugar
⅓ cup all-purpose flour
1 cup finely chopped pecans

- Combine sweet potatoes, sugar, eggs, vanilla, milk and ½ cup butter. Using electric mixer, beat until smooth. Spread mixture in greased 13x9x2-inch baking dish.
- Combine brown sugar, flour, ⅓ cup butter and pecans, mixing to crumb consistency. Sprinkle on sweet potato mixture.
- Bake at 350° for 30 minutes.

*This is a Thanksgiving and Christmas tradition in our family. I have never found anyone who didn't like this dish—even those who don't like sweet potatoes love it!*

Serves 12

Per ½ cup serving _____

Calories 405  Protein 3.77 g  Carbohydrates 53.5 g  Fat 20.5 g  Cholesterol 66.5 mg  Sodium 158 mg

# Teresa's Holiday Yam Casserole
Lee Ann Lamb

½ cup all-purpose flour
½ cup firmly-packed brown
sugar
½ cup regular oats, uncooked
1 teaspoon cinnamon
⅓ cup butter
2 (17 ounce) cans yams
2 cups fresh cranberries

- Combine flour, brown sugar, oats, cinnamon and butter, mixing to crumb consistency.
- Mix 1 cup crumbs with yams and cranberries. Pour mixture into 1½-quart casserole. Top with remaining crumbs.
- Bake, uncovered, at 350° for 35 minutes.

*This is an unusual and wonderful holiday dish that turns yams into everyone's favorite food.*

Makes approximately 6 cups

Per ½ cup serving _____

Calories 188  Protein 2.78 g  Carbohydrates 32.9 g  Fat 5.5 g  Cholesterol 13.7 mg  Sodium 115 mg

# Yummy Apple Yams

*Jennie Hentges*

2 *pounds yams (5 or 6 yams)*
1½ *pounds Granny Smith apples*
¼ *cup plus 2 tablespoons butter*
1⅔ *cups firmly-packed brown sugar*
3 *tablespoons maple syrup*
½ *cup apple cider*
1 *tablespoon lemon juice*
1 *tablespoon cinnamon*
½ *teaspoon ground ginger*

- Place yams in saucepan, add water to cover and simmer for about 30 minutes or until just tender. Drain and let stand until cool to touch. Peel yams and cut in ½-inch slices.

- Core and quarter apples. Slice into ½-inch pieces. Arrange apples and yams in 13x9x2-inch baking dish.

- Melt butter in saucepan. Stir in brown sugar, maple syrup, cider, lemon juice, cinnamon and ginger. Simmer for 10 minutes, stirring frequently. Pour over apples and yams.

- Bake at 325° for 30 minutes, basting occasionally with glaze from baking dish.

Makes approximately 8 cups

Per ½ cup serving ────────────────────────────────

Calories 192  Protein 1.12 g  Carbohydrates 38.5 g  Fat 4.5 g  Cholesterol 11.6 mg  Sodium 56.1 mg

──────── ★ ────────

There is a difference between yams and sweet potatoes. Yams, which are more common, are darker orange, sweeter, and more moist than sweet potatoes.

## Elegant Spinach

*Nanci Norin Jordt*

2 (10 ounce) packages frozen
chopped spinach, thawed
½ pound fresh mushrooms
4 tablespoons butter, divided
1 tablespoon all-purpose flour
½ cup milk
½ teaspoon salt
⅛ teaspoon garlic powder
1 (14 ounce) can artichoke
hearts, drained and quartered
¾ cup sour cream
¾ cup mayonnaise
3 tablespoons fresh lemon juice

- Drain spinach, pressing to remove moisture. Set aside.

- Reserve several mushroom caps for garnish. Slice remaining mushrooms and sauté in 2 tablespoons butter until tender.

- Melt 2 tablespoons butter in heavy saucepan. Stir in flour and cook for 2 minutes. Add milk, whisking until thickened. Remove from heat and stir in salt, garlic powder, spinach and sliced mushrooms.

- Place artichokes in buttered 2-quart casserole. Cover with spinach mixture.

- Combine sour cream, mayonnaise and lemon juice. Spread on spinach mixture. Arrange mushroom caps for garnish.

- Bake at 375° for 15 to 20 minutes.

Serves 8

Per ½ cup serving _____

Calories 309  Protein 5.56 g  Carbohydrates 13.7 g  Fat 27.5 g  Cholesterol 39.4 mg  Sodium 423 mg

★

As a general rule, vegetables that grow underground should
be covered during cooking, while those that grow above
ground should be cooked uncovered.

# Spinach Casserole

Adele McGee Ely

2 (10 ounce) packages frozen
chopped spinach
2 cups sour cream
1 envelope onion soup mix
1 (14 ounce) can artichoke
hearts, drained and quartered

- Prepare spinach according to package directions, cooking just until done. Drain well.
- Combine sour cream and soup mix. Gently fold into spinach and artichokes. Spread in 2-quart casserole.
- Bake at 375° for 20 minutes.

*This dish is wonderful even without the artichokes!*

Makes approximately 5 cups

Per ½ cup serving _____

Calories 134  Protein 4.23 g  Carbohydrates 9.45 g  Fat 10 g  Cholesterol 20.4 mg  Sodium 163 mg

# Em's Summer Squash Casserole

Lee Ann Lamb

6 to 8 yellow squash (about 2
pounds), cut up
Salt and black pepper to taste
2 tablespoons butter
1 tablespoon grated onion
1 chicken bouillon cube
1 egg, beaten
1 cup sour cream
½ cup (2 ounces) grated
Cheddar cheese
½ cup crumbled cooked bacon

- Cook squash in small amount of boiling water for about 10 minutes or until nearly tender. Drain well. Mash, then drain again.
- Combine squash, salt, black pepper, butter, onion, bouillon, egg, sour cream and cheese, mixing well. Pour into 2-quart casserole and top with bacon.
- Bake, uncovered, at 350° for 30 minutes.

Serves 8

Per ½ cup serving _____

Calories 167  Protein 5.83 g  Carbohydrates 6.61 g  Fat 13.5 g  Cholesterol 7.82 g  Sodium 321 mg

## Bacon Squash Casserole

Barbara Stromberg Boyd

2 pounds yellow squash
Salt
3 or 4 slices bacon, diced
½ cup minced onion
¼ cup chopped green bell pepper
8 crackers, crushed
2 eggs, beaten
1 cup milk
Salt and black pepper to taste
1 to 2 teaspoons margarine
¼ cup (1 ounce) grated
Parmesan cheese

• Cook squash in small amount of salted boiling water until tender. Drain well and place in mixing bowl. Break any large pieces into bite-sized chunks.

• Fry bacon until crisp. Remove and drain well.

• Retain 2 tablespoons bacon drippings. Sauté onion in drippings until tender; do not brown.

• Add onion, bell pepper, bacon, cracker crumbs, egg, milk, salt and black pepper to squash. Mix well. Pour mixture into lightly greased 8x8x2-inch baking dish. Dot with margarine and sprinkle with cheese.

• Bake, uncovered, at 350° for 25 minutes or until lightly browned.

*Zucchini squash may be substituted for yellow squash.*

Serves 8

Per ½ cup serving _____

Calories 139  Protein 5.86 g  Carbohydrates 9.81 g  Fat 9 g  Cholesterol 59 mg  Sodium 222 mg

———— ★ ————

You can cut the fat and calories in most recipes calling for fried bacon and drippings by cooking the bacon in the microwave, on paper toweling to absorb the fat, and substituting olive oil or canola oil for the bacon drippings.

# Grandma Allison's Stuffed Squash

Sally Guyton Joyner

4 medium-sized yellow squash
1 egg
¼ cup chopped onion
¼ cup chopped celery
2 tablespoons chopped pimiento (optional)
2 tablespoons low-fat margarine
1 (8 ounce) can water chestnuts, drained and coarsely chopped
½ cup cracker crumbs
Salt and black pepper to taste

- Trim ends from squash, cut lengthwise in halves and place in Dutch oven with small amount of water. Simmer until tender. Drain squash. Scoop out centers with a spoon. Place in blender or food processor.

- Add egg and blend well. Pour mixture into mixing bowl. Arrange squash halves in 13x9x2-inch baking dish prepared with vegetable cooking spray.

- Sauté onion, celery and pimiento in margarine until onion is translucent. Add to squash mixture. Stir in water chestnuts.

- Spoon squash mixture into halves and sprinkle with cracker crumbs, salt and black pepper.

- Bake, uncovered, at 350° for 30 minutes.

Every Christmas and Thanksgiving, our family enjoys this recipe.

Serves 8

Per serving

Calories 66  Protein 1.84 g  Carbohydrates 8.78 g  Fat 3 g  Cholesterol 23.4 mg  Sodium 103 mg

# *Spiced Acorn Squash*

Pamela Jones

1 *acorn squash*
2 *tablespoons margarine*
2 *teaspoons cinnamon*
2 *teaspoons brown sugar*
*Salt to taste*

- Cut squash in halves. Remove and discard seeds.
- Place squash halves in casserole. Place 1 tablespoon margarine in each and sprinkle with 1 teaspoon cinnamon and 1 teaspoon brown sugar.
- Bake, covered with aluminum foil, at 350° for 1 hour.
- Season with salt. Acorn halves may be served in the shell or pulp may be removed and mashed.

*2 tablespoons crushed pineapple and 1 tablespoon chopped pecans may be added to each half before baking.*

Serves 2

Per serving _____

Calories 214  Protein 2.12 g  Carbohydrates 29.7 g  Fat 11.5 g  Cholesterol 0  Sodium 276 mg

★

There are two basic categories of squash: summer squash, like yellow crookneck and zucchini; and winter squash, such as acorn, butternut, and spaghetti. Summer squash have soft skins and tender, moist insides, while winter squash have hard shells and meatier insides.

# Spinach-Stuffed Squash Boats

Barbara Boyd

4 yellow squash
Salt
2 tablespoons margarine, melted
Salt and black pepper to taste
½ cup grated Parmesan cheese, divided
½ cup chopped onion
¼ cup margarine
2 (10 ounce) packages frozen chopped spinach, cooked
¾ teaspoon salt or to taste
1 cup sour cream
2 teaspoons red wine vinegar
½ cup breadcrumbs
Margarine

• Cook whole squash in salted boiling water for 10 minutes or until tender. Carefully trim ends, cut lengthwise in halves and scoop out seeds.

• Sprinkle melted margarine, salt, black pepper and ¼ cup cheese into shells.

• Sauté onion in ¼ cup margarine until tender.

• Drain spinach in colander, pressing with paper towel to remove excess moisture.

• Add spinach, salt, sour cream and wine vinegar to onion, mixing well. Spoon mixture into each squash shell. Sprinkle with ¼ cup cheese and breadcrumbs. Dot with margarine. Place stuffed shells in lightly greased 8x8x2-inch baking dish.

• Bake, uncovered, at 350° for 15 minutes or until hot and bubbly.

Serves 8

Per serving _____

Calories 238  Protein 7.27 g  Carbohydrates 13.1 g  Fat 18.5 g  Cholesterol 25.4 mg  Sodium 594 mg

# Stuffed Summer Squash
*Ann Bommarito Armstrong*

*4 summer squash*
*1 cup (4 ounces) grated Romano cheese*
*½ cup breadcrumbs*
*¼ teaspoon black pepper*
*¼ to ½ teaspoon garlic salt*
*½ teaspoon basil leaves*
*½ teaspoon oregano*
*2 tablespoons parsley*
*Grated mozzarella or American cheese for garnish (optional)*
*Sliced mushrooms for garnish (optional)*
*Pimiento for garnish (optional)*
*Sliced tomatoes for garnish (optional)*

- Cut squash lengthwise in halves. Scoop seeds and pulp into saucepan, leaving shell thick enough to retain shape when cooked. Chop any large chunks of pulp to ½-inch cubes. Set aside.

- Place squash shells in Dutch oven and add water to cover. Bring to a boil, reduce heat and simmer for about 5 minutes or until tender but not softened. Drain shells.

- Combine Romano cheese, breadcrumbs, black pepper, garlic salt, basil, oregano and parsley.

- Add water to just cover seed and pulp in saucepan. Cook, stirring occasionally, until small chunks are tender and most of water has evaporated. Add enough breadcrumb mixture to form thick, moist stuffing.

- Spoon stuffing into squash shells. Garnish with mozzarella or American cheese, mushrooms slices, pimiento and tomato. Place on broiler-safe pan.

- Broil until golden.

*Use leftover stuffing mixture to fill mushroom caps, drizzle with olive oil and broil. Serve with stuffed squash.*

Serves 4

Per serving _____

Calories 136  Protein 9.73 g  Carbohydrates 9.05 g  Fat 7 g  Cholesterol 26.2 mg  Sodium 533 mg

# Fried Green Tomatoes

Donna Earle Crain

2 firm medium-sized green
tomatoes
½ teaspoon salt
½ teaspoon black pepper
½ cup white cornmeal
¼ cup bacon drippings

• Cut tomatoes in ¼-inch slices. Sprinkle with salt and black pepper. Dredge slices in cornmeal.

• Fry tomatoes in bacon drippings in heavy skillet over medium heat, turning once to brown on both sides.

Serves 4

Per serving ───────────────────────────────────────────

Calories 186  Protein 2.01 g  Carbohydrates 15 g  Fat 13.5 g  Cholesterol 12.1 mg  Sodium 280 mg

# Tomato Toppers

Jane Miller Sanders

4 large tomatoes
½ teaspoon salt
⅛ teaspoon black pepper
1 teaspoon crushed basil, divided
1 tablespoon minced green onion
¾ cup (3 ounces) shredded
Cheddar cheese, divided
2 tablespoons butter, melted
2 cups crispy rice cereal, crushed
to measure about ¾ cup

• Peel tomatoes and cut in halves. Blot cut surface with paper towel to remove excess moisture. Place, cut side up, in shallow baking dish.

• Combine salt, black pepper and ½ teaspoon basil. Sprinkle on tomatoes.

• Combine onion and ½ cup cheese. Sprinkle on tomatoes.

• Combine melted butter and remaining ½ teaspoon basil. Add cereal and ¼ cup cheese, mixing well. Spoon mixture on tomatoes.

• Bake at 350° for 15 to 20 minutes or until tomatoes are thoroughly heated and tops are lightly browned.

Serves 8

Per serving ───────────────────────────────────────────

Calories 109  Protein 3.71 g  Carbohydrates 9.29 g  Fat 6.5 g  Cholesterol 18.9 mg  Sodium 318 mg

# Fresh Tomato and Zucchini Casserole

*Nanci Norin Jordt*

4 *large tomatoes*
4 *small or 2 large zucchini squash*
½ *teaspoon basil*
1 *to 2 teaspoons whole oregano*
1 *to 2 teaspoons salt*
*Black pepper to taste*
1 *to 2 tablespoons olive or vegetable oil*
¼ *cup (1 ounce) grated Parmesan cheese*

- Peel tomatoes; cut in ¼-inch slices. Cut zucchini into ¼-inch slices. Layer half of tomatoes and then half of zucchini in large saucepan. Top with half of basil, oregano, salt, pepper, oil and cheese.

- Add remaining zucchini. Repeat layer by adding remaining tomatoes, basil, oregano, salt, pepper, oil and cheese.

- Cover and cook over medium heat for 15 to 20 minutes, or until zucchini just tender.

Serves 4

Per ½ cup serving _____

Calories 89  Protein 4.15 g  Carbohydrates 6.84 g  Fat 6 g  Cholesterol 4.92 mg  Sodium 661 mg

★

Always store tomatoes at room temperature until completely ripened, then refrigerate. Colder temperatures halt the ripening process.

# Vegetable Medley Casserole

Linda Moore

1 (11 *ounce*) *can white corn,
drained*
1 (16 *ounce*) *can French-style
green beans, drained*
½ *cup chopped celery*
½ *cup chopped green bell pepper*
½ *cup chopped onion*
½ *cup* (2 *ounces*) *grated
Cheddar cheese*
½ *cup sour cream*
1 (10¾ *ounce*) *can cream of
celery soup, undiluted*
*Salt and black pepper to taste*
½ *cup margarine, melted*
1½ *cups crushed round buttery
crackers*

• Combine corn, beans, celery, bell pepper, onion, cheese, sour cream and soup. Season with salt and black pepper. Pour mixture into 13x9x2-inch baking dish or 2-quart casserole.

• Combine melted margarine and cracker crumbs. Sprinkle on vegetable mixture.

• Bake, uncovered, at 350° for 45 minutes.

Makes approximately 6 cups

Per ½ cup serving ───────────────────────────

Calories 178  Protein 3.44 g  Carbohydrates 12.2 g  Fat 13.5 g  Cholesterol 12 mg  Sodium 553 mg

# Veggie Extravaganza

Joyce Moeller

2 *tablespoons margarine*
2 *tomatoes, cut in wedges*
1 *zucchini squash, sliced*
1 *yellow squash, sliced*
2 *carrots, sliced*
1 *onion, thinly sliced*
1 *green bell pepper, thinly sliced*
½ *cup broccoli flowerets*
½ *cup cauliflowerets*
⅓ *cup* (1⅓ *ounces*) *grated
Parmesan cheese*

• Stir fry in margarine all ingredients except Parmesan cheese, cooking just until tender.

• Pour vegetables into serving dish. Sprinkle with cheese.

*This recipe may be varied by adding or substituting other fresh vegetables. For more tender vegetables, place sautéed vegetables in casserole, sprinkle with cheese and bake, uncovered, at 300° for 10 to 15 minutes. Drain excess liquid and serve immediately.*

Makes approximately 6 cups

Per ½ cup serving ───────────────────────────

Calories 51  Protein 2.12 g  Carbohydrates 5.04 g  Fat 3 g  Cholesterol 2.16 mg  Sodium 82.8 mg

# *Vegetable* **Quesadillas**

*Barbara Bittner*

¼ cup seeded, diced tomato
¼ cup diced yellow or red bell
pepper
2 tablespoons chopped green
onion
1 teaspoon seeded, chopped hot
chili pepper
1 teaspoon chopped cilantro
2 (6 inch) flour tortillas
½ cup (2 ounces) shredded
Monterey Jack cheese
1 teaspoon vegetable oil or
margarine

- Combine tomato, bell pepper, green onion, chili pepper and cilantro. Set aside.

- In 10-inch non-stick skillet over medium heat, cook each tortilla about 1 minute on each side or until flexible. Place on plate.

- Sprinkle ¼ cup cheese on ½ of each tortilla. Top with ½ of vegetable mixture. Fold tortilla over to cover filling.

- Repeat with second tortilla.

- Heat oil in skillet and cook folded tortillas for 1 to 2 minutes on each side or until cheese is melted. Cut tortillas in halves to serve.

Serves 2

Per serving

Calories 220  Protein 9.73 g  Carbohydrates 17.4 g  Fat 12.5 g  Cholesterol 25.3 mg  Sodium 298 mg

★

Cilantro has become a staple in Texas kitchens. This fresh herb adds its distinctive flavor to a variety of foods. If it is not available fresh in your area, it is also known as coriander on the dried herb shelf.

# Italian Zucchini Pie

Mary Francis

1 tablespoon Dijon mustard
1 unbaked 9-inch pastry shell
4 cups thinly sliced zucchini
squash
1 cup chopped mushrooms
1 cup chopped onion
⅓ cup margarine
½ teaspoon salt
½ teaspoon black pepper
¼ teaspoon basil leaves
2 tablespoons parsley flakes
¼ teaspoon oregano
3 eggs, beaten
1 (5 ounce) can evaporated milk
2 cups (8 ounces) shredded
Swiss cheese

• Spread mustard in bottom of pastry shell.

• Sauté zucchini, mushrooms and onion in margarine in skillet until just tender. Stir in salt, black pepper, basil, parsley and oregano.

• Combine eggs, milk and cheese, blending well. Add vegetable mixture. Pour into pastry shell.

• Bake at 375° for 20 to 25 minutes. Let stand for 10 minutes before cutting to serve.

Serves 8

Per ⅛ wedge

Calories 374  Protein 14 g  Carbohydrates 20.2 g  Fat 27 g  Cholesterol 101 mg  Sodium 503 mg

# Mushroom-Stuffed Zucchini   Barbara Stromberg Boyd

4 medium zucchini squash
Boiling water
3 tablespoons minced onion
1 tablespoon olive oil
3 cups chopped fresh mushrooms
½ cup (2 ounces) grated
Parmesan cheese, divided
Salt and black pepper to taste
¼ teaspoon marjoram
3 slices bacon, diced, cooked and
drained

- Trim ends from zucchini. Cut in halves lengthwise and scoop out seeds. Drop zucchini into boiling water deep enough to cover. Simmer, covered, for 4 minutes or until just tender. Drain zucchini, cut side down.

- Sauté onion in olive oil until tender. Remove from skillet. Sauté mushrooms until tender, adding more oil if necessary.

- Combine mushrooms, onion, ¼ cup cheese, salt, black pepper and marjoram, mixing gently. Spoon mixture into each zucchini shells and sprinkle with ¼ cup cheese. Top with bacon. Place zucchini in greased 13x9x2-inch baking dish.

- Bake at 350° for 15 minutes or until thoroughly heated.

*Either ¼ teaspoon basil or thyme may be substituted for marjoram.*

Serves 8

Per serving _____

Calories 85  Protein 5.53 g  Carbohydrates 5.78 g  Fat 5 g  Cholesterol 6.94 mg  Sodium 193 mg

# Spinach-Stuffed Zucchini
Kathy Gordon

1 (10 ounce) package frozen
chopped spinach
4 zucchini squash
3 tablespoons chopped onion
3 tablespoons margarine
3 tablespoons all-purpose flour
1 cup milk
½ cup (2 ounces) shredded Swiss
cheese
Salt and black pepper to taste
1 tablespoon grated Parmesan
cheese

- Prepare spinach according to package directions. Drain well and press to remove excess moisture.

- Cook whole zucchini in boiling water for 5 minutes. Drain. Trim ends and cut in halves lengthwise. Remove and discard pulp, leaving ¼-inch thick shells. Place in 13x9x2-inch baking dish.

- Sauté onion in margarine until tender. Add flour and cook for 1 minute. Add milk, stirring until thickened.

- Add spinach, Swiss cheese, salt and black pepper to mixture. Spoon mixture into zucchini shells and sprinkle with Parmesan cheese.

- Bake, uncovered, at 350° for 25 minutes.

Serves 8

Per serving _____

Calories 126  Protein 5.48 g  Carbohydrates 10.6 g  Fat 7.5 g  Cholesterol 10.9 mg  Sodium 150 mg

# Zucchini Gondolas

Michelle Just-Linder

2 zucchini squash (about 1 pound)
½ cup chopped tomato
2 tablespoons chopped green bell pepper
2 tablespoons chopped green onion
1 clove garlic, minced
Salt to taste
½ teaspoon dried or 1 teaspoon fresh basil
½ teaspoon marjoram
¼ cup (1 ounce) grated low-fat mozzarella cheese

- Cut zucchini in halves lengthwise. Remove pulp and set aside. Steam zucchini shells over boiling water for 5 minutes.

- Chop ½ of reserved zucchini pulp. Add tomato, bell pepper, green onion, garlic, salt, basil and marjoram. Spoon zucchini mixture into shells. Place in 9x9x2-inch baking dish.

- Bake at 400° for 15 minutes. Sprinkle with cheese and bake for additional 5 minutes or until browned. Serve warm.

Either 1 teaspoon oregano or dill may be substituted for basil.

Serves 4

Per serving _____

Calories 42  Protein 3.4 g  Carbohydrates 5.38 g  Fat 1.5 g  Cholesterol 4.08 mg  Sodium 106 mg

★

Fresh zucchini is very perishable. Keep it refrigerated and use it as soon as possible. For a quick side dish, slice and steam zucchini, sprinkle with salt, pepper and freshly grated Parmesan cheese and enjoy.

# Stir Fried Zucchini

Nanci Norin Jordt

1 pound small zucchini squash,
cut julienne
1 medium-sized onion, sliced
3 tablespoons vegetable oil
2 tablespoons sesame seed
1 tablespoon soy sauce
½ teaspoon salt

- Stir fry zucchini and onion in oil in large skillet over medium heat for 5 to 10 minutes or until crisp tender.
- Immediately add sesame seed, soy sauce and salt, tossing to mix well.

Serves 6

Per ½ cup serving

Calories 105  Protein 3.05 g  Carbohydrates 5.61 g  Fat 8.5  Cholesterol 0  Sodium 352 mg

# Zucchini Mushroom Casserole

Stephanie O'Neil

2 zucchini squash, cubed
2 eggs
1 cup mayonnaise
1 cup (4 ounces) shredded
Cheddar cheese
½ cup chopped onion
½ cup chopped green bell pepper
½ pound fresh mushrooms,
sliced
4 slices bacon, cooked and
crumbled

- Parboil zucchini for about 2 minutes. Drain well.
- Combine zucchini with remaining ingredients, mixing well. Pour into buttered 2-quart casserole.
- Bake at 350° for 20 to 30 minutes or until center is firm.

Yellow squash may be substituted for zucchini.

Serves 8

Per ½ cup serving

Calories 311  Protein 7.28 g  Carbohydrates 5.89 g  Fat 29.5 g  Cholesterol 80.6 mg  Sodium 312 mg

# Pasta, Rice and On the Grill

What better way to end a day on Lake Austin than by pulling a grill to the water's edge. **Grilled Red Pepper Shrimp** and **Simply the Best Pork Tenderloin** served with **Island Salsa** are just as easy to prepare as burgers, and much more appealing. To re-energize add **Light Pasta Primavera** and **Lemon Cilantro Rice**. With this simple menu even the cook doesn't have to miss that final run around the lake.

*Thank you to Pier 1 Imports for the colorful serving pieces.*

# Fettuccine with Asparagus
*Laurie Shaw Davis*

1 (8 ounce) package fettuccine
½ pound asparagus, tough ends
discarded and cut in 1-inch
pieces
2 tablespoons unsalted
margarine
Pinch of white pepper
¼ cup grated Parmesan cheese

- Prepare fettuccine according to package directions. While pasta cooks, prepare asparagus.
- Sauté asparagus in margarine in skillet over medium heat for 5 minutes or until tender. Season with white pepper and cook for 3 to 5 minutes.
- Drain pasta and rinse with warm water. Place pasta in serving dish, add asparagus and Parmesan cheese, tossing to mix.

Serves 4

Per serving

Calories 302  Protein 11.2 g  Carbohydrates 45.2 g  Fat 8.5 g  Cholesterol 4.92 mg  Sodium 122 mg

# Light Pasta Primavera
*Dayna Beikirch*

1 (8 ounce) package angel hair
pasta
2 cups chopped broccoli
1 cup thinly sliced carrots
½ cup sliced green onion
2 cloves garlic
1 tablespoon dried basil
3 tablespoons low-fat margarine
2 cups sliced fresh mushrooms
½ teaspoon salt
½ teaspoon black pepper
½ cup red wine
2 tablespoons freshly grated
Parmesan cheese

- Prepare pasta according to package directions. While pasta cooks, prepare sauce.
- Sauté broccoli, carrots, onion, garlic and basil in margarine for 5 minutes or until vegetables are crisp tender. Add mushrooms, salt, black pepper and wine. Simmer for 2 minutes or until mushrooms are tender.
- Drain pasta. Serve vegetables and sauce over warm pasta, sprinkling each serving with Parmesan cheese.

Serves 4

Per serving

Calories 379  Protein 12.7 g  Carbohydrates 61 g  Fat 8 g  Cholesterol 2.46 mg  Sodium 416 mg

# Garden Fresh Pasta Marinara

Vicki Ashley Atkins

*Capellini or linguini works best*

1 (8 ounce) package pasta
1 tablespoon olive oil
2 cloves garlic, minced
¼ large onion, chopped
½ pound fresh mushrooms, sliced
2 large vine ripened tomatoes, peeled and coarsely chopped
½ cup tomato sauce
⅛ teaspoon Italian seasoning
1 tablespoon chopped fresh basil or ⅛ teaspoon dried basil
¼ cup dry white wine (optional)
Salt and black pepper to taste
Freshly grated Parmesan cheese (optional)

- Prepare pasta according to package directions while chopping vegetables for sauce.

- Heat a sauté pan at medium temperature. Add olive oil. Sauté garlic and onion in oil just until onions begin to soften.

- Add mushrooms and continue sautéing until onions are translucent.

- Add tomatoes and sauté 2 minutes more.

- Stir in the remaining ingredients (excluding Parmesan cheese) and simmer for 5 to 8 minutes, covered. (Be careful not to overcook the tomatoes! They should be soft but not mushy.) Ladle sauce over warm pasta.

- Sprinkle with freshly grated Parmesan cheese, if desired.

*For variety, add ½ pound peeled and deveined fresh shrimp and simmer until opaque, or add 2 grilled and sliced chicken breasts and simmer until chicken is thoroughly heated.*

Serves 4

Per serving
Calories 281  Protein 9.54 g  Carbohydrates 51.2 g  Fat 5 g  Cholesterol 0  Sodium 264 mg

# Spinach Cannelloni

Vicki Ashley Atkins

8 *cannelloni shells*
1 *(10 ounce) package frozen chopped spinach, thawed*
¾ *cup diced fresh mushrooms*
¼ *cup diced onion*
3 *cloves garlic, minced*
¼ *cup egg substitute*
2 *tablespoons freshly grated Parmesan cheese*
½ *teaspoon dried oregano*
¼ *teaspoon dried basil*
2 *cups low-fat spaghetti sauce*
*Chopped fresh parsley for garnish (optional)*

## Parmesan Sauce

1½ *tablespoons low-fat margarine*
1½ *tablespoons all-purpose flour*
1 *cup low-fat milk*
⅓ *cup freshly grated Parmesan cheese*
¼ *teaspoon nutmeg*
¼ *teaspoon white pepper*

- Prepare cannelloni shells according to package directions. While shells cook, prepare stuffing and sauce.
- Drain spinach, pressing to remove excess moisture. Set aside.
- Coat a large non-stick skillet with cooking spray. Place over medium heat until hot. Sauté mushrooms, onions and garlic for 2 minutes.
- Add spinach and sauté until mushrooms are tender and liquid evaporates. Remove from heat and cool slightly.
- Stir in egg substitute, Parmesan cheese, oregano and basil. Stuff each cannelloni shell with an equal part of mixture.
- Spread 1 cup of spaghetti sauce in bottom of baking dish and place stuffed shells on top of sauce. Spread remaining 1 cup spaghetti sauce over top of shells.
- Spoon Parmesan sauce down the middle of the casserole.
- Cover and bake at 375° for 30 minutes.
- Sprinkle with chopped fresh parsley if desired.

Parmesan Sauce

- Melt margarine in a saucepan over medium heat.
- Add flour and cook 1 minute, stirring constantly.
- Gradually add milk and cook until thickened, stirring constantly with a wire whisk.
- Add remaining ingredients and cook until cheese melts, stirring constantly.

Serves 8

Per serving _____

Calories 184  Protein 8.35 g  Carbohydrates 22.7 g  Fat 7.5 g  Cholesterol 6.84 mg  Sodium 484 mg

# Vegetarian Lasagna

Michelle Just-Linder

1 onion, chopped
2 cloves garlic, minced
3 cups sliced fresh mushrooms
6 cups diced fresh tomatoes
¼ cup chopped parsley
2 bay leaves
1½ teaspoons oregano
1½ teaspoons basil or more to taste
½ teaspoon thyme
1 (8 ounce) package whole wheat lasagna noodles
2 (10 ounce) packages frozen chopped spinach
1 cup low-fat ricotta cheese, thinned with ½ cup skim milk
1 (8 ounce) package thinly sliced low-fat mozzarella cheese
¼ cup grated Parmesan cheese

- Cook onion and garlic in large saucepan coated with vegetable cooking spray until onion is translucent.

- Add mushrooms, tomatoes, parsley, bay leaves, oregano, basil and thyme to onion and garlic. Simmer for 30 minutes. Add water as needed to prevent sticking. Remove bay leaf.

- While sauce is cooking, prepare lasagna noodles according to package directions. Drain and rinse in cold water to prevent sticking.

- Prepare spinach according to package directions. Drain well and press to remove excess moisture.

- Spread thin layer of sauce on the bottom of 13x9x2-inch baking dish, prepared with vegetable cooking spray. Layer noodles, sauce, spinach, ricotta and mozzarella. Repeat. Top with remaining noodles, sauce and mozzarella.

- Bake, covered, at 375° for 30 minutes. Remove cover and bake until browned. Let stand for 15 minutes before serving. Sprinkle with Parmesan cheese.

Serves 8

Per serving _____

Calories 323 Protein 22.9 g Carbohydrates 41.2 g Fat 9.5 g Cholesterol 27.5 mg Sodium 605 mg

# Shells and Cheddar Florentine
*Vicki Ashley Atkins*

2 cups uncooked shell pasta
1 cup low-fat cottage cheese
1 tablespoon Dijon mustard
⅔ cup low-fat sour cream
½ teaspoon black pepper
2 cups (8 ounces) shredded low-fat Cheddar cheese, divided
1 (10 ounce) package frozen chopped spinach, thawed and well drained
3 tablespoons chopped chives

- Prepare pasta according to package directions. While pasta cooks, prepare sauce.

- Combine cottage cheese and mustard in food processor. Process until smooth. Place in large bowl. Stir in sour cream and black pepper.

- Drain pasta well. Add to cottage cheese mixture.

- Blend 1½ cups Cheddar cheese, spinach and chives into pasta mixture. Pour into 13x9x2-inch baking dish prepared with butter-flavored cooking spray. Sprinkle with ½ cup Cheddar cheese.

- Bake at 350° for 25 minutes or until lightly browned.

*Chopped frozen broccoli or frozen peas can be substituted for spinach. Non-fat sour cream can be substituted for low-fat sour cream.*

Serves 12

Per serving _____

Calories 136  Protein 10.3 g  Carbohydrates 15.6 g  Fat 3.5 g  Cholesterol 9.92 mg  Sodium 121 mg

★

One cup of dried pasta yields approximately two cups of cooked pasta. Dried spaghetti must be measured by weight. Two ounces of dried spaghetti yields approximately one cup.

# Manicotti with Walnuts

Charlotte Woods Lipscomb

1 (8 ounce) package manicotti shells
1 (8 ounce) carton cottage cheese
1 (15 ounce) carton low-fat ricotta cheese
½ cup (2 ounces) shredded low-fat mozzarella cheese
¼ cup grated Parmesan cheese
2 tablespoons chopped parsley
½ teaspoon salt
¼ teaspoon black pepper
½ cup coarsely chopped walnuts
1 egg, beaten
1 (15 ounce) jar marinara sauce

- Prepare manicotti according to package directions. Drain and place in single layer on waxed paper or aluminum foil to prevent shells from sticking together.

- Combine cottage, ricotta, mozzarella and Parmesan cheeses, parsley, salt, black pepper, walnuts and egg, mixing well. Spoon mixture into cooled manicotti shells.

- Spread thin layer of marinara sauce in 13x9x2-inch baking dish. Arrange stuffed manicotti in single layer on sauce and top with remaining sauce.

- Bake, covered with aluminum foil, at 350° for about 25 minutes. Remove foil and bake for additional 15 minutes.

*For color, reduce ricotta cheese by ½ cup and add ½ cup grated carrot or chopped spinach. This vegetarian dish makes a hearty dinner when served with garlic bread and salad.*

Serves 8

Per serving _____

Calories 353  Protein 20.5 g  Carbohydrates 34.7 g  Fat 15 g  Cholesterol 53.4 mg  Sodium 698 mg

# Chicken in Bow Ties

*Pamela Jones*

1 (12 ounce) package bow tie
pasta
2 tablespoons pine nuts
3 skinless, boneless chicken
breast halves, thinly sliced
1 tablespoon olive oil, divided
Salt and black pepper to taste
2 small red bell peppers, thinly
sliced
2 shallots, minced
2 cloves garlic, minced
1 cup low-salt chicken broth
¼ cup balsamic vinegar
2 teaspoons chopped rosemary or
1 teaspoon dried rosemary
1 (9 ounce) package frozen
artichoke hearts, thawed

- Prepare pasta according to package directions, cooking until tender but firm. Drain and rinse with cold water. Set aside.

- Toast pine nuts in small skillet over medium heat for 3 to 4 minutes or until golden brown and fragrant, stirring almost constantly. Set aside.

- Sauté chicken in 2 teaspoons oil in non-stick skillet over high heat for 2 to 3 minutes or until just cooked through. Season with salt and black pepper. Using slotted spoon, remove from skillet and set aside.

- Sauté bell pepper, shallots and garlic in 1 teaspoon oil in skillet for 2 minutes or until bell pepper is tender. Using slotted spoon, remove from skillet and set aside.

- Pour broth and vinegar into skillet. Add rosemary. Bring to a boil.

- Add artichokes and cooked pasta to hot liquid. Cook for 2 minutes or until thoroughly heated.

- Add chicken and vegetables to pasta and toss to mix. Pour into serving dish and sprinkle with pine nuts. Serve warm.

Serves 6

Per serving _____

Calories 379 Protein 25.6 g Carbohydrates 50.5 g Fat 9 g Cholesterol 34.2 mg Sodium 187 mg

# Italian Artichokes and Chicken
Patsy Eppright

1 (12 ounce) package tricolor rotini pasta
1 clove garlic, minced
2 tablespoons butter or margarine
6 skinless, boneless chicken breast halves
1 (10¾ ounce) can cream of chicken soup, undiluted
1 cup low-fat sour cream
½ cup (2 ounces) shredded mozzarella cheese
¼ cup dry white wine
2 tablespoons grated Parmesan cheese
1 (6 ounce) jar marinated artichoke hearts, drained and cut in halves
2 tablespoons snipped parsley (optional)

- Prepare pasta according to package directions. While pasta cooks, prepare chicken and sauce.

- Sauté garlic in butter or margarine in 12-inch skillet for 15 seconds. Add chicken and cook for 5 minutes or until lightly browned, turning once.

- Combine soup, sour cream, mozzarella cheese and wine. Pour soup mixture over chicken. Cook, covered, for 7 to 10 minutes or until chicken is tender and done.

- Remove chicken to serving dish and keep warm.

- Add artichoke hearts to sauce in skillet. Cook, covered, for a few minutes or until thoroughly heated.

- Serve artichokes with sauce and chicken over well drained hot pasta. Garnish with parsley.

*Low-fat yogurt can be substituted for sour cream.*

Serves 6

Per serving _____

Calories 584  Protein 36.9 g  Carbohydrates 48.6 g  Fat 25.5 g  Cholesterol 95.8 mg  Sodium 562 mg

# Conchiglie Con Spinaci

Kari J. Tobias

1 (32 ounce) can tomatoes, undrained
1 teaspoon sugar
1 teaspoon salt
½ teaspoon black pepper
24 jumbo pasta shells
1 pound ground chicken
1 tablespoon vegetable oil
1 (15 ounce) carton low-fat ricotta cheese
1 (10 ounce) package frozen chopped spinach, thawed and well drained

- Combine tomatoes, sugar, salt and black pepper in saucepan. Bring to a boil, stirring to break up tomatoes; reduce heat and simmer, covered, for 20 minutes.
- While sauce is cooking, prepare pasta shells according to package directions.
- Sauté chicken in oil in 12-inch skillet over medium heat for about 10 minutes or until browned, stirring to crumble. Remove from heat.
- Drain spinach and press to remove excess liquid. Add spinach and ricotta cheese to chicken.
- Spread ½ of tomato sauce in 13x9x2-inch baking dish.
- Drain pasta shells. Spoon chicken mixture into shells and place on sauce in dish. Spoon remaining sauce over shells.
- Bake, covered with aluminum foil, at 375° for 40 minutes.

Serves 8

Per serving

Calories 317  Protein 23.2 g  Carbohydrates 29.3 g  Fat 12 g  Cholesterol 52.7 mg  Sodium 580 mg

# Cajun Chicken with Pasta

Patsy Eppright

½ (8 ounce) package fettuccine or linguine
2 (4 ounce) skinless, boneless chicken breast halves
⅓ medium-sized red bell pepper
⅓ medium-sized green bell pepper
1 teaspoon chopped shallots
2 tablespoons butter
½ teaspoon Cajun spice
½ cup whipping cream
Salt and black pepper to taste

- Prepare pasta according to package directions. While pasta is cooking, prepare sauce.
- Slice chicken and peppers into strips.
- Sauté chicken, red and green bell pepper and shallots in butter in large skillet over medium heat for 5 to 10 minutes or until chicken is just done.
- Sprinkle Cajun spice on chicken mixture. Stir in cream. Season with salt and black pepper. Keep warm.
- Drain pasta and rinse to prevent sticking. Add to chicken sauce and toss to mix thoroughly. Serve immediately.

Red and green bell peppers make this spicy and very colorful. Serve with salad, French bread and wine.

Serves 4

Per serving _____

Calories 371  Protein 16.7 g  Carbohydrates 26.8 g  Fat 22 g  Cholesterol 90.7 mg  Sodium 109 mg

# Cajun Chicken Spaghetti

Julie Strait

### Seasoning Mix
2 teaspoons dried thyme
1 teaspoon cayenne pepper
1 teaspoon white pepper
½ teaspoon black pepper
½ teaspoon dried basil

### Chicken Seasoning Mix
1 teaspoon salt
½ teaspoon white pepper
½ teaspoon black pepper
¼ to ½ teaspoon cayenne pepper
1½ teaspoons garlic powder
1 teaspoon ground cumin
½ teaspoon dried basil

### Sauce
1 cup chopped yellow onion
2 cloves garlic, minced
¼ cup butter, divided
2½ cups chicken broth
2 tablespoons Worcestershire sauce
2 (16 ounce) cans tomato sauce
2 tablespoons sugar
1 cup chopped green onion
2 pounds skinless, boneless chicken breasts, cubed
1 (16 ounce) package spaghetti

- Combine Seasoning Mix ingredients and set aside.
- Combine Chicken Seasoning Mix ingredients and set aside.
- Sauté onion and garlic in 2 tablespoons butter in large skillet until softened. Stir in Seasoning Mix and cook over medium heat for 8 to 10 minutes or until onion is dark brown; do not burn.
- Add broth and Worcestershire sauce to onion and garlic. Simmer for 8 minutes, stirring often.
- Add tomato sauce to broth mixture. Bring to a boil. Stir in sugar and green onion. Simmer for 40 minutes.
- Coat chicken with Chicken Seasoning Mix, rubbing to coat thoroughly. In a separate skillet, sauté chicken in 2 tablespoons butter for about 10 minutes or until cooked.
- While sauce and chicken are cooking, prepare spaghetti according to package directions.
- Add chicken to tomato sauce and continue cooking for 10 minutes.
- Drain spaghetti. Serve sauce over warm spaghetti.

*This spaghetti dish is very spicy but low in fat. To reduce intensity of flavor, use ½ amount of peppers.*

Serves 8

Per serving _____

Calories 536  Protein 34.8 g  Carbohydrates 59 g  Fat 18 g  Cholesterol 88.1 mg  Sodium 1374 mg

## Aunt Adeline's Asparagus Pasta

Ann Bommarito Armstrong

½ pound lean ground beef
1 tablespoon parsley
2 slices white bread, soaked in water
1 egg
1 clove garlic, pressed
⅓ cup (1⅓ ounces) grated Romano cheese
Salt and black pepper to taste
1 medium-sized onion, chopped
2 tablespoons olive oil
3 cups sliced fresh asparagus
1 tomato, chopped
2 cups water
1 (8 ounce) package fettuccine, linguine or other pasta, broken in 1½-inch pieces

- Combine beef, parsley, bread, egg, garlic, Romano cheese, salt and black pepper. Shape into ½-inch meatballs.
- Sauté onion in oil until tender. Add asparagus and sauté until lightly browned. Season with salt and black pepper.
- Add tomato and water to vegetables. Bring to a boil.
- Drop meatballs into sauce. Reduce heat and simmer for 20 to 25 minutes or until thoroughly cooked.
- While meatballs are cooking, prepare pasta according to package directions. Drain well and place in serving bowl.
- Add sauce to pasta, toss to mix and serve immediately.

*This recipe has been in my family since time began. My great-grandfather came to America from Sicily in the early 1900's and was convinced that unless you ate pasta at least once a day, you had not eaten!*

Serves 8

Per serving _____

Calories 299  Protein 16.7 g  Carbohydrates 32.7 g  Fat 11.5 g  Cholesterol 59.1 mg  Sodium 152 mg

# Meatballs and Wagon Wheels
Mary Lou Cindrich

1 pound lean ground beef
⅓ cup milk
⅓ cup breadcrumbs
1 egg
2 tablespoons chopped onion
½ teaspoon Worcestershire sauce
½ teaspoon salt
Dash of black pepper
1 (16 ounce) package wagon wheel pasta
1 (10 ounce) can cream of mushroom soup, undiluted
1 (8 ounce) package cream cheese, cubed
½ cup water

- Combine beef, milk, breadcrumbs, egg, onion, Worcestershire sauce, salt and black pepper. Shape into meatballs.

- Sauté meatballs in skillet until browned. Reduce heat to low and cook, covered, for 15 minutes. Remove meatballs from skillet and discard drippings.

- While meatballs are cooking, prepare pasta according to package directions.

- Combine soup, cream cheese and water in skillet and heat thoroughly, mixing to blend, until cheese is melted and sauce is smooth.

- Add meatballs to sauce and heat thoroughly. Serve over warm pasta.

Serves 8

Per serving _____

Calories 568  Protein 28.4 g  Carbohydrates 55.8 g  Fat 25 g  Cholesterol 114 mg  Sodium 629 mg

★

Both fresh and dried pastas can be found in a variety of shapes and flavors. Take a break from the same old spaghetti and macaroni - try lemon-pepper fettuccine or wagon wheel pasta instead.

# Mimi's Spaghetti

Vera Alexander Dufour

1 pound ground beef
1 medium-sized onion, chopped
2 cloves garlic, minced
3 carrots, diced
3 stalks celery, chopped
1 (16 ounce) can tomatoes, diced
2 (15 ounce) cans tomato sauce
1 (6 ounce) can tomato paste
1 (12 ounce) can cocktail
vegetable juice
½ cup water
½ cup dry red wine
2 tablespoons parsley
1 tablespoon sugar
1 teaspoon Italian seasoning
Dash of chili powder
Salt and black pepper to taste
1 (16 ounce) package spaghetti

- Sauté meat in Dutch oven until lightly browned, stirring to crumble. Drain all fat.

- Add onion, garlic, carrots and celery to meat. Cook for about 10 minutes or until vegetables are tender.

- Stir tomatoes, tomato sauce and paste, vegetable juice, water, wine, parsley, sugar, Italian seasoning and chili powder into meat mixture. Season with salt and black pepper. Bring to a boil, reduce heat and simmer for 45 minutes to 1 hour.

- While sauce is cooking, prepare spaghetti according to package directions.

- Serve topped with sauce.

*This delicious, easy and healthy recipe has been in an Italian family for several generations. Cooked chicken, sausage or ham may be substituted for beef.*

Serves 8

Per serving _____

Calories 482  Protein 27.7 g  Carbohydrates 65 g  Fat 12 g  Cholesterol 56.2 mg  Sodium 1154 mg

# Linguine in White Clam Sauce Barbara Stromberg Boyd

2 (6 ounce) cans minced clams
1 small white onion
4 cloves garlic
2 tablespoons olive oil
½ cup dry white wine or dry vermouth
¼ cup minced parsley
Salt and black pepper to taste
1 (8 ounce) package linguine
¼ cup grated Parmesan cheese

- Drain liquid from clams into blender. Add onion and garlic and process until vegetables are liquefied.

- Heat oil in large skillet over low heat. Add vegetable mixture and simmer for 5 to 10 minutes.

- Add clams, wine, parsley, salt and black pepper to vegetable mixture. Simmer, uncovered, for 30 to 45 minutes.

- While sauce cooks, prepare linguine according to package directions. Drain well.

- Serve sauce over warm linguine. Sprinkle with Parmesan cheese.

Serves 6

Per serving _____

Calories 296  Protein 15.3 g  Carbohydrates 36.9 g  Fat 7 g  Cholesterol 23.4 mg  Sodium 219 mg

# Shrimp in Champagne Sauce with Pasta

*Ginny Ashley*

1 cup sliced fresh mushrooms
1 tablespoon olive oil
1 pound shelled and deveined medium shrimp
1½ cups champagne
¼ teaspoon salt
2 tablespoons minced shallots
2 plum tomatoes, diced
1 cup whipping cream, divided
1 (8 ounce) package angel hair pasta
3 tablespoons chopped parsley

- Sauté mushrooms in oil in medium saucepan over medium-high heat until tender. Remove mushrooms from pan and set aside.

- In same saucepan, combine shrimp, champagne and salt. Over high heat, bring to a boil; when liquid boils, shrimp will be done. Remove with slotted spoon and set aside.

- Add shallots and tomatoes to cooking liquid. Boil for about 8 minutes or until liquid is reduced to ½ cup. Stir in ¾ cup cream and boil for 2 minutes until slightly thickened and reduced.

- Add shrimp and mushrooms to sauce and heat thoroughly.

- Prepare pasta according to package directions. Drain well. Toss pasta with ¼ cup cream and parsley.

- To serve, spoon shrimp and sauce over individual servings of pasta.

Serves 4

Per serving _____

Calories 659  Protein 33.3 g  Carbohydrates 52 g  Fat 28.5 g  Cholesterol 254 mg  Sodium 340 mg

# Fried Rice

Linda Uchiyama Kelley

4 slices bacon, diced
¼ pound chopped shrimp
½ cup chopped onion
1 cup bean sprouts
4 cups cold cooked rice
2 eggs, beaten
1 tablespoon soy sauce
2 green onions, chopped

- Fry bacon in large skillet until crisp.
- Add shrimp, onion and bean sprouts to bacon and cook until onion is translucent.
- Add rice to shrimp mixture and cook until thoroughly heated. Using spatula, push mixture to one side of skillet, leaving space for eggs. Add eggs and cook until set, stirring to crumble. Mix with rice and stir in soy sauce, blending well.
- Garnish with chopped green onion.

*For variety, substitute 1 cup shredded cooked chicken, 1 cup slivered ham or 1 cup slivered roast beef instead of bacon. Heat meat in 3 tablespoons oil in skillet.*

Makes approximately 5 cups

Per ½ cup serving _____

Calories 176  Protein 7.13 g  Carbohydrates 25.2 g  Fat 5 g  Cholesterol 64 mg  Sodium 186 mg

# Green Rice

Laura Pankonien

1 cup thinly sliced green onion with tops
½ cup vegetable oil
1 ½ cups uncooked regular rice
⅔ cup finely chopped green bell pepper
⅓ cup minced parsley
3 cups chicken broth
Salt to taste
¼ teaspoon black pepper

- Sauté onion in oil until softened; do not brown.
- Add rice, bell pepper, parsley, broth, salt and black pepper to onion, stirring to blend. Pour mixture into 2-quart casserole.
- Bake, covered, at 350° for 45 minutes. Fluff with fork before serving.

Bell pepper may be omitted.

Serves 8

Per serving _____

Calories 269  Protein 4.68 g  Carbohydrates 29.3 g  Fat 14.5 g  Cholesterol 0  Sodium 328 mg

# Lemon Cilantro Rice

Barbara Pate Bannister

4 cups chicken broth
2 cups uncooked regular rice
2 teaspoons salt or to taste
1 teaspoon cracked black pepper
2 medium-sized onions, minced
1 tablespoon vegetable oil
Zest of 1 lemon
Juice of 1 lemon
3 to 4 tablespoons chopped cilantro

- Pour broth into large saucepan. Bring to a boil. Stir in rice, salt and black pepper. Reduce heat and simmer for 18 to 20 minutes.
- Sauté onion in oil until translucent. Stir in lemon zest.
- Add onion mixture, lemon juice and cilantro to cooked rice, fluffing with fork. Let stand for 4 to 5 minutes to blend flavors before serving.

Instant rice can be used. Follow package directions, substituting broth for water.

Makes approximately 8 cups

Per ½ cup serving _____

Calories 105  Protein 2.99 g  Carbohydrates 19.4 g  Fat 1.5 g  Cholesterol 0  Sodium 462 mg

# Mushroom and Brown Rice Pilaf   Vicki Ashley Atkins

1 tablespoon all-purpose flour
1 tablespoon vegetable oil
2½ cups sliced fresh mushrooms
½ cup chopped onion
¼ cup chopped red bell pepper
2¼ cups chicken broth
1½ cups water
½ teaspoon salt
¾ teaspoon dried whole thyme
½ teaspoon garlic powder
¼ teaspoon ground red pepper
1 (14 ounce) package instant
brown rice

- Combine flour and oil in large saucepan prepared with vegetable cooking spray. Cook over medium heat, stirring constantly, until lightly browned.
- Add mushrooms, onion and bell pepper to flour paste. Cook, stirring constantly, until vegetables are tender.
- Stir broth, water, salt, thyme, garlic powder and red pepper into vegetable mixture. Bring to a boil.
- Add rice to vegetables and liquid. Simmer, covered, for 10 minutes or until liquid is absorbed and rice is tender. Remove from heat and let stand for 5 minutes.

Makes approximately 8 cups

Per ½ cup serving _____

Calories 115  Protein 3.26 g  Carbohydrates 21.2 g  Fat 2 g  Cholesterol 0  Sodium 179 mg

# Parsley Rice Casserole   Nanci Norin Jordt

1 cup uncooked regular rice
1 cup milk
¼ cup butter, melted
½ cup (2 ounces) grated
American cheese
½ medium-sized onion, minced
1 cup chopped parsley
1 egg, beaten
½ teaspoon salt
¼ teaspoon paprika

- Combine all ingredients. Pour mixture into buttered casserole.
- Bake at 350° for 45 minutes.

Serves 8

Per ½ cup serving _____

Calories 137  Protein 4.28 g  Carbohydrates 8.46 g  Fat 9.5 g  Cholesterol 49.7 mg  Sodium 261 mg

# Pecan Rice
*Jeanne Cassidy*

1 cup uncooked brown rice
2¼ cups chicken broth
½ cup diced green onion
1 cup diced celery
2 tablespoons margarine
1 cup toasted pecans
1 teaspoon Worcestershire sauce
¼ teaspoon salt or to taste
Black pepper to taste

- Combine rice and broth in saucepan. Bring to a boil, reduce heat and simmer, covered, for 35 minutes. Let stand for 10 minutes after heat has been turned off.
- Sauté onion and celery in margarine until vegetables are tender. Add pecans and Worcestershire sauce, tossing to mix.
- Combine rice and vegetable mixture. Season with salt and black pepper.

Makes 5½ cups

Per ½ cup serving _____

Calories 158  Protein 3.29 g  Carbohydrates 15.7 g  Fat 9.5 g  Cholesterol 0  Sodium 248 mg

# Wild Rice and Almond Casserole
*Kathy Clay*

½ pound sliced fresh mushrooms
1 cup uncooked wild rice
2 tablespoons sliced green onion
2 tablespoons chopped green bell pepper
½ cup butter
2½ cups chicken broth
1 teaspoon salt
¼ teaspoon black pepper
½ cup slivered almonds

- Sauté mushrooms, rice, onion and bell pepper in butter for about 5 minutes or until rice is golden.
- Add broth, salt and black pepper to rice mixture. Pour into greased 1½-quart casserole.
- Bake covered at 350° for 1 hour or until liquid is absorbed, adding almonds for final 15 minutes of baking time.

Makes approximately 5 cups

Per ½ cup serving _____

Calories 204  Protein 5.81 g  Carbohydrates 16.8 g  Fat 13.5 g  Cholesterol 24.9 mg  Sodium 505 mg

## Shelley's Barley Pilaf

*Martha Rife*

1 cup pearl barley
⅓ cup pine nuts, cashews or pecans
¼ cup butter
1 cup chopped green onion
½ cup chopped parsley
¼ teaspoon salt
¼ teaspoon black pepper
3⅓ cups boiling chicken broth

- Rinse barley in cold water and drain.
- Sauté nuts in butter until lightly browned. Remove nuts with slotted spoon and set aside.
- Sauté onion and barley in butter until lightly toasted. Remove from heat.
- Add parsley, salt, black pepper, nuts and broth to barley mixture. Pour into buttered 2-quart casserole.
- Bake at 350° for 1 hour and 10 minutes.

Makes approximately 4 cups

Per ½ cup serving

Calories 211  Protein 5.96 g  Carbohydrates 22.7 g  Fat 12 g  Cholesterol 15.5 mg  Sodium 461 mg

## Jalapeño Grits

*Pamela Jones*

¾ cup uncooked regular grits
3½ cups water
Dash of salt
2 eggs or ½ cup egg substitute
½ cup margarine
1½ cups (6 ounces) shredded jalapeño cheese

- Combine grits and salted water in saucepan. Bring to a boil and cook for 5 minutes. Remove from heat.
- Stir eggs, margarine and jalapeño cheese into grits mixture. Pour into 1½-quart casserole prepared with vegetable cooking spray.
- Bake at 325° for 45 minutes.

Makes approximately 4 cups

Per ½ cup serving

Calories 260  Protein 8.26 g  Carbohydrates 12.2 g  Fat 20 g  Cholesterol 75.4 mg  Sodium 318 mg

# Grilled Corn on the Cob

*Sally Guyton Joyner*

6 ears fresh or frozen corn
¼ cup plus 2 tablespoons
margarine, softened
1½ teaspoons lemon pepper
¼ teaspoon garlic salt

- Rinse corn and blot with paper towel to dry.
- Combine margarine, lemon pepper and garlic salt. Spread mixture on each ear of corn.
- Separately wrap ears of corn in squares of heavy-duty aluminum foil, twisting ends to seal.
- Grill, with cover closed, over medium coals for 10 minutes, turn and grill an additional 10 minutes.

Serves 6

Per serving _____

Calories 147  Protein 2.73 g  Carbohydrates 19.8 g  Fat 8 g  Cholesterol 0  Sodium 212 mg


# Grilled Zucchini Fans

*Sally Guyton Joyner*

2 tablespoons canola oil
¼ teaspoon garlic salt
½ teaspoon lemon pepper
6 small zucchini squash

- Combine oil, garlic salt and lemon pepper.
- Cut each zucchini lengthwise several times without slicing through stem end, creating a "fan."
- Place on hot grill with slices arranged as fan. Brush with seasoned oil.
- Grill, with lid closed, for 5 minutes on each side, basting when turning.

Serves 6

Per serving _____

Calories 61  Protein 1.69 g  Carbohydrates 4.31 g  Fat .5 g  Cholesterol 0  Sodium 4.36 mg

# Grilled Eggplant

*Jeanne Cassidy*

1 *large eggplant*
*Salt*
¼ *cup pesto*
2 *tablespoons olive oil*
4 *or* 5 *Roma tomatoes, cut in* 20 *thin slices*
1 *cup (4 ounces) shredded provolone cheese*

- Peel eggplant, if desired, and cut into 10 equal slices.
- Generously season eggplant with salt. Let stand for 30 minutes, rinse slices and blot with paper towel to dry.
- Combine pesto and oil. Brush mixture on both sides of each eggplant slice.
- Grill over medium coals, turning several times, for 8 to 10 minutes or until golden and tender.
- Place 2 thin tomato slices on each slice of eggplant and top with provolone cheese. Close grill lid and allow cheese to melt. Serve hot.

Makes 10 slices

Per slice

Calories 127  Protein 5.26 g  Carbohydrates 6.58 g  Fat 9.5 g  Cholesterol 10.9 mg  Sodium 163 mg

★

There are several varieties of eggplant, but the large, tapered, deep purple kind are the ones most often referred to in recipes. Keep them refrigerated and use them as soon as possible.

# Grilled Cajun Potatoes

Sally Guyton Joyner

4 *large potatoes, cut in ½-inch slices*
½ *teaspoon minced garlic*
⅓ *cup margarine, melted*
½ *teaspoon salt*
¼ *teaspoon black pepper*
¼ *teaspoon red pepper*
¼ *teaspoon oregano*
¼ *teaspoon paprika*
2 *tablespoons chopped parsley*

- Combine potatoes, garlic, margarine, salt, black pepper, red pepper, oregano and paprika, tossing to mix. Pour into 13x9x2-inch microwave-safe dish. Cover with plastic wrap, vented slightly.
- Microwave on high (100 percent) setting for 6 to 8 minutes, stirring halfway through cooking time. Let stand for 3 minutes.
- Place potato slices on hot grill, reserving butter mixture.
- Grill potatoes for 5 minutes on each side.
- Place potatoes in serving bowl. Add reserved butter mixture and parsley, tossing to mix. Serve immediately.

Serves 8

Per serving _____

Calories 169  Protein 2.26 g  Carbohydrates 23.5 g  Fat 7.5 g  Cholesterol 0  Sodium 210 mg

★

Allow about 30 minutes for coals to become hot enough for cooking. They should be covered in a layer of white ash. Before grilling, use a long meat fork, or tongs, to brush away the ash and your food will cook more evenly.

# Barbecued Lemon Chicken

LaNyce Whittemore

*Must be marinated at least 6 hours*

2 (2 to 3 pound) broiler-fryers,
halved or quartered, or 4 to 6
pounds chicken pieces
1 cup vegetable oil
½ cup fresh lemon juice
1½ teaspoons salt
2 teaspoons basil
2 teaspoons onion powder
1 teaspoon paprika
½ teaspoon dried thyme
1 clove garlic, chopped

- Place chicken in large heavy plastic zipper-lock bag or baking dish.

- Combine oil, lemon juice, salt, basil, onion powder, paprika, thyme and garlic in a jar and shake well.

- Pour marinade over chicken. Marinate, covered, in refrigerator overnight or for at least 6 hours.

- Remove from refrigerator 1 hour before cooking. Drain and reserve marinade.

- Grill chicken over low heat, skin side up, for 20 to 25 minutes, brushing with marinade. Turn chicken and grill, skin side down, for 20 minutes or until done.

Serves 10

Per serving _____

Calories 479  Protein 34.28 g  Carbohydrates .775 g  Fat 37 g  Cholesterol 138 mg  Sodium 533 mg

★

Before squeezing fresh lemons or limes for their juice, puncture them with the tip of a knife and heat them in the microwave for 20 seconds. They will yield more juice than when squeezed cold.

# Citrus Ginger Grilled Chicken     La Nyce Whittemore

½ cup fresh lime juice
2 tablespoons orange or lime marmalade
2 teaspoons minced ginger
1 large clove garlic, minced
¼ cup dry white wine
¼ cup safflower oil
⅛ teaspoon freshly ground black pepper
6 skinless, boneless chicken breast halves
3 tablespoons butter, softened
Lime wedges for garnish

- Combine lime juice, marmalade, ginger, garlic, wine, oil and black pepper in jar with tight-fitting lid. Shake to blend well. Reserve 1 tablespoon.

- Place chicken in shallow glass dish or plastic bag and add marinade. Marinate for 2 to 6 hours.

- Blend reserved marinade and butter, mixing with wooden spoon. Place on waxed paper or plastic wrap and roll to cylinder shape. Chill until firm.

- Grill chicken over medium heat for 7 to 10 minutes, turn and grill for additional 7 to 10 minutes, basting occasionally with marinade.

- As chicken completes cooking, bring remaining marinade to a boil and cook for 45 seconds.

- Place chicken on individual serving plates. Cut chilled butter mixture into ¼-inch slices and place on chicken. Garnish with lime wedges and serve immediately with heated marinade as sauce.

Serve chicken with steamed fresh vegetables and rice pilaf.

Serves 6

Per serving _____

Calories 295 Protein 23.7 g Carbohydrates 2.61 g Fat 19.5 g Cholesterol 88.1 mg Sodium 131.75 mg

# Chicken à la Marsha

LaNyce Whittemore

*Must marinate at least 8 hours*

¼ cup chopped cilantro
2 jalapeño peppers, seeded
3 cloves garlic
1 cup olive oil
1 cup honey
½ cup fresh lime juice
1½ tablespoons salt
2 tablespoons dried oregano or 6 tablespoons chopped fresh oregano
1½ teaspoons cumin
8 skinless, boneless chicken breast halves
1 green bell pepper, cut in rings
1 red bell pepper, cut in rings
1 yellow bell pepper, cut in rings
1 red onion, cut in rings
1 pineapple (optional), cut in rings
1 small eggplant (optional), peeled and sliced or fanned
1 lime, sliced
Cilantro

- Using food processor, chop cilantro, jalapeño peppers and garlic. With blade running, add oil, honey, lime juice, salt, oregano and cumin.

- Pour over chicken. Marinate, covered, in refrigerator overnight or for at least 8 hours.

- Drain and reserve marinade.

- Grill chicken slowly over low heat, basting frequently with marinade. Do not overcook or use high heat.

- About 5 minutes before chicken is cooked, add bell peppers, onion, pineapple and eggplant to grill, basting with marinade.

- Bring remaining marinade to a boil, cook for several minutes and serve as sauce.

- Place chicken in center of large platter, surround with vegetables and garnish with lime and cilantro.

Serves 8

Per serving _____

Calories 334  Protein 25.08 g  Carbohydrates 23.43 g  Fat 16.5 g  Cholesterol 72.6 mg  Sodium 321.2 mg

# Grilled Sherry Apricot Chicken     Cookbook Board

*Must marinate for 4 hours*

¼ cup apricot jam
2 tablespoons vegetable oil
¼ cup soy sauce or teriyaki
sauce
¼ cup dry sherry or white wine
2 tablespoons minced scallions
2 tablespoons minced garlic
2 tablespoons minced ginger
1 tablespoon fresh lemon juice
Salt and freshly ground black
pepper to taste
6 chicken breast halves

- Combine all ingredients except chicken in large bowl, mixing well.
- Add chicken to marinade, turning to coat. Marinate in refrigerator for 4 hours.
- Grill chicken over low to medium coals for 30 minutes, turning frequently and basting with marinade.

Serves 6

Per serving _____

Calories 234  Protein 24 g  Carbohydrates 5.25 g  Fat 12.5 g  Cholesterol 72.6 mg  Sodium 261 mg

──────── ★ ────────

Just before sundown on the Fourth of July, Austinites of all ages pack picnic baskets and head downtown to the banks of Town Lake for the Austin Symphony Orchestra's traditional holiday concert. The performance concludes with the playing of the 1812 Overture, the firing of the cannons signalling the beginning of an awesome fireworks display over the water.

# Pesto Grilled Chicken with Pasta       Patti Shields

2 (8 ounce) packages fresh cheese tortellini
1 cup pesto sauce
½ cup mayonnaise
¼ cup minced purple onion
4 plum tomatoes, sliced
½ cup pitted ripe olives
1 large yellow bell pepper, cut in chunks
4 (4 ounce) skinless, boneless chicken breast halves

- Prepare tortellini according to package directions. Drain well.
- Combine pesto sauce and mayonnaise, blending thoroughly. Combine ¾ cup pesto mixture, pasta, onion, tomatoes, olives and bell peppers, tossing to combine. Spoon into 8 individual serving dishes.
- Grill chicken over medium-hot coals for 8 minutes, turning once. Brush with remaining pesto mixture during final 4 minutes of grilling.
- Cut chicken into strips and place on individual pasta servings. Serve warm or chilled.

*For variety, ¼ cup red wine vinegar may be substituted for mayonnaise.*

Serves 8

Per serving _____

Calories 501  Protein 26.9 g  Carbohydrates 23.4 g  Fat 34 g  Cholesterol 160 mg  Sodium 592 mg

★

Always start with a clean grilling rack, coated in non-stick vegetable cooking spray. Position the rack about six inches above the coals.

# Rotisserie Chicken

Vicki Ashley Atkins

*Skinning the chickens is the tricky part of this recipe, but it really allows the meat to absorb the basting sauce; and, it reduces the fat and calories*

½ cup ketchup
½ cup low-fat margarine, melted
½ cup vinegar
½ cup Worcestershire sauce
½ cup fresh lemon juice
2 whole chickens, skin removed
Black pepper to taste

- Combine ketchup, margarine, vinegar, Worcestershire sauce and lemon juice, blending well.

- Place chickens on rotisserie attachment of grill. As chickens turn, generously sprinkle with black pepper.

- Grill, with lid closed, for 1 hour. Begin basting chickens with sauce and continue cooking for additional 1 hour, basting frequently. Serve any remaining sauce with chicken.

*Cooked chickens can be frozen by wrapping in heavy duty foil; thaw and reheat in same foil by baking at 350° for 1 hour. Sauce can be used as marinade for cut-up chicken or thick-sliced pork chops. Marinate for 3 to 6 hours and grill as usual. For a great moonlight dinner on a boat, serve with sweet and sour slaw, a loaf of crusty French bread and a bottle of chilled Chardonnay wine for a happy crew with no on-board cooking!*

Serves 12

Per serving _____

Calories 147  Protein 23.57 g  Carbohydrates 1.98 g  Fat 4.5 g  Cholesterol 76.7 mg  Sodium 182.1 mg

─────── ★ ───────

Most butchers will gladly skin whole chickens for you if you ask. It saves time and keeps you from having to deal with all that messy chicken skin, and removes most of the fat from your chicken.

# Basil Burgers

Jeanne Cassidy

1½ pounds ground sirloin beef
¼ cup basil pesto
1 large clove garlic, minced
¼ cup oil-packed sun-dried
tomatoes, drained and minced
Salt and freshly ground black
pepper to taste
6 slices provolone cheese
6 slices tomato
Thin purple onion slices
6 bagels, onion rolls or seed
buns, split

- Combine beef, pesto, garlic, tomatoes, salt and black pepper, mixing thoroughly. Shape into four patties.

- Brush grill rack with oil. Grill burgers to desired doneness, topping with cheese slices as cooking is completed.

- Serve burgers, topped with tomato slices and onion, on bagels, rolls or buns.

Serves 6

Per burger

Calories 602  Protein 38 g  Carbohydrates 44.2 g  Fat 30 g  Cholesterol 90.6 mg  Sodium 825 mg

# Grilled Basil-Garlic Steak

Kari J. Tobias

Must marinate for 8 hours or overnight

2 tablespoons olive oil
½ cup red wine
1 small clove garlic, minced
1 tablespoon minced onion
¼ teaspoon salt
½ teaspoon black pepper
1 bay leaf
¼ teaspoon leaf oregano
¼ teaspoon dried basil
1 (1½ pounds) boneless sirloin
steak, 1-inch thick

- Combine all ingredients except steak.

- Trim fat from steak. Place steak in dish with tight fitting lid. Pour marinade over steak and chill, covered, for 8 hours or overnight, turning steak several times.

- Grill steak for about 5 minutes on each side for medium rare.

- Thinly slice steak across grain to serve.

Serves 6

Per serving

Calories 183  Protein 23.07 g  Carbohydrates .467 g  Fat 8.5 g  Cholesterol 67.4 mg  Sodium 99 mg

## Marinated Flank Steak

Pamela Jones

*Must marinate overnight*

¼ cup red wine vinegar
¼ cup canola or extra virgin
olive oil
1 onion, minced
2 cloves garlic, pressed
½ teaspoon dried basil
½ teaspoon dry mustard
¼ teaspoon hot pepper sauce
2 (1 pound) flank steaks

- Combine all ingredients except steak and stir until well blended.
- Place steak in dish. Pour marinade over steak and chill, covered, overnight, turning a few times.
- Grill steak to medium rare, approximately 4 to 5 minutes per side.
- Thinly slice steak across grain to serve.

Serves 8

Per serving _____

Calories 230  Protein 23.32 g  Carbohydrates 1.61 g  Fat 14 g  Cholesterol 57.2 mg  Sodium 72.28 mg

## Simply the Best Pork Tenderloin

Vicki Ashley Atkins

*Marinate 8 hours or overnight*

1 cup teriyaki sauce
2 large cloves garlic, pressed
2 pork tenderloins, trimmed

- Combine teriyaki sauce and garlic in large plastic zipper bag.
- Add tenderloins. Marinate overnight in refrigerator or for at least 8 hours, turning bag occasionally.
- Remove tenderloins. Grill over hot coals or over medium high heat on gas grill for 8 to 10 minutes on each side or to desired doneness. Tenderloins may be baked at 400° for 30 to 40 minutes.

*For added zip, add 1 teaspoon freshly grated ginger to marinade.*

Serves 6

Per serving _____

Calories 202  Protein 33.8 g  Carbohydrates 2.98 g  Fat 5.5 g  Cholesterol 89.6 mg  Sodium 752 mg

# Grilled Lamb Chops

Pamela Jones

¼ cup unsalted margarine, softened
1½ tablespoons Dijon mustard
1 shallot, minced
1 tablespoon chopped parsley
1 tablespoon chopped chervil or tarragon
1 tablespoon chopped chives
Black pepper to taste
4 lamb chops, 1½-inch thick, fat trimmed

- Combine margarine, mustard, shallot, parsley, chervil, chives and black pepper, mixing well by hand or in food processor. Set aside.

- Grill lamb chops on cold grill over hot coals, turning every 2 minutes and brushing with herbed mustard. Chops will be medium rare after 5 minutes.

*For pork chops, grill for 16 minutes, basting at 4 minute intervals. For veal chops or beef, grill for 10 to 12 minutes, basting at 2 to 3 minute intervals.*

Serves 4

Per serving _____

Calories 248  Protein 26 g  Carbohydrates .904 g  Fat 15 g  Cholesterol 80.8 mg  Sodium 115 mg

★

When choosing lamb, look for bright pink flesh, pink bones, and white fat. Spring lamb is the choicest and most tender.

# Halibut with Papaya Corn Salsa
Jeanne Cassidy

## Papaya Corn Salsa

½ fresh papaya, peeled, seeded and diced
¼ cup minced red bell pepper
¼ cup minced purple onion
½ cup cooked fresh, frozen or canned corn
1 small avocado, chopped
3 tablespoons lime juice
1 tablespoon olive oil
¼ teaspoon salt

4 (4 ounce) halibut steaks or any firm fish fillets
2 tablespoons olive oil
½ teaspoon salt
¼ teaspoon freshly ground white pepper or gourmet blend pepper
½ teaspoon crumbled thyme

• Combine all salsa ingredients. Chill until ready to serve with grilled fish.

• Brush fish with oil on both sides. Season with salt, white pepper and thyme.

• Grill fish over medium-hot coals for 10 to 12 minutes, turning several times. Serve with salsa.

Serves 4

Per 4-ounce fillet with ¼ cup salsa _____

Calories 260  Protein 24.64 g  Carbohydrates 6.84 g  Fat 15 g  Cholesterol 36.3 mg  Sodium 399.4 mg

## Seafood Kabobs

Jeanne Cassidy

*Must marinate for 1 to 2 hours*

⅓ cup lime juice
3 tablespoons orange juice
⅓ cup olive oil
1 clove garlic, minced
2 tablespoons minced parsley or cilantro
1 jalapeño pepper, seeded and minced (optional)
¼ teaspoon salt
1 teaspoon brown sugar
12 medium to large shrimp
12 scallops
2 salmon steaks, cut in 2-inch pieces

- Combine all ingredients except seafood.
- Place seafood on 4 skewers, alternating shrimp, scallops and salmon. Place in a shallow dish. Pour marinade over kabobs, cover and chill for 1 to 2 hours.
- Grill over medium hot coals, turning several times, for 12 to 15 minutes, basting kabobs with marinade.

Serves 4

Per serving _____

Calories 139  Protein 15.77 g  Carbohydrates 1.65 g  Fat 7.5 g  Cholesterol 61.3 mg  Sodium 111 mg

## Grilled Shrimp Oregano

Denise Ouellette Forwood

*Must marinate at least 2 hours*

2 pounds large shrimp, peeled and deveined
¼ cup lemon juice
½ cup vegetable oil
1 tablespoon minced onion
1 teaspoon salt
1 teaspoon black pepper
1 teaspoon garlic powder
1 tablespoon oregano

- Place shrimp in bowl. Combine remaining ingredients and pour over shrimp. Cover and chill for at least 2 hours.
- Place shrimp, facing same direction, on skewers.
- Grill over low heat for 3 to 4 minutes on each side. Serve immediately.

Serves 6

Per serving _____

Calories 233  Protein 30.8 g  Carbohydrates 2.35 g  Fat 10.5 g  Cholesterol 230 mg  Sodium 377 mg

# Grilled Red Pepper Shrimp

Jeanne Cassidy

*Marinate several hours before grilling*

2 tablespoons fresh lemon or lime juice
3 tablespoons olive oil
2 large cloves garlic, minced
½ teaspoon salt
1 teaspoon cayenne pepper
⅛ teaspoon crushed red pepper flakes
1 teaspoon paprika
1 pound peeled large shrimp

- Combine all ingredients except shrimp in a sealable container.
- Add shrimp to marinade. Marinate for several hours in refrigerator, stirring several times.
- Place shrimp on 8-inch skewers.
- Grill over medium heat for 5 to 10 minutes or until shrimp are curled and firm. Serve hot or cold.

Serves 4

Per serving _____

Calories 183  Protein 23.11 g  Carbohydrates 1.86 g  Fat 9 g  Cholesterol 173 mg  Sodium 346 mg

# Grilled Tuna Mediterranean Style

Jeanne Cassidy

⅓ cup olive oil
2 tablespoons balsamic vinegar
2 tablespoons sherry or dry white wine
1 tablespoon chopped parsley
2 bay leaves, broken
2 cloves garlic, minced
2 tablespoons chopped oregano or 1 teaspoon dried oregano
¼ teaspoon salt
2 tuna, redfish, pompano or any firm lean fish steaks

- Combine all ingredients except fish. Let stand for 30 minutes to blend flavors.
- Pour marinade over fish steaks. Marinate for 30 minutes.
- Grill fish over medium heat for 15 minutes, turning several times and basting with marinade.

Serves 2

Per 4-ounce fillet _____

Calories 219  Protein 26.46 g  Carbohydrates .478 g  Fat 11.5 g  Cholesterol 43.1 mg  Sodium 89.2 mg

## Grilled Snapper Mexicana
Jeanne Cassidy

4 (6 ounce) snapper or redfish fillets
¼ cup olive oil, divided
¼ teaspoon salt
¼ teaspoon freshly ground black pepper
⅛ to ¼ teaspoon cayenne pepper (optional)
¼ teaspoon ground cumin
2 cloves garlic, minced
1 large green bell pepper, cut in ¼-inch strips
1 large onion, cut vertically in ¼-inch strips
6 Roma tomatoes, quartered, or 1 (16 ounce) can diced tomatoes, undrained
1 avocado, peeled and sliced
1 cup (4 ounces) shredded Monterey Jack cheese

- Season fillets by rubbing 2 tablespoons oil, salt, black pepper, cayenne pepper and cumin on both sides.
- Grill fish over medium coals for about 10 minutes or until done, turning several times. Place in broiler-proof serving dish and keep warm.
- Sauté garlic in 2 tablespoons oil in saucepan over medium heat for 1 minute. Add onion and bell pepper and sauté for 2 to 3 minutes. Add tomatoes and cook for additional 2 minutes.
- Pour vegetables and pan juices over fish. Top each fillet with avocado slices and ¼ cup cheese.
- Broil until cheese is melted.

Serves 4

Per serving

Calories 514  Protein 44.2 g  Carbohydrates 12.4 g  Fat 32.5 g  Cholesterol 88.2 mg  Sodium 409 mg

## Easy Marinade for Beef
Nanci Norin Jordt

1 cup vegetable oil
¾ cup soy sauce
½ cup lemon juice
¼ cup Worcestershire sauce
3 tablespoons prepared mustard
2 cloves garlic, pressed or minced
2 teaspoons coarsely ground black pepper

- Combine all ingredients, mixing well. Let stand for several hours.
- To use, pour marinade over beef. Marinate in refrigerator overnight.

Makes approximately 2¾ cups

Per tablespoon

Calories 49  Protein .495 g  Carbohydrates .893 g  Fat 5 g  Cholesterol 0  Sodium 249 mg

# All-Purpose Oriental Marinade
*Sherrie Smith*

1 cup soy sauce
1 cup sherry wine
1 cup pineapple juice
1 cup firmly-packed brown sugar
2 cloves garlic, pressed

- Combine all ingredients. Let stand for several hours or overnight.

*Delicious with any meat or fish.*

Makes approximately 4 cups

Per tablespoon _____

Calories 16  Protein .259 g  Carbohydrates 3.21 g  Fat 0  Cholesterol 0  Sodium 258 mg

# Tarragon Cider Basting Sauce
*Pamela Jones*

½ cup apple cider or juice
¼ cup vinegar
2 tablespoons honey
2 tablespoons butter
¼ cup sliced green onion
2 tablespoons prepared steak sauce
1 teaspoon salt
¼ teaspoon black pepper
1 teaspoon crushed dried tarragon

- Combine all ingredients in 1½-quart saucepan.
- Bring to a boil, then reduce heat and simmer for 20 minutes, stirring occasionally.
- Baste meat or vegetables during final 15 to 20 minutes of grilling. Heat remaining sauce to serve at table.

*Tarragon Cider Sauce has au jus consistency, ideal for basting because bold sauce flavors can penetrate and blend with food. Sauce is great for beef, poultry, pork or fish entrees and glorifies vegetable accompaniments such as grilled potatoes, mushrooms, green bell peppers, tomatoes, onions and squash.*

Makes approximately 1 cup

Per tablespoon _____

Calories 27  Protein .114 g  Carbohydrates 3.79 g  Fat 1.5 g  Cholesterol 3.88 mg  Sodium 177 mg

# The Best Barbecue Sauce Ever
Jennie Hentges

2 (32 ounce) bottles ketchup
½ cup cider vinegar
2 tablespoons Worcestershire sauce
¼ cup plus 2 tablespoons liquid smoke
4 to 6 tablespoons hot pepper sauce
¾ cup sugar
1½ cups firmly-packed brown sugar
2 tablespoons minced garlic
1 onion, chopped, or ¼ cup onion flakes
2¼ tablespoons chili powder
2½ tablespoons barbecue spice
1½ teaspoons dry mustard

• Combine all ingredients in 4-quart saucepan. Simmer for 45 minutes, stirring often.

Makes 10 cups

Per tablespoon

Calories 22  Protein .215 g  Carbohydrates 5.63 g  Fat .5 g  Cholesterol 0  Sodium 141 mg

# Island Salsa
Vicki Ashley Atkins

1 cup chopped pineapple
1 mango, peeled and chopped
1 papaya, peeled and chopped
1 medium-sized red bell pepper, chopped
2 kiwi, peeled and chopped
½ cup chopped purple onion
¼ cup chopped cilantro
2 mild jalapeño peppers, seeds removed and chopped
Juice of 1 lime
Ground white pepper to taste

• Toss all ingredients together gently. May be prepared up to 3 hours in advance but no more.

*Wonderful with grilled meats or fish.*

Makes approximately 5½ cups

Per ¼ cup serving

Calories 23  Protein .395 g  Carbohydrates 5.86 g  Fat .5 g  Cholesterol 0  Sodium 1.51 mg

# Southwest Chili Sauce

Culinary Arts Catering, Inc.

*Wear rubber gloves when handling chilies*

1 *dried guajillo chili pepper*
1 *dried ancho chili pepper*
2 *plum tomatoes*
½ *cup chopped onion*
2 *cloves garlic*
¼ *bunch cilantro, leaves only*
¼ *cup peach juice*
¼ *cup apricot juice*
¼ *cup frozen orange juice concentrate, thawed*
½ *cup water*
¼ *teaspoon cinnamon*
¼ *teaspoon ground cumin*
½ *cup toasted almonds*
¼ *cup olive oil*
¼ *cup peanut oil*
4 *teaspoons red wine vinegar*
2 *tablespoons honey or pancake syrup*
1 *teaspoon kosher salt*

- Wearing rubber gloves, stem and seed chilies. Toast in cast iron skillet over medium high heat for about 30 seconds, stirring to prevent scorching. Remove from skillet and set aside.

- Toast whole tomatoes, onion and garlic in skillet, cooking until tomato skin is blistered and lightly charred and onion and garlic are golden brown.

- Add chilies to tomato mixture. Stir in cilantro, peach, apricot and orange juices, water, cinnamon and cumin. Bring to a boil, reduce heat and simmer for 15 to 20 minutes or until consistency of syrup.

- Pour warm liquid into blender container. Add almonds, olive and peanut oils, vinegar, syrup and kosher salt. Puree until smooth.

- After sauce is prepared, 1 or 2 more chilies may be added until you find the "heat" you desire. May be served with chicken, beef or pork.

*This wonderful sauce was served over grilled chicken for lunch in the Tearoom of Austin Junior Forum's 1993 "Christmas at the Caswell House."*

Makes approximately 2 cups

Per ¼ cup serving _____

Calories 225  Protein 2.35 g  Carbohydrates 15.8 g  Fat 18 g  Cholesterol 0  Sodium 340 mg

# Soups and Sandwiches

The leaves are turning, the air is crisp and pigskin time is here. What better way to kick off the season than with a tailgate party. University of Texas fans no longer feel tied to the traditional, time-consuming fried chicken and baked beans before the game. Score a touchdown with family and friends by planning your next tailgate party around hearty, warm soups and mouth-watering sandwiches. Create a pre-game menu that allows your guests to choose either hearty **Black Bean Soup with Poblano Cream** or the lighter **Chunky Minestrone**. The choice of sandwiches can range from the filling **Greg's Favorite Sub** to **Chutney Chicken Croissants** or refreshing **Town Lake Sandwiches**.

*Photo of the University of Texas at Austin Memorial Stadium taken from the grounds of the Lyndon Baines Johnson Library.*

# Chilled Cucumber Soup

*Linda Uchiyama Kelley*

½ cup chopped green onion with some tops
2 tablespoons butter or margarine
2 cups diced seeded cucumber
1 cup chopped watercress or leaf spinach
½ cup diced peeled potatoes
2 cups chicken broth
¾ teaspoon salt
½ teaspoon white pepper
1 cup light or heavy whipping cream
Thinly sliced radishes for garnish

- Sauté green onion in butter or margarine in 4-quart saucepan over medium heat for 5 minutes; do not brown butter or onion.
- Add cucumber, watercress, potatoes, broth, salt and white pepper to onion. Bring to a boil, reduce heat and simmer for 15 minutes or until vegetables are tender. Let stand to cool slightly.
- Puree, about 1½ cups of vegetable mixture at a time, in blender until smooth. Pour into large bowl. Stir in cream.
- Chill, covered, for several hours or overnight.
- When ready to serve, float several thin radish slices on top of each serving.

*Instead of radishes, soup servings may be garnished with sprinkle of paprika or curry powder, chopped chives or cucumber slice.*

Makes approximately 6 cups

Per ½ cup serving
Calories 97  Protein 1.8 g  Carbohydrates 4.13 g  Fat 8.5 g  Cholesterol 27.3 mg  Sodium 292 mg

★

Chilled soups make a delightfully refreshing first course for spring and summer luncheons.

# Tequila Gazpacho

*Vera Alexander Dufour*

8 cups tomato juice
¼ cup tequila
4 or 5 cloves garlic, minced
1½ bunches green onion,
chopped
1 large red bell pepper, chopped
2 green bell peppers, chopped
4 cups grated zucchini squash
1 stalk celery, chopped
2 teaspoons ground cumin
Salt and black pepper to taste

• Combine tomato juice and tequila in large bowl. Add remaining ingredients, mixing well.

• Chill, covered, for 4 hours.

*For easy preparation, use food processor to chop vegetables to medium-fine consistency.*

Makes approximately 16 cups

Per ½ cup serving _____

Calories 22  Protein .865 g  Carbohydrates 4.25 g  Fat .1 g  Cholesterol 0  Sodium 256 mg

# Blackeyed Pea Soup

*Sally Guyton Joyner*

3 cups dry blackeyed peas
1 ham bone or ham hock
12 cups water
3 cups finely chopped celery
3 cups minced onion
3 cups finely chopped carrots
2 pounds smoked sausage, diced
2 cups shredded cabbage
(optional)
2 tablespoons chili powder
2 tablespoons Worcestershire
sauce
Salt and black pepper to taste
Cayenne pepper to taste

• Combine blackeyed peas, ham bone and water in stock pot. Bring to a boil, reduce heat and simmer until peas are softened. Discard ham bone.

• Add celery, onion and carrots. Cook for 1 hour.

• Add sausage to vegetables. Cook for 30 minutes.

• Add cabbage for last 15 minutes of cooking time.

• Stir in chili powder and Worcestershire sauce. Season with salt, black pepper and cayenne pepper.

*If needed, add water during cooking time. To lower fat content, slice and lightly brown sausage in skillet, drain on paper towel and add to soup.*

Makes 16 cups

Per ½ cup serving _____

Calories 152  Protein 7.12 g  Carbohydrates 10.3 g  Fat 9.5 g  Cholesterol 21.9 mg  Sodium 372 mg

# Black Bean Soup with Poblano Cream

Linda Simmons

2 cups dry black beans
1 ham hock
4 cups beef broth
2 medium-sized onions, diced
1 green bell pepper, seeds removed and diced
2 medium carrots, diced
3 stalks celery, diced
6 cloves garlic, diced
1 poblano chili pepper
1 cup low-fat sour cream
¼ cup red wine (optional)

- Soak beans according to package directions. Drain well. Combine beans, ham hock and broth in stock pot. Cook until beans are tender. Discard ham hock.

- Add onion, bell pepper, carrots, celery and garlic to beans. Simmer for about 1 hour or until vegetables are tender. Add red wine 10 minutes before serving.

- Remove stem, seeds and membrane of poblano pepper. Puree the pepper. Mix with sour cream.

- Ladle soup into individual serving bowls and garnish each with 1 teaspoon sour cream mixture.

Makes approximately 8 cups

Per ½ cup serving

Calories 109  Protein 6.32 g  Carbohydrates 14.6 g  Fat 3 g  Cholesterol 9.24 mg  Sodium 223 mg

★

Austinites don't give up their outdoor lifestyle when the weather turns cool. After a crisp, cool autumn day of sailing, nothing says "welcome home" like the smell of something simmering on the stove. And, nothing warms the soul like hearty, homemade soups and stews.

# Cheesy Chowder

*Cheryl Briggs Patton*

1 (16 ounce) package bacon, chopped
2 medium-sized onions, chopped
3 or 4 carrots, coarsely chopped
3 medium potatoes, peeled and diced
2½ to 3 cups chicken broth
1 cup milk
3 cups (12 ounces) grated American cheese
3 to 4 tablespoons all-purpose flour
Salt and freshly ground black pepper to taste
Chopped parsley for garnish

• Fry bacon in 4-quart saucepan until crisp. Remove bacon and set aside.

• Retain 2 tablespoons bacon drippings in saucepan. Add onion and sauté until translucent.

• Add bacon, carrots, potatoes and broth. Bring to a boil, reduce heat and simmer, covered, for 15 minutes or until potatoes are tender.

• Stir in milk.

• Combine cheese and flour, tossing to coat cheese. Add to soup and stir until cheese is melted. Season with salt and black pepper.

• Ladle soup into individual bowls and garnish each serving with parsley.

*This is a wonderful soup for a cold winter's night (if Texas ever has any!).*

Makes approximately 12 cups

Per ½ cup serving _____

Calories 121  Protein 5.79 g  Carbohydrates 6.63 g  Fat 8 g  Cholesterol 17.7 mg  Sodium 431 mg

# Cheesy Chicken Vegetable Soup

*Barbara Stromberg Boyd*

1 (3 pound) chicken, cut up
9 cups water
½ teaspoon salt
½ teaspoon black pepper
½ to ¾ cup chopped onion
2 cups diced celery
2 cups diced carrots
2 cups diced potatoes
1 cup cooked rice
4 chicken bouillon cubes
1 (16 ounce) package pasteurized process cheese spread, cut in chunks

- Combine chicken, water, salt, black pepper, onion and celery in stock pot. Simmer, covered, for 45 minutes or until chicken is tender.
- Remove chicken from broth. Remove and discard skin and bones. Coarsely chop chicken and return to broth.
- Add carrots, potatoes, rice and bouillon. Simmer, covered, for 1¼ to 1½ hours, stirring occasionally.
- Add cheese to soup. Stirring gently, heat until cheese is melted.

Makes approximately 18 cups

Per ½ cup serving _____

Calories 150  Protein 10.4 g  Carbohydrates 4.73 g  Fat 10 g  Cholesterol 40.3 mg  Sodium 370 mg

★

It is simple to remove the fat from stocks and broths. Simply chill the liquid in the refrigerator or freezer until the fat congeals on the surface where it can be easily lifted or spooned off. You now have a delicious, almost fat-free base for your homemade soup.

# Cheesy Zucchini Soup

Nanci Norin Jordt

2 slices bacon
½ cup chopped green onion
¼ cup chopped green bell pepper
2½ cups diced zucchini
1½ teaspoons salt, divided
1 cup chicken broth
¼ cup butter
¼ cup all-purpose flour
2½ cups milk
½ teaspoon black pepper
½ teaspoon Worcestershire sauce
1 cup (4 ounces) cubed old English or sharp Cheddar cheese spread
¼ teaspoon cayenne pepper

- Fry bacon in skillet until crisp. Remove, crumble and set aside.
- Sauté onion and green pepper in bacon drippings until vegetables are tender.
- Puree zucchini, ½ teaspoon salt and broth in blender. Add puree to onion and green pepper. Simmer, covered, for 10 minutes.
- Melt butter in heavy saucepan. Whisk in flour and cook for 2 minutes over medium heat. Whisk in milk, 1 teaspoon salt, black pepper and Worcestershire sauce. Continue to cook over medium heat.
- Stir in cheese. Cook, stirring constantly, until cheese is melted. Stir in cayenne pepper and zucchini mixture and heat thoroughly.
- Ladle soup into individual bowls and garnish each serving with bacon bits.

Makes approximately 6 cups

Per ½ cup serving _____

Calories 149  Protein 6.48 g  Carbohydrates 7.62 g  Fat 10.5 g  Cholesterol 29.4 mg  Sodium 689 mg

# Curried Cauliflower Soup

*Pam Brown*

1½ teaspoons curry powder
1 tablespoon butter
3½ cups well-seasoned chicken or
turkey broth (homemade
preferred; if canned, undiluted)
1 large head cauliflower, cut in
flowerets
1 small onion, minced
1 stalk celery, diced
½ cup half and half
Worcestershire sauce to taste
Salt to taste
Freshly grated nutmeg to taste
2 tablespoons chopped parsley for
garnish (optional)

- Cook curry powder in butter in heavy 4-quart saucepan for a few minutes, stirring constantly, to release its flavor.

- Add broth, cauliflower, onion and celery. Cook, covered, for 20 minutes or until cauliflower is very tender.

- Puree, a portion at a time, in blender or food processor until very smooth.

- Pour puree into saucepan. Add half and half, mixing well. Heat thoroughly.

- Season to taste with Worcestershire sauce, salt and nutmeg.

- Ladle soup into individual bowls and garnish with parsley.

*Soup may be prepared up to 4 days in advance. Store in refrigerator. Reheat in heavy saucepan. This fragrant, spicy soup may be served hot or chilled.*

Makes approximately 6 cups

Per ½ cup serving _____

Calories 45  Protein 2.43 g  Carbohydrates 3.24 g  Fat 2.5 g  Cholesterol 6.31 mg  Sodium 345 mg

# Mexican Chicken Soup

*Beverly Irick*

1 (3 pound) chicken, skin
removed and cut up
8 cups water
2 cups canned tomatoes, chopped
1 clove garlic, minced
½ cup chopped onion
2 (4 ounce) cans chopped green
chilies, drained
2 cups cooked pinto beans,
drained, (or 1 pound can
drained)
½ cup frozen corn
1 teaspoon cumin
½ teaspoon black pepper
6 corn tortillas, cut in narrow
strips (optional)

- Combine chicken and water in heavy saucepan. Simmer for about 25 minutes or until tender.

- Remove chicken from broth. Remove and discard bones. Coarsely chop chicken and return to broth.

- Add remaining ingredients, except tortillas. Simmer until thoroughly heated, about 15 minutes. Add tortilla strips during last few minutes of cooking.

Makes about 14 cups

Per ½ cup serving _____

Calories 107  Protein 14.4 g  Carbohydrates 4.48 g  Fat 3.5 g  Cholesterol 40.3 mg  Sodium 225 mg

★

Canned beans should be drained and rinsed before adding to soups and stews. Rinsing prevents the taste of the canning liquids from interfering with the flavor of your homemade stock.

# Aztec Corn and Shrimp Soup

Chez Z Café

1 yellow onion, diced
4 stalks celery, diced
4 cloves garlic, minced
½ cup margarine
¼ cup chopped parsley
1 teaspoon seasoned salt
1 teaspoon celery salt
½ teaspoon white pepper
2 cups all-purpose flour
3 bouillon cubes
8 cups water
2 (12 ounce) cans tomato sauce
1 tablespoon Worcestershire sauce
1 tablespoon hot pepper sauce
2 bay leaves
1 small package crab boil
1 (8 ounce) package frozen cream style corn
1 (8 ounce) package frozen whole kernel corn
2 pounds small peeled and deveined shrimp (fresh or frozen and defrosted)

- Sauté onion, celery and garlic in margarine until tender.
- Add parsley, seasoned salt, celery salt, white pepper and flour to vegetables and cook 10 minutes, stirring frequently with wire whisk.
- Dissolve bouillon cubes in 8 cups water. Add to vegetable mixture.
- Add remaining ingredients except the corn and shrimp and bring to a boil.
- Add corn and shrimp and cook until shrimp is done.
- Remove crab boil bag and bay leaves before serving.

Makes approximately 20 cups

Per ½ cup serving

Calories 93  Protein 6.18 g  Carbohydrates 10.9 g  Fat 3 g  Cholesterol 34.6 mg  Sodium 443 mg

# Tom's Roasted Corn Chowder   Beverly Woldhagen James

6 ears corn, in husks
3 large potatoes, peeled and diced, divided
3 cups half and half
6 slices bacon
1 large onion, diced
3 stalks celery, diced
2 cups chicken broth
1 teaspoon sugar
1 bay leaf
Dill sprigs for garnish

- Place corn in husks on preheated grill or in oven for broiling. Grill for 20 to 25 minutes, turning occasionally; outside will be charred. Let stand until cool. Remove husk, then cut corn from cob and set aside.

- Place ⅔ of potatoes in saucepan and add water to cover. Simmer for 15 to 20 minutes or until potatoes are tender. Drain well. Combine ½ of cooked potatoes and half and half, beating until smooth liquid.

- Mash remaining cooked potatoes and set aside.

- Fry bacon until crisp. Crumble and set aside. Discard all but 2 tablespoons bacon fat.

- Sauté onion, celery and remaining diced potatoes in bacon drippings until vegetables are tender.

- Add corn and sauté.

- Combine sautéed vegetables, broth, mashed potatoes, sugar and bay leaf in 4-quart saucepan. Bring to a boil, reduce heat and simmer for 15 minutes.

- Remove bay leaf. Stir in half and half mixture and bacon. Heat thoroughly.

- Ladle soup into individual bowls and garnish with dill sprigs.

Makes approximately 12 cups

Per ½ cup serving _____

Calories 103  Protein 3.29 g  Carbohydrates 13.2 g  Fat 5 g  Cholesterol 12.5 mg  Sodium 113 mg

# Crab Bisque

Mary Lou Cindrich

1 medium-sized onion, diced
½ cup butter
½ cup all-purpose flour
1 teaspoon garlic salt
1 drop hot pepper sauce
1 teaspoon dry mustard
1 tablespoon paprika
1 tablespoon chicken bouillon granules
White pepper to taste
5 cups milk or half and half
1 cup dry vermouth or dry white wine
2 cups crab meat
Splash of dry sherry
¼ cup chopped parsley

- Sauté onion in butter in heavy saucepan until onion is transparent.
- Add flour and cook until bubbly.
- Combine garlic salt, hot pepper sauce, mustard, paprika, bouillon, white pepper and milk. Add to onion mixture. Bring to a boil, stirring constantly.
- Add wine. Bring to a boil, reduce heat and simmer for 20 to 30 minutes, stirring occasionally.
- Stir in crab meat and sherry. Heat thoroughly but do not boil.
- Add parsley just before serving.

Makes approximately 8 cups

Per ½ cup serving _____

Calories 149  Protein 6.11 g  Carbohydrates 7.83 g  Fat 9.5 g  Cholesterol 39.7 mg  Sodium 454 mg

# French Country Lentil Soup

Jeanne Cassidy

*Freezes well*

1 (16 ounce) package dried lentils
1 large onion, chopped
2 tablespoons olive oil
4 carrots, coarsely grated
1 teaspoon fines herbes
1 (29 ounce) can tomatoes, chopped, with juice
4 (10½ ounce) cans beef consommé
2 cloves garlic, minced
3 tablespoons brown sugar
⅔ cup dry red wine
½ cup chopped parsley
Salt and black pepper to taste

- Rinse lentils. Soak in water to cover for several hours or overnight. Drain.
- Sauté onion in olive oil in stock pot for 5 minutes.
- Add lentils, carrots, fines herbes, tomatoes, consommé, garlic and brown sugar to onion. Simmer for 45 minutes to 1 hour or until lentils are tender.
- Add wine and parsley. Season with salt and black pepper. Simmer for 5 minutes, adding water if needed for desired consistency.

*Great with French bread and a glass of red wine. Favorite dried herbs may be substituted for fines herbes, or a combination of thyme, oregano, rosemary, sage and basil to measure 1 teaspoon.*

Makes approximately 10 cups

Per ½ cup serving _____

Calories 131  Protein 9.67 g  Carbohydrates 19.1 g  Fat 1.5 g  Cholesterol 0  Sodium 490 mg

# Chunky Minestrone

*Vicki Ashley Atkins*

1½ cups chopped onion
2 medium carrots, sliced
1 clove garlic, minced
2 teaspoons olive oil
½ cup uncooked long grain rice
1 teaspoon Italian seasoning
3 cups water
1 (29 ounce) can chopped
tomatoes, undrained
2 (10½ ounce) cans beef
consommé
2 tablespoons ketchup
2 medium zucchini squash, cut
in halves lengthwise, then sliced
1 (15½ ounce) can garbanzo
beans, drained
1 (10 ounce) package frozen
chopped spinach, thawed and
drained
¼ teaspoon salt
¼ teaspoon black pepper
⅔ cup (2⅔ ounces) freshly
grated Parmesan cheese

- Sauté onion, carrots and garlic in olive oil in stock pot over medium-high heat for 3 minutes.

- Add rice, Italian seasoning, water, tomatoes, consommé and ketchup to vegetables. Bring to a boil, reduce heat and simmer, covered, for 20 minutes.

- Add zucchini, garbanzo beans, spinach, salt and black pepper to vegetables. Cook for 5 minutes.

- Ladle soup into individual bowls and sprinkle with Parmesan cheese.

Makes approximately 15 cups

Per ½ cup serving ⎯⎯⎯⎯⎯⎯⎯⎯⎯⎯⎯⎯⎯⎯⎯⎯⎯⎯⎯

Calories 67  Protein 4.08 g  Carbohydrates 9.93 g  Fat 1.5 g  Cholesterol 1.75 mg  Sodium 229 mg

# Gourmet Mushroom Soup

*Donna Earle Crain*

1 *medium-sized onion, chopped*
2 *teaspoons butter*
½ *pound fresh mushrooms,
sliced*
2 *to 3 tablespoons all-purpose
flour*
4 *cups beef consommé*
1 *cup whipping cream*
*Dash of black pepper*
*Pinch of nutmeg*
¼ *cup vermouth or sherry
(optional)*

• Sauté onion in butter in 4-quart saucepan until onion is browned.

• Add mushrooms to onion and sauté until tender.

• Stir in flour, mixing to coat mushrooms. Cook for 5 minutes over medium-high heat, stirring occasionally to prevent burning.

• Add consommé, stirring constantly.

• Add cream, black pepper and nutmeg, blending well; do not boil. Reduce heat and simmer for 10 minutes.

• Stir in vermouth just before serving.

Makes approximately 6 cups.

Per ½ cup serving

Calories 97  Protein 2.84 g  Carbohydrates 3.83 g  Fat 8 g  Cholesterol 28.9 mg  Sodium 227 mg

———★———

To lower the fat and calories in your favorite cream soup recipes, try replacing the cream with equal parts of lowfat milk and cottage cheese processed until smooth in a blender or food processor. This mixture should also allow you to eliminate any butter and flour used for thickening.

# Mushroom Cheese Soup
Nanci Norin Jordt

4 (10¾ ounce) cans cream of
mushroom soup, undiluted
2 cups half and half
2 cups milk
1 cup sour cream
2 cups (8 ounces) cubed
pasteurized process cheese spread
½ teaspoon cayenne pepper
1 pound fresh mushrooms,
trimmed and sliced
¼ cup dry white wine

- Combine soup, half and half, milk, sour cream, cheese and cayenne pepper in stock pot, stirring well. Cook over medium heat until cheese is melted, stirring constantly.
- Add mushrooms to soup. Simmer for 20 to 30 minutes, stirring frequently.
- Stir in wine just before serving.

*To prepare in advance, omit wine. Set soup aside to cool, then refrigerate. Reheat and add wine just before serving. To reduce calories, substitute skim milk for half and half and use low-fat sour cream.*

Makes approximately 14 cups

Per ½ cup serving _____

Calories 131  Protein 4.18 g  Carbohydrates 6.05 g  Fat 10 g  Cholesterol 20.4 mg  Sodium 489 mg

# Mushroom Rice Soup
Gwen Walden Irwin

2 medium-sized onions, chopped
½ pound fresh mushrooms,
sliced
3 tablespoons butter
2 tablespoons all-purpose flour
5 cups chicken broth
1 tablespoon uncooked long
grain rice
1 bay leaf
Salt and black pepper to taste

- Sauté onion and mushrooms in butter in 4-quart saucepan over medium heat until vegetables are softened.
- Sprinkle flour on vegetables and stir until smooth.
- Add broth, stirring constantly, and bring to a boil. Stir in rice and bay leaf. Reduce heat and simmer, covered, for 15 to 20 minutes.
- Remove bay leaf. Season with salt and black pepper.

Makes approximately 8 cups

Per ½ cup serving _____

Calories 47  Protein 2.19 g  Carbohydrates 3.57 g  Fat 2.5 g  Cholesterol 5.82 mg  Sodium 399 mg

# French Onion Soup

*Debbie Harris*

5 pounds yellow onions, thinly
sliced
6 tablespoons butter
2 tablespoons olive oil
½ teaspoon sugar
2 teaspoons salt
¼ cup plus 1 tablespoon all-
purpose flour
14 cups boiling beef broth
1½ cups dry white wine
⅓ cup cognac
2 (8 inch) French baguettes, cut
in 1-inch slices and toasted
4 cups (16 ounces) coarsely
grated Swiss and Parmesan
cheese, mixed

- Simmer onions in butter and olive oil in stock pot for 2 hours, stirring frequently and adding sugar and salt after 15 minutes of cooking time. Onions will become golden brown.

- Sprinkle flour on onions and cook for 5 minutes.

- Add boiling broth and wine. Simmer for 45 minutes, skimming if necessary.

- Just before serving, bring to a boil. Add cognac.

- Ladle soup into heated individual bowls. Top each serving with bread rounds and generous sprinkling of cheese.

Makes approximately 16 cups

Per ½ cup serving _____

Calories 168  Protein 7.44 g  Carbohydrates 15.1 g  Fat 7.5 g  Cholesterol 17.9 mg  Sodium 646 mg

★

Do not store garlic or onions in the refrigerator. They should be stored in an open container in a dry, dark place where air can circulate around them.

# Baked Potato Soup

Gwen Waldin Irwin

4 large baking potatoes
⅔ cup butter or margarine
⅔ cup all-purpose flour
6 cups milk
¾ teaspoon salt
½ teaspoon black pepper
4 green onions, chopped, divided
12 slices bacon, cooked and crumbled, divided
1¼ cups (5 ounces) shredded Cheddar cheese, divided
1 cup sour cream

- Pierce potato skins several times with fork. Bake at 400° for 1 hour or until tender. Let stand until cool. Cut potatoes into halves lengthwise, scoop out pulp and set aside; discard skins.
- Melt butter in heavy saucepan over low heat. Add flour, stirring until smooth. Cook for 1 minute, stirring constantly.
- Gradually add milk. Cook over medium heat, stirring constantly, until mixture is thickened and bubbly.
- Add potato pulp, salt, pepper and 2 tablespoons green onion, ½ cup bacon and 1 cup cheese. Cook until thoroughly heated.
- Stir in sour cream.
- Ladle soup into individual bowls and garnish with remaining onion, bacon and cheese. Chopped tomatoes and chopped jalapeño peppers may also be used.

*Potato skins may be left on potatoes. Add extra milk for thinner consistency if desired. Low-fat milk and low-fat sour cream may be substituted.*

Makes approximately 12 cups

Per ½ cup serving

Calories 186  Protein 5.77 g  Carbohydrates 12.7 g  Fat 12.5 g  Cholesterol 35.2 mg  Sodium 242 mg

# Minnesota Wild Rice Soup
Barbara Stromberg Boyd

½ cup minced onion
¼ cup finely chopped celery
¼ cup finely chopped carrots
2 tablespoons butter
1½ cups sliced fresh mushrooms
(about ¼ pound)
¼ cup all-purpose flour
¾ teaspoon salt
¼ teaspoon freshly ground white
pepper
2 cups beef broth
1 cup half and half or whipping
cream
1 cup cooked wild rice (not
instant or precooked)
⅛ teaspoon bitters
1 tablespoon fresh chervil or ¾
teaspoon dried chervil
2 tablespoons brandy or dry
white wine
¼ cup blanched sliced almonds

- Sauté onion, celery and carrots in butter in 3-quart saucepan for 3 minutes or until onion is softened.

- Add mushrooms and cook over low heat for 3 to 4 minutes.

- Stir flour, salt and pepper into vegetables. Cook, while stirring, until mixture is bubbly and golden brown.

- Add broth and half and half, whisking to blend and cooking over low heat until thickened and smooth.

- Stir in wild rice, bitters, chervil, brandy and almonds. Heat thoroughly over low heat; do not scorch.

*For variety, 2 cups sliced cooked duck may be added to soup.*

Makes approximately 6 cups

Per ½ cup serving ————————————————————

Calories 94  Protein 2.66 g  Carbohydrates 7.58 g  Fat 5.5 g  Cholesterol 12.6 mg  Sodium 296 mg

## Carmelita's Tortilla Soup
Cheryl Briggs Patton

1 (2 to 3 pound) chicken or 6 chicken breast halves
1½ large onions, diced
1 (4 ounce) can diced green chilies, drained
1 tablespoon vegetable oil
2 fresh serrano peppers, finely chopped
1 (10 ounce) can tomatoes with green chilies, undrained
8 cups chicken broth
2 large tomatoes, chopped
2 cloves garlic, mashed
Salt to taste
Ground cumin to taste
Juice of 2 limes
8 corn tortillas, cut in strips
¼ cup (1 ounce) grated Monterey Jack cheese (optional)

- Boil chicken in 3 quarts of water until tender. Remove chicken and set aside.

- Strain broth and set aside. Discard skin and bones from chicken. Chop into bite-sized pieces and add to broth.

- Sauté onion and green chilies in oil until tender. Stir in serrano peppers.

- Reheat broth and chicken. Add sautéed vegetables, tomatoes and garlic. Season with salt and cumin. Stir in lime juice. Simmer soup until thoroughly heated, adding tortilla strips just before serving.

- Ladle soup into individual bowls and sprinkle each serving with cheese.

Makes approximately 12 cups

Per ½ cup serving _____

Calories 83  Protein 8.48 g  Carbohydrates 7.35 g  Fat 2 g  Cholesterol 19.2 mg  Sodium 489 mg

## Sopa de Tortilla

*Rhonda Copeland Gracely*

1 ½ cups chopped onion
1 (4 ounce) can diced green
chilies, drained
2 cloves garlic, minced
1 tablespoon margarine
1 (16 ounce) can tomatoes,
chopped
2 cups beef broth
2 cups chicken broth
1 cup water
1 ½ cups tomato juice
1 teaspoon salt
¼ teaspoon black pepper
1 teaspoon cumin seed
1 tablespoon chili powder
2 tablespoons Worcestershire
sauce
1 tablespoon picanté sauce or
more to taste
1 ½ cups shredded cooked chicken
6 corn tortillas, cut in small
pieces
1 ½ cups (6 ounces) shredded
Cheddar cheese

- Sauté onion, chilies and garlic in margarine in heavy saucepan until vegetables are tender.
- Add tomatoes and liquids. Stir in seasonings, Worcestershire sauce and picanté sauce, mixing well. Simmer, covered, for 15 to 20 minutes.
- Stir in chicken, tortillas and cheese. Simmer for 10 minutes more.

*A great recipe for satisfying the "Mexican food" urge without a lot of calories. Cheese may be omitted to further reduce calories.*

Makes approximately 12 cups

Per ½ cup serving _____

Calories 93  Protein 7.23 g  Carbohydrates 6.88 g  Fat 4.5 g  Cholesterol 19.2 mg  Sodium 453 mg

# Texas Turkey and Dumplings

Vicki Ashley Atkins

1 *pound ground turkey*
1 *cup chopped onion*
1 *cup chopped green bell pepper*
¼ *teaspoon salt*
¼ *teaspoon coarsely ground black pepper*
¼ *cup chili powder*
1 *teaspoon dried oregano*
¼ *to* ½ *teaspoon cayenne pepper (or to taste)*
3 *cups water*
1 *(29 ounce) can whole tomatoes, undrained*
1 *(15 ounce) can black beans, drained*
1 *(10 ounce) package frozen corn*
1 *(6 ounce) can tomato paste*
⅔ *cup all-purpose flour*
⅔ *cup yellow cornmeal*
2 *teaspoons baking powder*
¼ *teaspoon salt*
2 *tablespoons chilled margarine, diced*
2 *tablespoons minced parsley*
⅔ *cup low-fat milk*

- Prepare Dutch oven with vegetable cooking spray. Place over medium heat until hot.
- Place turkey, onion, bell pepper and seasonings in Dutch oven. Cook until turkey is browned and vegetables are tender.
- Add water, tomatoes, beans, corn and tomato paste. Bring to a boil, reduce heat and simmer, uncovered, for 30 minutes, stirring occasionally.
- Combine flour, cornmeal, baking powder and salt. Cut in margarine until mixture resembles coarse meal. Stir in parsley. Add milk, stirring just until moistened.
- Drop batter by tablespoonfuls into hot soup. Do not stir. Simmer, uncovered, for 10 minutes. Cover, cook for 10 minutes more or until dumplings are done.

Makes approximately 12 cups soup and 12 dumplings

Per 1 cup serving with 1 dumpling _____

Calories 260  Protein 16.8 g  Carbohydrates 32.5 g  Fat 8 g  Cholesterol 39.6 mg  Sodium 1055 mg

# Baked Cheese Sandwiches
Judy Fitzgerald Fincannon

4 cups (16 ounces) grated
longhorn Cheddar cheese
1 cup butter or margarine,
softened
2 medium-sized onions, grated
Hot pepper sauce to taste
Worcestershire sauce to taste
Garlic powder to taste
Horseradish to taste
1½ (16 ounce) loaves thin sliced
sandwich bread

- Combine cheese, butter and onion, mixing well. Add hot pepper and Worcestershire sauces, garlic powder and horse-radish, blending thoroughly.
- Spread cheese mixture on ½ of bread slices. Top with remaining slices.
- Trim crusts and cut sandwiches into desired sizes. Place on baking sheet.
- Bake, uncovered at 400° for 10 to 15 minutes.

*Sandwiches may be assembled, frozen, thawed and baked.*

Serves 18

Per sandwich _____
Calories 347  Protein 11.4 g  Carbohydrates 29.5 g  Fat 20.5 g  Cholesterol 55.8 mg  Sodium 549 mg

──────── ★ ────────

Make a plain sandwich extra-special by starting with a wonderfully textured whole-grain bread. Or, try tucking your fillings into French bread slices or Greek pita pockets.

# Mozzarella and Roasted Pepper Sandwiches

*Jane Miller Sanders*

4 *pitted Greek style black olives*
1 *tablespoon fresh lemon juice*
¼ *cup olive oil*
½ *clove garlic*
⅛ *teaspoon cayenne pepper*
4 (4 *inch*) *pieces Italian bread*
1 *large yellow or red bell pepper,*
  *roasted and quartered*
1 (8 *ounce*) *package sliced*
  *mozzarella cheese*
1 *cup loosely-packed fresh basil*
  *leaves*

- In a blender, blend olives, lemon juice, oil, garlic and cayenne pepper until mixture is smooth.
- Slice the bread horizontally into thirds and remove the middle bread slices and discard (or save for breadcrumbs or croutons).
- Brush the cut sides of the bread tops and bottoms with olive mixture (dressing).
- Layer the roasted pepper, mozzarella cheese and basil leaves on the bottom halves of the bread.
- Cover the sandwiches with the top halves of the bread and press firmly.
- Serve immediately.

*Sandwich may be heated slightly to melt cheese, if desired. To prepare roasted peppers, secure pepper on long handled fork. Singe over gas flame or roast under a broiler, singeing or burning skin evenly. Place pepper in small paper bag and close securely. Let stand 5 to 10 minutes to steam pepper. Remove from bag. Remove skin, seed and inner membranes from pepper. Slice remaining portion.*

Serves 4

Per sandwich _____

Calories 456  Protein 16.8 g  Carbohydrates 33.7 g  Fat 28.5 g  Cholesterol 44.5 mg  Sodium 590 mg

# Swiss Sandwich Loaf

*Barbara Bittner*

3 cups (12 ounces) shredded
Swiss cheese
⅔ cup chopped tomato
½ cup chopped green onion
⅔ cup mayonnaise
1 (7 inch) round loaf
pumpernickel

- Combine cheese, tomato, onion and mayonnaise.
- Slice bread crosswise to form 11 slits; do not cut completely through bottom of loaf.
- Spread filling in alternate slits. Wrap loaf in aluminum foil.
- Bake at 325° for about 30 minutes or until cheese is melted.
- Separate into 6 sandwiches.

*Loaf may be left intact and separated just before serving. The filling is also very good for grilled sandwiches.*

Serves 6

Per sandwich _____

Calories 272  Protein 10.8 g  Carbohydrates 17.2 g  Fat 18 g  Cholesterol 31.9 mg  Sodium 357 mg

# Chutney Chicken Croissants

*Lori Hamilton Cooke*

1 (8 ounce) carton whipped
cream cheese
3 tablespoons chopped chutney
1½ teaspoons curry powder
2 cups chopped cooked chicken
6 croissants, split horizontally
¾ cup alfalfa sprouts

- Combine cream cheese, chutney and curry powder, mixing well.
- Add chicken and stir thoroughly.
- Spread chicken mixture on bottom halves of croissants. Top with alfalfa sprouts and tops of croissants.

Serves 6

Per sandwich _____

Calories 487  Protein 21.4 g  Carbohydrates 30.9 g  Fat 29 g  Cholesterol 126 mg  Sodium 595 mg

# Creamy Chicken and Ham Sandwiches

*Vicki Ashley Atkins*

½ cup sliced fresh mushrooms
¼ cup diced green onion
¼ cup diced red bell pepper
1 tablespoon low-fat margarine
3 tablespoons cornstarch
1 cup low-fat (2 percent) milk, divided
¼ cup dry white wine
½ cup chicken broth
½ teaspoon dried thyme
¼ teaspoon white pepper
¼ teaspoon dried rosemary
1 cup diced cooked chicken breast
1 cup diced cooked lean ham
½ cup (2 ounces) grated low-fat Swiss cheese
3 English muffins, split and toasted
Parsley for garnish

- Sauté mushrooms, green onion and bell pepper in margarine until vegetables are just tender.
- Combine cornstarch with ¼ cup milk, blending well. Add cornstarch liquid, ¾ cup milk, wine, broth, thyme, white pepper and rosemary to vegetables. Simmer, stirring constantly, until thickened.
- Add chicken, ham and cheese to sauce. Heat, stirring constantly, until cheese is melted.
- Spread chicken mixture on toasted muffin halves. Garnish with parsley.

Serves 6

Per muffin half _____

217 calories  Protein 20.1 g  Carbohydrates 20.5 g  Fat 5 g  Cholesterol 39.7 mg  Sodium 607 mg

★

It is best to assemble sandwiches just before serving, but if you must prepare them ahead, wrap each sandwich individually in plastic wrap or foil, creating an airtight package. If you are using lettuce and tomato, wrap them separately and add just before eating.

# Corned Beef on Onion Rolls

Nanci Norin Jordt

1 cup chopped cooked corned beef
½ cup mayonnaise or salad dressing
⅓ cup minced celery
1 tablespoon minced onion
2 tablespoons prepared mustard
4 onion hard rolls, split

- Combine all ingredients except hard rolls and mix well.
- Spread corned beef mixture on bottom halves of onion rolls. Cover with top halves of rolls.

Thousand Island dressing may be substituted for mayonnaise.

Serves 4

Per sandwich _____

Calories 397  Protein 13.1 g  Carbohydrates 20.3 g  Fat 29.5 g  Cholesterol 46.3 mg  Sodium 791 mg

# Rachel Sandwiches

Nanci Norin Jordt

Prepare and chill slaw several hours before assembling

2½ cups shredded cabbage
½ cup chopped celery
¼ cup diced green bell pepper
¼ cup diced cucumber
3 tablespoons minced onion
¼ teaspoon salt
Dash of black pepper
12 slices rye bread
1 (8 ounce) package sliced Swiss cheese
½ pound sliced cooked corned beef
½ cup mayonnaise or salad dressing
2 to 3 tablespoons half and half
½ cup toasted slivered almonds

- Combine cabbage, celery, bell pepper, cucumber, onion, salt and black pepper. Chill until ready to assemble sandwiches.
- Layer cheese and corned beef on 6 slices bread.
- Blend mayonnaise with half and half. Add dressing and almonds to chilled cabbage mixture and toss to mix thoroughly.
- Spoon on top of corned beef slices. Cover with remaining bread slices.

Sandwiches can be grilled for best flavor. Butter both sides of assembled sandwiches and grill until lightly browned.

Serves 6

Per sandwich _____

Calories 571  Protein 26.6 g  Carbohydrates 31.8  Fat 40 g  Cholesterol 84.4 mg  Sodium 1553 mg

# Hot Ham Sandwiches
*Carla Fisher*

½ cup butter, melted
2 tablespoons mustard
½ teaspoon Worcestershire sauce
1 teaspoon minced onion
1 tablespoon poppy seeds
8 sandwich buns, split
1 pound thinly sliced ham
1 (8 ounce) package sliced Swiss,
Cheddar or American cheese

- Combine melted butter, mustard, Worcestershire sauce, onion and poppy seed, mixing well.
- Spread on buns. Layer ham and cheese on buns.
- Wrap for freezing. Freeze.
- To serve, bake sandwiches in foil at 350° for 20 minutes.

Serves 8

Per sandwich

Calories 406  Protein 21.4 g  Carbohydrates 25 g  Fat 24 g  Cholesterol 80.9 mg  Sodium 1671 mg

# Greg's Favorite Sub
*Nanci Norin Jordt*

1 (16 ounce) loaf French bread
Butter or margarine, softened, or
mayonnaise
1 tablespoon wine vinegar
1 tablespoon olive oil
¼ teaspoon garlic salt
4 or 5 crisp lettuce leaves
½ pound sliced salami
2 tomatoes, sliced
Salt and black pepper
1 (4 ounce) package sliced Swiss
cheese
½ pound sliced boiled ham
½ cucumber, thinly sliced
1 large onion, sliced

- Cut bread in thirds horizontally. Set center third aside for croutons or breadcrumbs. Spread cut surface of bottom third with butter.
- Combine vinegar, olive oil and garlic salt, blending well.
- Dip lettuce leaves in dressing. Layer lettuce leaves, salami and tomato slices on buttered bread. Season with salt and black pepper.
- Layer cheese, ham, cucumber and onion on tomatoes. Cover with bread top. Secure with wooden picks.
- Cut assembled loaf crosswise into 6 sandwiches.

Serves 6

Per sandwich

Calories 471  Protein 24.8 g  Carbohydrates 45.9 g  Fat 20.5 g  Cholesterol 62.3 mg  Sodium 1968 mg

# Sub Sandwich Deluxe

Millie Warden Skidmore

1 loaf fresh French bread
Low-fat mayonnaise-type salad
dressing to taste
Prepared mustard to taste
¼ pound thinly sliced cooked
turkey breast
¼ pound thinly sliced honey
baked ham
¼ pound thinly sliced roast beef
1 (4 ounce) package cojack
cheese, thinly sliced
1 tomato, thinly sliced
¼ to ½ green bell pepper, thinly
sliced
1 or 2 green onions, thinly sliced
3 or 4 medium lettuce leaves

- Cut French bread in half lengthwise.
- Spread salad dressing and mustard on both sides of the bread to your taste.
- Layer meats on half of bread.
- Layer cheese on meat.
- Layer tomato, bell pepper, onion and lettuce on top of the cheese.
- Place the other half of the bread on top to make a very large sandwich.
- Slice into smaller portions to serve.

Serves 8

Per sandwich

Calories 319  Protein 20.4 g  Carbohydrates 31.9 g  Fat 12 g  Cholesterol 46.5 mg  Sodium 680 mg

# Curried Tuna Sandwich

Michelle Beauchat Zogas

2 (6⅛ ounce) cans water-packed
light tuna, drained and flaked
1 medium apple, chopped
½ cup mayonnaise
½ cup low-fat plain yogurt
2 teaspoons lemon juice
2 tablespoons minced onion
2 teaspoons curry powder
4 whole wheat pitas
3 carrots, grated

- Combine tuna, apple, mayonnaise, yogurt, lemon juice, onion and curry powder, mixing well.
- Cut pitas in halves crosswise. Spoon tuna mixture into each half. Stuff grated carrots into pitas.

Serves 8

Per half pita

Calories 247  Protein 15.3 g  Carbohydrates 19.8 g  Fat 12.5 g  Cholesterol 22.9 mg  Sodium 374 mg

# Tuna Dill Sandwich
Kari J. Tobias

½ cup non-fat mayonnaise-type
salad dressing
¼ teaspoon black pepper
½ teaspoon dillweed
1 (6⅛ ounce) can water-packed
tuna, drained
½ cup chopped purple onion
2 tablespoons shredded carrot
2 English muffins, split
4 lettuce leaves
4 slices non-fat American cheese

- Combine salad dressing, black pepper and dillweed. Add tuna, onion and carrots, mixing well.
- Place lettuce leaf on each muffin half, add cheese slice and top with tuna mixture.

Serves 4

Per muffin half _____

Calories 196  Protein 20.9 g  Carbohydrates 24.9 g  Fat 1 g  Cholesterol 18.1 mg  Sodium 1046 mg

# Pam's Tuna Sandwiches
Martha Rife

1 (6⅛ ounce) can water-packed
light tuna, drained and flaked
4 ounces cream cheese, softened
½ cup mayonnaise
1 tablespoon Worcestershire
sauce
1 teaspoon lemon juice
½ cup chopped pecans
1 (4 ounce) can chopped black
olives, drained
12 slices sandwich bread

- Combine all ingredients except the bread. Chill.
- Serve on your favorite sandwich bread.

Serves 6

Per sandwich _____

Calories 475  Protein 14.9 g  Carbohydrates 33.2 g  Fat 32 g  Cholesterol 42 mg  Sodium 702 mg

## Smoked Salmon and Avocado with Lemon Caper Butter

Jane Miller Sanders

¼ cup plus 1 tablespoon unsalted butter, softened
1½ tablespoons fresh lemon juice, divided
1 tablespoon bottled capers, drained
1 avocado
8 slices pumpernickel bread
½ pound thinly sliced smoked salmon
1 small purple onion, thinly sliced
1 cup alfalfa sprouts
Salt and black pepper to taste

- Combine butter, 1 tablespoon lemon juice and capers, creaming until smooth.
- Peel avocado, remove pit and cut into 12 wedges. Sprinkle with ½ tablespoon lemon juice to prevent darkening.
- Spread butter mixture on 1 side of each bread slice. Layer salmon, onion, avocado slices and alfalfa sprouts on 6 slices bread. Cover with remaining bread slices, butter side down, pressing firmly.

Serves 4

Per sandwiches _____

Calories 447  Protein 17.7 g  Carbohydrates 36.8 g  Fat 26.5 g  Cholesterol 51.9 mg  Sodium 1027 mg

# Calzones

Jane Miller Sanders

1 cup low-fat ricotta cheese
1 cup (4 ounces) shredded mozzarella cheese
¼ pound cooked ham, finely chopped
2 teaspoons oregano
1 (10 count) can refrigerated biscuits

- Combine ricotta and mozzarella cheese, ham and oregano.
- Separate biscuits. Place each between sheets of wax paper and roll to form 6-inch circles.
- Spoon cheese mixture into center of each biscuit. Lightly moisten edges of dough with water. Fold each (like a turnover) to form semi-circle, a "calzone." Press edges with fork tines to seal. Place on baking sheet prepared with vegetable cooking spray.
- Bake at 400° for 10 to 12 minutes or until golden brown. Serve immediately.

*These can be assembled in advance, stored in refrigerator and baked just before serving. Leftovers can be refrigerated and reheated.*

Serves 10

Per serving

Calories 172  Protein 8.98 g  Carbohydrates 14.2 g  Fat 4 g  Cholesterol 21.8 mg  Sodium 548 mg

# Crostini

Sandy Wyatt Niederstadt

1 pound ground beef
1 (14 ounce) jar pizza sauce
¼ cup (1 ounce) grated
Parmesan cheese
½ teaspoon Italian seasoning
1 loaf Italian bread
1 (6 ounce) package sliced
mozzarella cheese
Sliced olives (optional)
Sliced mushrooms (optional)
Sliced green onion (optional)
Other pizza toppings (optional)

- Cook beef in large skillet until browned, stirring to crumble. Drain excess fat.
- Add pizza sauce, Parmesan cheese and Italian seasoning to beef. Simmer for 10 minutes.
- Cut lengthwise slice from top of bread. Scoop bread from bottom of loaf, reserving for croutons or breadcrumbs.
- Line bottom ½ of loaf with ½ of mozzarella cheese slices. Spoon beef mixture into loaf and top with olives, mushrooms, green onion or other pizza ingredients. Arrange remaining mozzarella slices on filling and cover with top of bread loaf. Wrap in aluminum foil.
- Bake at 400° for 8 to 10 minutes. Slice crosswise to serve.

Serves 8

Per serving _____

Calories 423  Protein 27.3 g  Carbohydrates 34.1 g  Fat 19.5 g  Cholesterol 76.4 mg  Sodium 779 mg

# Greek Pocket Steaks

*Jennie Hentges*

2 tablespoons olive or vegetable oil, divided
1 tablespoon red wine vinegar
¾ teaspoon salt, divided
½ teaspoon dried oregano, crushed
1 small cucumber, seeds removed and chopped
1 small tomato, chopped
2 pita bread rounds
1 medium-sized onion, sliced
4 cubed beef steaks (about 1 pound total)
Salt and black pepper
1 cup shredded lettuce
Pimiento-stuffed olives (optional)

- Combine 1 tablespoon oil, vinegar, ¼ teaspoon salt and oregano. Add cucumber and tomato.

- Cut bread rounds crosswise in halves. Place on baking sheet. Warm in oven at 250°.

- Sauté onion in 1 tablespoon oil, cooking until tender but not browned. Remove from skillet.

- Sauté steaks in skillet for 2 minutes, turn and cook for 2 minutes or until done. Remove steaks and season with salt and black pepper. Place 1 steak and portion of onion in each bread half.

- Toss lettuce with remaining cooked onion and cucumber mixture. Spoon into bread halves with steak.

- Serve with olives.

Serves 4

Per serving _____

Calories 418  Protein 30.4 g  Carbohydrates 7.44 g  Fat 29.5 g  Cholesterol 95.6 mg  Sodium 805 mg

# Italian Sausage Broils

Patti Shields

½ pound bulk Italian sausage
½ teaspoon dried basil
½ teaspoon dried oregano
1 (8 ounce) can plain tomato sauce or sauce with mushrooms
1½ cups (6 ounces) shredded mozzarella cheese
4 English muffins, split, toasted and buttered

- Brown sausage in skillet, stirring to crumble. Drain excess fat.
- Add basil, oregano and tomato sauce. Simmer until thoroughly heated.
- Sprinkle 1 tablespoon cheese on each half of muffin. Spoon on sausage mixture and sprinkle with remaining cheese.
- Broil 3 inches from heat source until cheese is melted. Serve immediately.

Serves 8

Per muffin half

Calories 254  Protein 12.3 g  Carbohydrates 16.4 g  Fat 15.5 g  Cholesterol 44 mg  Sodium 720 mg

# Town Lake Sandwiches

Ann Bommarito Armstrong

1 tablespoon low-fat cream cheese, softened
1 sandwich roll, cut lengthwise in half
1 ounce turkey pastrami or turkey ham
⅛ cucumber, peeled and thinly sliced
¼ cup bean sprouts
¼ avocado, peeled and sliced

- Spread cream cheese on bottom half of roll.
- Roll up pastrami and place on cream cheese. Add cucumber, bean sprouts and avocado. Cover with top of roll.

*Sandwich can be stored in sealed container until served.*

Serves 1

Per sandwich

Calories 334  Protein 15.6 g  Carbohydrates 35.4 g  Fat 15.5 g  Cholesterol 23.7 mg  Sodium 621 mg

## Sandwiches Del Rio

*Mary Lou Cindrich*

*4 slices rye, light wheat or white bread*
*2 tablespoons mayonnaise*
*2 ripe avocados, peeled and thinly sliced*
*1 medium-sized onion, thinly sliced*
*1 (4 ounce) can whole green chilies, drained and cut in strips*
*1 or 2 tomatoes, sliced*
*8 slices bacon, crisply cooked*
*4 ounces thinly sliced Cheddar cheese*

- Spread bread with mayonnaise.
- Layer each slice with avocado, onion, chilies, tomato and 2 strips bacon. Top with cheese slices.
- Broil for about 5 minutes or until cheese is melted.

Serves 4

Per sandwich _____

Calories 395  Protein 14.6 g  Carbohydrates 19.6 g  Fat 30 g  Cholesterol 44.6 mg  Sodium 922 mg

★

Make sure your greens are completely dry before adding them to a sandwich. Even the best of ingredients can't overcome soggy bread.

# Cucumber Tea Sandwiches

*Donna Earle Crain*

1 medium cucumber, peeled
1 small onion
1 (8 ounce) carton softened cream cheese
¼ teaspoon salt
Dash of hot pepper sauce or cayenne pepper
½ cup butter, softened
1 (16 ounce) loaf sandwich bread

- Place cucumber and onion in food processor. Process with several brief off/on pulses until finely chopped. Drain vegetables in sieve, pressing with back of spoon to remove excess liquid.

- Combine drained vegetables, cream cheese, salt and hot pepper sauce, mixing well.

- Lightly butter a piece of bread and top with cucumber mixture. Butter a second piece of bread and place it butter side down on top of the sandwich.

- Trim crusts and cut into triangles, bars or other shapes with cookie cutters.

*I made these as part of a real English tea at 3:30 in the morning for my daughter and her friends while we watched Prince Charles and Princess Diana's wedding (in the days before VCRs).*

Serves 12

Per sandwich ─────────────────────────────────
Calories 293  Protein 6.73 g  Carbohydrates 30.6 g  Fat 16 g  Cholesterol 43.2 mg  Sodium 466 mg

# Main Dishes

Experience Thanksgiving with a Hill Country twist. Still warm enough in November for a by-the-creek gathering of family and friends, sometimes Texans forego the traditional turkey and trimmings for a more varied menu. Recently guests at artist Daryl Howard's ranch on the banks of the Big Bear Creek, enjoyed a menu of lighter main dishes such as **Italian Potroast** with vegetables, herbed **Cornish Hens Rosé** basted in a light wine, and **Portuguese Roughy Fillets** sautéed in tomatoes, black olives, onions and capers. These dishes reflected the eclectic mixture of people and lifestyles that gathered to celebrate the occasion.

*Serving pieces courtesy of Clarksville Pottery and Gallery, Austin, Texas.*

# Black Bean Burritos

*Patti Shields*

1 cup chopped red bell pepper
6 green onions with tops, chopped
4 cloves garlic, minced
1 tablespoons vegetable oil
1 (15 ounce) can black beans
⅔ cup picanté sauce
1 tablespoon minced cilantro
2 teaspoons ground cumin
8 hard-cooked eggs, chopped
8 flour tortillas
1 cup (4 ounces) grated Monterey Jack cheese
2 cups shredded lettuce
1 cup low-fat sour cream
Picanté sauce

- Cook bell pepper, onion and garlic in oil in covered saucepan over medium heat, stirring occasionally, for 8 to 10 minutes or until vegetables are tender.
- Drain and lightly mash beans. Add beans, picanté sauce, cilantro, cumin and eggs to vegetable mixture. Heat thoroughly.
- Spread ½ cup bean mixture on each tortilla, sprinkle with 2 tablespoons cheese and roll up. Top each burrito with chopped lettuce, 2 tablespoons sour cream and picanté sauce.

Serves 8

Per serving _____

Calories 391  Protein 19.2 g  Carbohydrates 38.1 g  Fat 18 g  Cholesterol 236 mg  Sodium 429 mg

★

Dried beans are nutritious, filling, and inexpensive, and when served in combination with rice, provide a complete protein.

# Black Bean-Tortilla Casserole

Jeanne Cassidy

2 tablespoons vegetable oil
1½ cups chopped onion
½ cup chopped green bell pepper
1 (14½ ounce) can tomatoes, chopped, with juice
¾ cup mild or medium hot picanté sauce
2 cloves garlic, minced
1 teaspoon ground cumin
2½ cups cooked black beans, drained and rinsed
10 (6 inch) corn tortillas
2½ cups (10 ounces) shredded Cheddar or Monterey Jack cheese

- Sauté onion and bell pepper in oil for several minutes.
- Add undrained tomatoes, picanté sauce, garlic and cumin.
- Simmer for 10 minutes and add beans.
- In 13x9x2-inch casserole dish, spread ⅓ of the bean mixture over the bottom.
- Top with half of the tortillas, then half the cheese.
- Add another layer of beans, the remainder of the tortillas and cover with the rest of the bean mixture.
- Cover and bake for 30 minutes at 350°.
- Remove and sprinkle with remaining cheese and let stand for 5 minutes.
- Cut into squares and serve with sliced olives, green onions, sour cream and jalapeño slices.

Serves 10

Per serving _____

Calories 281  Protein 13.4 g  Carbohydrates 30.4 g  Fat 12.5 g  Cholesterol 25.5 mg  Sodium 367 mg

# Coquille St. Jacques

Carol Darilek

1 pound scallops, well rinsed
1 cup dry white wine
Water
2 onions, chopped, divided
¼ cup chopped parsley
Salt and black pepper to taste
1 bay leaf
2 cups sliced mushrooms
3 tablespoons butter or
margarine, divided
3 tablespoons all-purpose flour
½ cup cream
1 cup (4 ounces) grated Swiss
cheese

- Place scallops in large saucepan with wine and enough water to cover. Add 1 onion, parsley, salt, black pepper and bay leaf. Simmer for 5 minutes. Drain, reserving 1 cup liquid. Set aside.

- Sauté remaining onion and mushrooms in 1 tablespoon butter until tender. Remove from skillet and set aside.

- Prepare roux by melting remaining 2 tablespoons butter in skillet and blending in flour. Cook over low heat until bubbly. Add 1 cup reserved scallop liquid and ¼ cup cream. Continue to cook, gradually adding remaining cream. Cook for 3 minutes, stirring constantly.

- Add scallops, onions and mushrooms to sauce. Pour into 4 broiler-proof ramekins and top with Swiss cheese.

- Broil until cheese is golden.

Serves 4

Per serving _____

Calories 421  Protein 30.1 g  Carbohydrates 19.3 g  Fat 21 g  Cholesterol 96.6 mg  Sodium 628 mg

# Scallops and Shallots

Pamela Jones

1 medium-sized onion, chopped
4 shallots, chopped
¼ cup margarine
20 scallops
½ cup dry white wine
2 tablespoons parsley
1 clove garlic, minced
½ teaspoon celery leaves
¼ teaspoon thyme
¼ teaspoon marjoram
¼ bay leaf, crushed

- Sauté onion and shallots in margarine for 5 minutes.
- Add remaining ingredients. Simmer for 10 minutes, or until scallops are done. Pour scallop mixture into broiler-safe ramekins.
- Broil for 4 minutes or until scallops are lightly browned.

Serves 4

Per serving _____

Calories 229  Protein 20 g  Carbohydrates 8.82 g  Fat 12.5 g  Cholesterol 37.4 mg  Sodium 321 mg

# Shrimp Cerveza

Mary Francis

1 pound shrimp in shell
1 lemon, sliced
15 to 20 peppercorns
1 bay leaf
Salt to taste
2 dashes of allspice
1 (12 ounce) can beer

- Place all ingredients in large saucepan.
- Add enough water to cover shrimp.
- Bring to a boil, turn off heat, and let stand until cool.
- Drain shrimp and serve.

Serves 2

Per serving _____

Calories 322  Protein 47 g  Carbohydrates 12.1 g  Fat 4 g  Cholesterol 345 mg  Sodium 878 mg

# Skillet Barbecued Shrimp

Pamela Jones

½ cup unsalted margarine, divided
1 tablespoon minced garlic
Salt to taste
½ teaspoon freshly ground black pepper
½ teaspoon fresh rosemary leaves, crushed
½ teaspoon dried oregano
1 teaspoon cayenne pepper
1 bay leaf, crushed
3 to 5 sprigs thyme, chopped, or ½ teaspoon dried thyme
2 pounds unpeeled large shrimp, rinsed in cold water
1 cup dry white wine

- Melt ¼ cup margarine in large skillet. Add garlic, salt, black pepper, rosemary, oregano, cayenne pepper, bay leaf and thyme.
- Add shrimp. Cook over medium heat, stirring and shaking pan, for about 5 minutes.
- Add remaining ¼ cup margarine and wine to shrimp. Cook, stirring and shaking pan, for 5 minutes more.
- Serve with rice and French bread.

Serves 6

Per serving
Calories 314  Protein 31 g  Carbohydrates 2.73 g  Fat 18 g  Cholesterol 230 mg  Sodium 404 mg

★

Two pounds of shrimp, uncooked with shells intact, will yield approximately one pound after cooking, peeling and deveining.

# Shrimp Tetrazzini

*Donna Earle Crain*

1 (8 ounce) package thin spaghetti
1 medium-sized onion, chopped
¼ cup butter or margarine
1 pound shrimp, peeled and deveined
½ pound fresh mushrooms, sliced
¼ cup all-purpose flour
¼ cup mayonnaise
1 teaspoon salt
¼ teaspoon cayenne pepper
2 cups milk
¼ cup sherry
3 tablespoons grated Parmesan cheese

- Prepare spaghetti according to package directions. Drain and set aside.
- Sauté onion in butter until tender.
- Add shrimp and mushrooms. Cook, stirring often, for 5 minutes. Remove from skillet.
- In the same skillet, blend flour, mayonnaise, salt and cayenne pepper. Add liquids, mixing well, and cook until thickened. Remove from heat and combine with shrimp mixture. Add spaghetti and toss well to coat.
- Pour into 1½-quart casserole. Top with Parmesan cheese.
- Bake at 350° for 30 minutes.

Serves 4

Per serving _____

Calories 565  Protein 34.4 g  Carbohydrates 35.7 g  Fat 30.5 g  Cholesterol 232 mg  Sodium 1048 mg

★

Shrimp should be cooked only until they turn pink. If they are being used in a sauce or casserole, never cook them first or they will become rubbery.

# Wild Rice Shrimp Creole
*Mary Francis*

½ cup chopped onion
⅓ green bell pepper, chopped
¼ cup margarine
1 (16 ounce) can chopped
   tomatoes, undrained
1¾ cups water
½ teaspoon salt
¼ teaspoon black pepper
¼ teaspoon paprika
¼ teaspoon garlic salt
¼ teaspoon rosemary
Hot pepper sauce to taste
¾ cup uncooked wild rice
1 pound shrimp, peeled

- Sauté onion and bell pepper in margarine in 3-quart saucepan until tender.
- Add tomatoes, water, salt, black pepper, paprika, garlic salt, rosemary and hot pepper sauce. Stir in rice. Simmer, covered, for 20 minutes.
- Add shrimp. Simmer, covered, for 10 minutes.

Serves 6

Per serving _____

Calories 255  Protein 18 g  Carbohydrates 24.1 g  Fat 9.5 g  Cholesterol 115 mg  Sodium 506 mg

# Shrimp Okra Gumbo
*Mary Francis*

3 cups cut okra
2 tablespoons bacon fat
1½ cups diced onion
1 (16 ounce) can tomatoes
2 cloves garlic, crushed
1 teaspoon salt
1 teaspoon black pepper
Dash of red pepper
1 bay leaf
2 cups water
2 pounds peeled shrimp

- Sauté okra in bacon fat until browned. Add onion and cook until onion is translucent.
- Add tomatoes, garlic, salt, black pepper, red pepper, bay leaf and water. Bring to a boil, reduce heat and simmer, covered, for 30 minutes.
- Stir in shrimp. Simmer, covered, for 15 minutes more.

*Serve with rice, salad and garlic bread.*

Serves 6

Per serving _____

Calories 261  Protein 33.4 g  Carbohydrates 14.5 g  Fat 7.5 g  Cholesterol 235 mg  Sodium 735 mg

# Shellfish Supreme

Kathy Marsh

1 pound crab meat, shredded
1 pound shrimp, peeled and deveined
2 cups cooked rice
½ green bell pepper, chopped
⅓ cup chopped parsley
2 (10 ounce) packages frozen peas
1½ cups mayonnaise
Salt
Black pepper
Cayenne pepper

- Combine crab, shrimp, rice, bell pepper, parsley, peas and mayonnaise, mixing well.
- Season to taste with salt, black pepper and cayenne pepper. Pour into a greased 13x9x2-inch baking dish.
- Bake, covered, at 350° for 1 hour.

Serves 8

Per serving

Calories 539  Protein 28.6 g  Carbohydrates 26.8 g  Fat 35.5 g  Cholesterol 167 mg  Sodium 674 mg

# Oysters Mediterranean

Geri Francis

¾ pound fresh spinach, chopped
¼ cup plus 1 tablespoon butter or margarine, divided
2 shallots, chopped
½ cup chopped parsley
Dash of hot pepper sauce
2 tablespoons ouzo liqueur
½ cup (2 ounces) crumbled feta cheese
½ cup Italian-seasoned breadcrumbs
Dash of cayenne pepper
12 oysters on the half shell
Rock salt

- Sauté spinach in 1 tablespoon butter until wilted. Remove from skillet and set aside.
- Sauté shallots and parsley in ¼ cup butter until parsley is wilted. Add to spinach. Stir in hot pepper sauce and ouzo. Set aside.
- Combine feta cheese, breadcrumbs and cayenne, mixing to crumb consistency.
- Place oysters in the half shell on a bed of rock salt in a baking pan. Top each oyster with a mounded spoonful of spinach mixture and sprinkle with cheese mixture.
- Bake at 450° for 10 to 12 minutes.

Serves 4

Per serving

Calories 372  Protein 15.2 g  Carbohydrates 20.5 g  Fat 24 g  Cholesterol 111 mg  Sodium 850 mg

# Quick Paella

Julie Wescott

1 medium-sized onion, chopped
2 tablespoons margarine
¼ teaspoon saffron or 1 teaspoon curry powder
Cayenne pepper to taste
1 cup uncooked long grain rice
2 cups chicken broth
1 pound fresh or frozen white fish, cut into pieces
Salt to taste
1 cup frozen peas
½ cup diced red bell pepper
1¼ cups frozen shrimp or chopped cooked chicken
Lemon wedges for garnish

- Sauté onion in margarine in large skillet over medium heat until onion is translucent. Sprinkle with saffron and cayenne pepper. Add rice to onion. Stir in broth and simmer, covered, for 10 minutes.

- Season fish with salt. Arrange on rice, pressing slightly. Place peas, bell pepper and shrimp on rice. Cover and cook for 10 minutes more.

- Garnish with lemon wedges.

Serves 6

Per serving

Calories 319  Protein 31  Carbohydrates 30.8 g  Fat 7 g  Cholesterol 118 mg  Sodium 517 mg

# Flounder in Spinach

Patti Shields

2 (10 ounce) packages frozen chopped spinach
1 cup sour cream
1 medium-sized onion, chopped
1½ tablespoons all-purpose flour
2 tablespoons lemon juice
1 teaspoon salt
1½ pounds flounder fillets
¼ pound fresh mushrooms, sliced
Paprika

- Prepare spinach according to package directions and drain well.

- Combine sour cream, onion, flour, lemon juice and salt. Add ½ of mixture to spinach, mixing well.

- Place spinach mixture in 13x9x2-inch baking dish. Arrange fish on spinach. Place mushrooms around fish. Top with remaining sour cream mixture and sprinkle with paprika.

- Bake at 375° for 20 minutes.

Serves 6

Per serving

Calories 235  Protein 26.4 g  Carbohydrates 11.8 g  Fat 10 g  Cholesterol 71.4 mg  Sodium 1261 mg

# Flounder Stuffed with Marinated Shrimp

*Mary Francis*

½ cup lemon juice
3 or 4 cloves garlic, minced
1 tablespoon parsley
½ teaspoon paprika
1 pound fresh shrimp, peeled and deveined
3 to 4 pounds fresh flounder, skin removed

- Combine lemon juice, garlic, parsley and paprika. Add shrimp, tossing to coat. Marinate, covered, in refrigerator for 45 minutes.
- Cut slit along recessed line in center of flounder. Spoon marinated shrimp into slit. Or omit slit, place shrimp on fillets and roll, securing with wooden pick. Place in shallow baking dish.
- Bake at 350° for 20 minutes.

Serves 6

Per serving _____

Calories 358  Protein 72.8 g  Carbohydrates 2.55 g  Fat 4.5 g  Cholesterol 292 mg  Sodium 415 mg

★

Fish should be cooked just until it turns completely opaque at its thickest part. Overcooking makes fish dry and robs it of its natural flavor.

# Flounder Casserole

Nanci Norin Jordt

2 cups cooked long grain rice
1½ pounds flounder or other white fish fillets
Salt and black pepper to taste
2 tablespoons dry white wine
¼ cup chopped black olives
2 tablespoons capers, rinsed and chopped
1½ cups canned whole tomatoes, well drained
½ cup butter
1 tablespoon minced shallots
1½ teaspoons minced garlic
1 cup breadcrumbs
Lemon wedges for garnish (optional)
Parsley sprigs for garnish (optional)

- Pour rice into shallow 2-quart microwave-safe casserole, spreading in an even layer.

- Season fish with salt and black pepper. Fold each fillet in half and place on rice with folded edge toward outside of dish.

- Sprinkle wine, olives and capers evenly over fish. Top with tomatoes.

- Place butter in microwave-safe bowl. Cook at 50 percent power for 3 minutes. Add breadcrumbs and toss to coat. Sprinkle breadcrumbs on top of casserole.

- Microwave, covered with wax paper, at 100 percent power for 3 minutes. Remove wax paper, rotate dish ¼ turn and cook at 50 percent power for 8 minutes.

- Garnish with lemon wedges and parsley, if desired.

Serves 6

Per serving

Calories 417  Protein 26.1 g  Carbohydrates 34.8 g  Fat 18.5 g  Cholesterol 95.8 mg  Sodium 705 mg

# Portuguese Roughy Fillets

*Vicki Ashley Atkins*

¼ cup chopped onion
1 clove garlic, crushed
1 tablespoon olive oil, divided
½ cup chopped green bell pepper
¾ cup chopped canned tomatoes
2 tablespoons white wine
2 tablespoons sliced black olives
10 ounces orange roughy
Salt and black pepper to taste
½ teaspoon Creole seasoning
1 tablespoon capers, rinsed

- In a saucepan, sauté onion and garlic in 1 teaspoon oil until softened. Add bell pepper and sauté for 3 minutes. Stir in tomatoes, wine and olives. Simmer, covered, for 10 minutes, stirring occasionally.

- Season fish on both sides with salt, black pepper and Creole seasoning.

- Heat remaining 2 teaspoons oil in 9-inch skillet. Add fish and cook for 3 minutes. Turn fish over and top with vegetable mixture. Add capers. Simmer, covered, for 5 minutes or until fish flakes easily; do not overcook.

- Serve over brown rice.

Serves 2

Per serving _____

Calories 240  Protein 28.2 g  Carbohydrates 8.4 g  Fat 9 g  Cholesterol 36.8 mg  Sodium 851 mg

# Red and More

*Catherine Newberger*

6 redfish fillets, split lengthwise
2 cups crab meat
2 cups small peeled shrimp
2 cups shredded mozzarella cheese
¼ cup garlic butter, divided

**Hollandaise Sauce**
2 egg yolks, beaten
3 tablespoons lemon juice
¼ cup margarine, softened

- Arrange ½ of each fillet in greased 13x9x2-inch baking dish. Spread each with 1 teaspoon garlic butter.
- Place ⅓ cup each of crab meat, shrimp and cheese on each fillet, and top with remaining ½ of fillet. Place 1 teaspoon garlic butter on each.
- Bake at 450° for about 20 minutes or until fish flakes and cheese is melted.
- In a saucepan, beat egg yolks and stir in lemon juice. Add margarine and beat vigorously.
- Cook over low heat, stirring constantly, until margarine is melted and sauce is thickened. Serve hot with stuffed fish fillets.

Serves 6

Per serving

Calories 512  Protein 46.8 g  Carbohydrates 3.14 g  Fat 34 g  Cholesterol 293 mg  Sodium 727 mg

★

Fish will keep for up to two days without freezing. It is best to store it on a bed of ice in the coldest part of the refrigerator.

# Sole Florentine

Mary Francis

1 (10 ounce) package frozen
chopped spinach
2 tablespoons minced onion
1 cup sliced mushrooms
1 tablespoon margarine
½ cup breadcrumbs
2 tablespoons parsley
1 (6 ounce) can crab meat
1 tablespoon lemon juice
1 tablespoon white wine
(optional)
6 thick fillets of sole or any mild
white fish

• Prepare spinach according to package directions. Drain well.

• Sauté onion and mushroom in margarine in small skillet over medium heat until onion is tender. Stir in spinach. Remove from heat. Add breadcrumbs, parsley, crab meat, lemon juice and wine.

• Slit each fillet and fill with crab mixture. Place in baking dish prepared with vegetable cooking spray.

• Bake at 350° for 15 to 20 minutes or until fish flakes easily.

Serves 6

Per serving

Calories 230  Protein 39.2 g  Carbohydrates 10.3 g  Fat 3 g  Cholesterol 107 mg  Sodium 325 mg

## Aunt Lucile's Trout Amandine
Vicki Stafford Bohls

¼ cup all-purpose flour
1 teaspoon seasoned salt
1 teaspoon paprika
2 pounds trout fillets, cut in 6 pieces
¼ cup butter or margarine, melted, divided
½ cup sliced almonds
2 tablespoons lemon juice
4 or 5 drops hot pepper sauce
1 tablespoon chopped parsley

- Combine flour, seasoned salt and paprika. Dredge fish in seasoned flour, rolling to coat all sides, and place in single layer, skin side down, in well-greased 13x9x2-inch broiler-safe baking dish.

- Drizzle 2 tablespoons butter over fish. Broil about 4 inches from heat source for 10 to 15 minutes.

- While fish cooks, sauté almonds in remaining 2 tablespoons butter.

- Blend lemon juice and hot pepper sauce, mixing well. Add parsley.

- Pour over cooked fish and sprinkle with almonds.

*Aunt Lucile is a wonderful cook and an even better fisher-woman!*

Serves 6

Per serving _____

Calories 308  Protein 30.8 g  Carbohydrates 6.28 g  Fat 17.5 g  Cholesterol 123 mg  Sodium 541 mg

# Chicken Breast Alouette

Donna Earle Crain

6 skinless, boneless chicken
breast halves
½ teaspoon salt
⅛ teaspoon black pepper
1 (17½ ounce) package puff
pastry sheets
1 (4 ounce) carton garlic and
spice flavored Alouette cheese
1 egg
2 tablespoons water

- Season chicken with salt and black pepper.

- Cut 1 pastry sheet into four 7x6-inch rectangles. Cut second sheet into two 7x6-inch rectangles and one 12x6-inch rectangle. Trim 7x6-inch rectangles into oval shapes.

- Spread each pastry oval with cheese. Place chicken breast on each oval. Fold pastry over chicken lengthwise, pressing seam to seal.

- Cut remaining pastry sheet into 12x¼-inch strips. Braid strips. Cover the seam with one braid and wrap another around the middle, like tying a package.

- Combine egg and water, beating well. Brush chicken bundles with egg wash.

- Bake at 400° for 25 minutes.

Serves 6

Per serving _____

Calories 760  Protein 39.1 g  Carbohydrates 37.6 g  Fat 49.5 g  Cholesterol 143 mg  Sodium 558 mg

# Asparagus Chicken Breasts
Linda Bush

12 stalks fresh or canned asparagus
6 skinless, boneless chicken breast halves, pounded flat
1 (8 ounce) package low-fat cream cheese, softened
½ cup minced green onion
3 tablespoons low-fat margarine
1 (10¾ ounce) can cream of asparagus soup, undiluted
¼ to ½ cup skim milk
¼ teaspoon paprika

- Blanch or steam fresh asparagus for a few minutes; drain and rinse canned spears.
- Spread each chicken breast half with cream cheese. Sprinkle green onion on cheese.
- Place 2 asparagus spears in center of chicken breast and roll tightly. Place seam side down in greased 13x9x2-inch baking dish. Dot each roll with margarine.
- Combine soup and milk, blending until smooth. Pour over chicken rolls.
- Bake at 400° for 45 minutes. Sprinkle with paprika before serving.

Serves 6

Per serving

Calories 419  Protein 37.1 g  Carbohydrates 8.33 g  Fat 25.5 g  Cholesterol 120 mg  Sodium 454 mg

# Chicken Bombers
Vicki Stafford Bohls

6 tablespoons cream cheese with chives
6 tablespoons butter
6 skinless, boneless chicken breast halves, pounded flat
6 slices bacon

- Place 1 tablespoon cream cheese and 1 tablespoon butter in center of each chicken breast. Roll tightly.
- Wrap 1 bacon slice around each chicken roll. Place in greased 13x9x2-inch baking dish.
- Bake, uncovered, at 350° for 45 minutes.

*Kids love these, especially because of their silly name!*

Serves 6

Per serving

Calories 353  Protein 33.2 g  Carbohydrates .424 g  Fat 23.5 g  Cholesterol 119 mg  Sodium 255 mg

# Chicken Bundles

Patti Shields

1 (2½ ounce) jar sliced
mushrooms, drained
¼ cup (1 ounce) shredded
mozzarella or Monterey Jack
cheese
⅓ cup plain yogurt
1 tablespoon chopped pimiento
2 teaspoons parsley flakes
4 skinless, boneless chicken
breast halves
1 tablespoon margarine or
butter, melted
Grated Parmesan cheese

- Combine mushrooms, cheese, yogurt, pimiento and parsley.
- Pound chicken to ¼-inch thickness.
- Spread 2 rounded tablespoons of mushroom mixture on each chicken piece, fold sides to enclose and secure with wooden picks. Place chicken rolls, pick side up, in 11x7x2-inch baking dish.
- Brush tops of rolls with margarine. Sprinkle with Parmesan cheese.
- Bake at 350° for 40 to 45 minutes.

Serves 4

Per serving _____

Calories 214  Protein 32.7 g  Carbohydrates 2.93 g  Fat 7.5 g  Cholesterol 77.1 mg  Sodium 325 mg

———— ★ ————

For pounding chicken, or any meat, slit open the sides of a large plastic
zipper top bag, place the meat between the plastic and pound away.
The bags are heavy enough not to tear or burst.

## Chicken and Chestnuts

*Pam Posey Brown*

2 tablespoons all-purpose flour
Salt and black pepper to taste
8 skinless, boneless chicken
breast halves
¼ cup vegetable oil
¾ cup sautérne or white wine
1 (10¾ ounce) can cream of
chicken soup, undiluted
1 (8 ounce) can water chestnuts,
drained and sliced
1 (4 ounce) can sliced
mushrooms, drained
2 tablespoons chopped green bell
pepper
¼ teaspoon thyme

- Combine flour, salt and black pepper. Dredge chicken pieces in seasoned flour.

- Sauté chicken in oil, turning to lightly brown on all sides. Place chicken in 3-quart casserole.

- Add wine to pan drippings. Stir in soup, water chestnuts, mushrooms, bell pepper and thyme. Simmer for 2 minutes. Pour sauce over chicken.

- Bake, covered, at 350° for 45 minutes. Remove cover and bake for 15 to 20 minutes or until tender.

Serves 8

Per serving _____

Calories 181  Protein 14.9 g  Carbohydrates 7.15 g  Fat 8.5 g  Cholesterol 35.6 mg  Sodium 319 mg

## Cheesy Chicken Marsala

Vicki Ashley Atkins

½ cup fine dry breadcrumbs
½ cup (2 ounces) grated
Parmesan cheese
1½ teaspoons parsley flakes
½ teaspoon paprika
8 skinless, boneless chicken
breast halves
¼ cup low-fat margarine
⅔ cup Marsala wine

- Combine breadcrumbs, cheese, parsley and paprika, mixing well.
- Press each chicken piece into breadcrumb mixture, coating both sides heavily. Place chicken in 13x9x2-inch baking dish prepared with non-stick vegetable cooking spray. Sprinkle remaining crumbs on chicken and dot with margarine.
- Bake, covered, at 350° for 30 minutes. Pour wine over chicken and bake, covered, for additional 15 minutes. Remove cover and bake 15 minutes more.

Serves 8

Per serving _____

Calories 175  Protein 17.1 g  Carbohydrates 5.7 g  Fat 6.5 g  Cholesterol 39.1 mg  Sodium 245 mg

## Chicken Dressed for Dinner

Kathy Marsh

8 skinless, boneless chicken
breast halves
8 slices Monterey Jack cheese
1 (10¾ ounce) can cream of
chicken soup, undiluted
½ cup white wine or water
1 cup herb-seasoned stuffing
mix, crushed
¼ cup butter or margarine,
melted

- Place chicken in greased 13x9x2-inch baking dish. Arrange cheese slices on chicken.
- Combine soup and wine, blending well. Spoon over chicken.
- Sprinkle with stuffing mix and drizzle with butter.
- Bake at 350° for 45 to 55 minutes.

Serves 8

Per serving _____

Calories 279  Protein 21.7 g  Carbohydrates 5.5 g  Fat 17.5 g  Cholesterol 60.9 mg  Sodium 496 mg

## Creamy Mushroom Chicken   Barbara Hoover McEachern

3 tablespoons margarine
1 tablespoon olive oil
3 tablespoons lemon juice
1 tablespoon paprika
Dash of cayenne pepper
6 skinless, boneless chicken breast halves
Garlic salt to taste
2 (4 ounce) cans sliced mushrooms, drained and diced
Salt to taste
⅔ cup low-sodium chicken broth
2 cups low-fat sour cream, at room temperature
¼ cup sherry

- Melt margarine. Add oil, lemon juice, paprika and cayenne pepper.
- Season chicken with garlic salt. Dip pieces in butter mixture and place in 13x9x2-inch baking dish.
- Bake at 375° for about 30 minutes or until chicken is tender.
- Season mushrooms with salt. Add broth and sour cream.
- Pour sour cream mixture over chicken. Add sherry.
- Bake at 375° for 30 to 35 minutes more or until sauce is bubbly.

Serves 6

Per serving _____

Calories 451  Protein 33.9 g  Carbohydrates 6.52 g  Fat 31.5 g  Cholesterol 124 mg  Sodium 605 mg

———— ★ ————

Buying boneless, skinless chicken breasts may seem more expensive than buying whole pieces, but remember, you will lose about one-third of the package weight when you discard the skin and bones. And think of the time you will save!

# Chicken Florentine with Mushroom Sauce

Ginny Ashley

½ cup minced onion
1 tablespoon margarine
2 (10 ounce) packages frozen chopped spinach, thawed and drained
1 cup (4 ounces) shredded Swiss cheese
½ teaspoon ground nutmeg
4 skinless, boneless chicken breast halves, pounded flat

**Mushroom Sauce**

2 cups sliced fresh mushrooms
1 tablespoon margarine
2 teaspoons lemon juice
1 cup chicken broth
1 cup milk
½ cup dry white wine
White pepper to taste

- Sauté onion in margarine. Remove from heat and add spinach, cheese and nutmeg.
- Spoon spinach mixture into 4 mounds in lightly-greased 13x9x2-inch baking dish. Place chicken piece over each mound.
- Bake at 350° for 20 to 30 minutes or until chicken is done.
- Sauté mushrooms in margarine until liquid evaporates.
- Add lemon juice, broth, milk, wine and white pepper to mushrooms. Bring to a boil and cook until liquid is reduced by ⅔ and sauce is slightly thickened.
- Spoon ¼ of sauce over each serving.

Serves 4

Per serving _____

Calories 540  Protein 47.6 g  Carbohydrates 19.2 g  Fat 29.5 g  Cholesterol 124 mg  Sodium 578 mg

# Chicken with Mustard Cream

Mary Lou Cindrich

4 skinless, boneless chicken breast halves, pounded flat
½ teaspoon salt
¼ teaspoon black pepper
3 tablespoons Dijon or spicy brown mustard, divided
½ cup all-purpose flour
3 tablespoons butter
1 cup half and half

- Season chicken with salt and black pepper. Spread each side of chicken breasts with mustard, using 2 tablespoons.

- Place flour in shallow dish. Press chicken into flour, coating on both sides and shaking to remove excess.

- Brown chicken in butter in 10-inch skillet over moderately high heat, cooking for about 3 minutes on each side. Remove and keep warm.

- Pour half and half into skillet. Bring to a boil and cook for about 2 minutes, scraping skillet to dislodge brown bits. Remove from heat.

- Stir in 1 tablespoon mustard. Add chicken and reheat briefly.

Serves 4

Per serving _____

Calories 350  Protein 31.4 g  Carbohydrates 15.4 g  Fat 17.5 g  Cholesterol 92mg  Sodium 572 mg

# Crunchy Pecan Chicken

Kathy Gordon

½ cup all-purpose flour
½ cup cornmeal
¾ cup finely chopped pecans
1 to 2 tablespoons Creole seasoning
2 eggs
¼ cup water
8 skinless, boneless chicken breast halves
½ cup vegetable oil

- Combine flour, cornmeal, pecans and Creole seasoning, mixing well.
- In separate bowl, blend eggs and water.
- Dip chicken in egg mixture, then into pecan mixture, coating each piece completely.
- Cook chicken in oil in heavy skillet over medium high heat for about 10 minutes on each side. Remove from skillet and drain.

Serves 8

Per serving _____

Calories 402  Protein 31.3 g  Carbohydrates 14.9 g  Fat 24.5 g  Cholesterol 121 mg  Sodium 96.3 mg

# Chicken Poppicotti

The Old Pecan St. Café

4 (6 ounce) skinless boneless whole chicken breasts
12 ounces cream cheese, softened
¼ cup plus 2 tablespoons cottage cheese
¼ cup grated Parmesan cheese
2 tablespoons ricotta cheese
½ teaspoon granulated garlic
2 pinches of white pepper
4 ounces fresh spinach, torn

- Pound rough side of chicken breasts until flattened.
- Thoroughly blend all remaining ingredients, except for spinach. Add spinach but do not overmix.
- Stuff each breast with mixture and fold over.
- Sauté stuffed chicken pieces in non-stick skillet prepared with vegetable cooking spray for 2 minutes on each side, turning carefully. Place in baking dish.
- Bake at 350° for 8 to 10 minutes or until chicken is done.

Serves 4

Per serving _____

Calories 661  Protein 49.1 g  Carbohydrates 4.81 g  Fat 49 g  Cholesterol 213 mg  Sodium 607 mg

# Sesame Chicken Supreme
Patsy Eppright

*To serve as an appetizer, use chicken tenders and serve with dipping sauces*

¼ cup plus 2 tablespoons all-
purpose flour, divided
½ teaspoon salt
¼ teaspoon black pepper
4 skinless, boneless chicken
breast halves
1 egg
2 tablespoons milk
3 tablespoons sesame seeds
2 cups vegetable oil for deep
frying

**Supreme Sauce**
2 tablespoons butter
1½ teaspoons all-purpose flour
1 cup chicken broth
Salt and black pepper to taste
1 egg yolk, beaten

- Combine 2 tablespoons flour, salt and black pepper in clean paper bag. Add chicken pieces and shake to coat.
- Beat egg with milk.
- Combine ¼ cup flour and sesame seeds.
- Dip each chicken piece in egg mixture, then in sesame seed mixture to coat.
- Deep fry chicken in oil heated to 350°, cooking for about 10 minutes or until golden and tender. Drain on paper towels. Keep chicken warm while preparing Supreme Sauce.
- Melt butter in saucepan. Add flour, stirring to form smooth paste.
- Gradually add broth, cooking until smooth. Season with salt and black pepper.
- Slowly add about ⅓ cup hot sauce to egg yolk, whisking to blend. Then gradually add yolk mixture to remaining sauce, cooking over low heat and whisking just until sauce is thickened and smooth.
- Serve sauce with chicken.

*Our traditional New Year's dinner, served with rice and blackeyed peas.*

Serves 4

Per serving, chicken _____

Calories 289  Protein 30.5 g  Carbohydrates 11.1 g  Fat 13 g  Cholesterol 120 mg  Sodium 361 mg

Per serving, sauce _____

Calories 79  Protein 2.1 g  Carbohydrates 1.16 g  Fat 7.5 g  Cholesterol 53 mg  Sodium 329 mg

# Chinese Chicken Rolls

Mary Francis

1 cup shredded cabbage
1 green onion, minced
¼ cup thinly sliced celery
1 teaspoon soy sauce
⅛ teaspoon ground ginger
2 skinless, boneless chicken breast halves
Salt and black pepper to taste
1 chicken bouillon cube
½ cup boiling water

- About 1 hour before serving, combine cabbage, onion, celery, soy sauce and ginger in a small bowl. Set aside.

- Cut chicken breasts in halves lengthwise. Pound to ¼-inch thickness. Season with salt and black pepper.

- Place ¼ of cabbage mixture on each chicken piece. Roll up, jelly roll fashion, and secure with wooden picks. Place in baking dish.

- Dissolve bouillon in boiling water. Pour over chicken rolls.

- Bake, covered with aluminum foil, at 350° for 30 minutes. Remove foil and bake for additional 15 minutes.

Serves 2

Per serving _____

Calories 155  Protein 28.9 g  Carbohydrates 4.45 g  Fat 2 g  Cholesterol 68.8 mg  Sodium 1363 mg

# Stir Fry Chicken

Julie Clark

⅓ cup sherry
2 to 3 tablespoons soy sauce
½ teaspoon sugar
Dash of ground ginger
Dash of mustard
4 skinless, boneless chicken
breast halves, cut in 2-inch strips
3 tablespoons vegetable oil
4 small carrots, thinly sliced
1 cup broccoli flowerets
2 cups bean sprouts
2 cups pea pods
1 (8 ounce) can sliced water
chestnuts, drained
½ pound fresh mushrooms,
sliced
1 cup chicken broth
1 tablespoon cornstarch

• Combine sherry, soy sauce, sugar, ginger and mustard, mixing well. Add chicken strips and chill for 1 hour.

• Drain chicken, reserving marinade. Heat oil to 350° in skillet. Add chicken and stir fry for 2 to 3 minutes. Remove chicken from skillet.

• Add cut vegetables and stir fry for 2 minutes. Remove vegetables from skillet and drain.

• Combine broth, reserved marinade and cornstarch, blending well. Pour into skillet. Add vegetables and cook, stirring often, until slightly thickened. Add chicken to vegetables and sauce and heat through.

*Serve over rice or Chinese noodles.*

Serves 4

Per serving _____

Calories 240  Protein 20.7 g  Carbohydrates 26.4 g  Fat 5 g  Cholesterol 34.2 mg  Sodium 1055 mg

# Walnut Chicken

*Patsy Eppright*

¼ cup plus 1 tablespoon
vegetable oil, divided
1 tablespoon plus 2 teaspoons
soy sauce, divided
1 tablespoon cornstarch, divided
4 skinless, boneless chicken
breast halves, cut in 1-inch pieces
½ cup chicken broth
½ teaspoon grated ginger root
½ teaspoon red pepper flakes
1 medium-sized onion, cut in 1-
inch pieces
1 clove garlic, minced
1 red bell pepper, cut in 1-inch
pieces
½ cup toasted chopped walnuts

- Combine 1 tablespoon oil, 2 teaspoons soy sauce and 1 teaspoon cornstarch in bowl. Add chicken, stirring to coat well. Marinate, covered, in refrigerator for 30 minutes.
- Combine broth, ginger, 1 tablespoon soy sauce and 2 teaspoons cornstarch. Set aside.
- Stir fry chicken with red pepper flakes in ¼ cup oil in large skillet or wok over medium high heat until chicken is no longer pink. Remove chicken.
- Stir fry onion, garlic and bell pepper until onion is tender.
- Add chicken and broth mixture to vegetables. Cook, stirring constantly, until thickened. Stir in walnuts.
- Serve over rice.

Serves 4

Per serving _____

Calories 414  Protein 20.7 g  Carbohydrates 9.83 g  Fat 33 g  Cholesterol 46.4 mg  Sodium 574 mg

# Salsa Chicken

Terre Churchill

1 small bunch broccoli
1½ cups chopped onion
3 large cloves garlic, minced
1 tablespoon olive oil
1 cup chopped red bell pepper
1 pound skinless, boneless chicken breast, cut in bite-sized chunks
2 large or 3 medium tomatoes, diced
1 (16 ounce) can kidney beans
1 cup medium hot salsa
¼ cup chopped cilantro (optional)
Salt and black pepper to taste

- Cut broccoli in bite-sized pieces and steam for 2 to 3 minutes, drain and set aside.

- Sauté onion and garlic in oil in large non-stick skillet or Dutch oven for 3 minutes or until softened. Add bell pepper and sauté for 2 minutes.

- Add chicken, tomatoes, broccoli, beans, salsa and cilantro to onion mixture. Over medium heat, bring to a boil, stir lightly, reduce heat and simmer, covered, just until chicken is cooked.

- Season with salt and black pepper.

*Serve over rice or angel hair pasta.*

Serves 6

Per serving _____

Calories 217  Protein 23.9 g  Carbohydrates 22.9 g  Fat 4 g  Cholesterol 43.8 mg  Sodium 656 mg

# Light Italian Chicken with Basil    Sally Guyton Joyner

4 skinless, boneless chicken breast halves
2 tablespoons all-purpose flour
½ teaspoon salt
½ teaspoon dried oregano
3 tablespoons low-fat margarine, divided
1 medium-sized onion, diced
2 medium zucchini, cut in bite-sized pieces
2 medium plum tomatoes, diced
2 teaspoons fresh lemon juice
Grated peel of 1 lemon
1½ teaspoons chicken bouillon granules
½ cup water
¼ cup sliced basil leaves or ½ teaspoon dried basil
Basil leaves or parsley sprigs for garnish

- Cut each piece of chicken in half and pound to ¼-inch thickness.
- Combine flour, salt and oregano. Dredge chicken pieces in seasoned flour to coat.
- Sauté chicken in 2 tablespoons margarine in non-stick 12-inch skillet, turning to brown on both sides. Remove and keep warm.
- Add 1 tablespoon margarine to skillet. Add onions and sauté until golden. Add zucchini and cook, stirring occasionally, until golden and tender-crisp.
- Add tomatoes, lemon juice, lemon peel, bouillon and water to vegetables. Over high heat, bring to a boil and cook for 1 minute, scraping skillet to dislodge browned bits. Stir in sliced basil.
- Arrange chicken on platter. Spoon sauce over chicken and garnish with basil leaves or parsley.

Serves 4

Per serving _____

Calories 202  Protein 29.2 g  Carbohydrates 10.5 g  Fat 5 g  Cholesterol 68.6 mg  Sodium 651 mg

# Orange Chicken Italiano

*Vicki Ashley Atkins*

4 skinless chicken breast halves
1 cup orange juice
½ cup white wine
Paprika to taste
½ tablespoon Italian seasoning
1 small onion, chopped
1 large tomato, chopped
¼ pound fresh mushrooms, sliced
1 teaspoon peanut, canola or olive oil

- Place chicken in shallow baking dish. Combine juice and wine and pour over chicken. Sprinkle with paprika and Italian seasoning.

- Bake, uncovered, at 350° for 30 minutes.

- While chicken bakes, sauté onion, tomatoes and mushrooms in oil until onion is translucent. Spoon vegetables over chicken and bake uncovered for 1 hour more.

*Serve over brown rice with a fresh steamed vegetable and crusty Italian bread.*

Serves 4

Per serving _____

Calories 207  Protein 28.9 g  Carbohydrates 10.9 g  Fat 3 g  Cholesterol 68.4 mg  Sodium 83.1 mg

★

Food has a sensual quality all its own. It should appeal not only to our sense of taste, but to sight, smell and touch as well. Nutritious food, beautifully presented, will nourish all our senses.

# Chicken Castillian

Jeanne Cassidy

Must marinate overnight

4 cloves garlic, minced
2 tablespoons dried oregano
Salt and black pepper to taste
½ cup red wine vinegar
½ cup olive oil
1 cup pitted prunes, cut in halves
½ to ¾ cup Spanish green olives
½ cup capers, rinsed
4 bay leaves
2 (2½ to 3 pound) broiler fryers,
quartered, or 4 chicken legs, 4
thighs and 4 breast halves
¾ cup firmly-packed brown
sugar
1 cup white wine
¼ cup chopped parsley

- Combine garlic, oregano, salt, black pepper, vinegar, oil, prunes, olives, capers and bay leaves.

- Pour over chicken, turning to coat pieces. Marinate, covered, in refrigerator overnight.

- Drain chicken, reserving marinade. Arrange chicken in single layer in large shallow baking dish. Spoon marinade over chicken. Sprinkle with brown sugar. Pour white wine around chicken.

- Bake at 350° for 1¼ hours, basting several times.

- Arrange chicken on platter. Spoon sauce over chicken and garnish with parsley. Serve with rice, couscous or polenta.

This dish was inspired by Chicken Marsella, a dish made famous by The Silver Palate, Manhattan's celebrated gourmet food shop.

Serves 8

Per serving _____

Calories 571  Protein 31.6 g  Carbohydrates 34.1 g  Fat 33 g  Cholesterol 115 mg  Sodium 694 mg

# Chicken Jerusalem

Sara Butler

2 pounds chicken pieces or 4
chicken breast halves
⅓ cup all-purpose flour
¼ cup butter
½ teaspoon salt
¼ teaspoon white pepper
¼ teaspoon ground nutmeg
¼ pound mushrooms, sliced
6 artichoke bottoms, quartered
1 cup sherry
1 pint cream
2 tablespoons minced chives
2 tablespoons minced parsley

- Dredge chicken in flour to coat. Sauté chicken in butter until lightly browned.

- Season with salt, white pepper and nutmeg. Add mushrooms and artichokes. Pour sherry over all.

- Simmer, covered, for about 15 minutes or until chicken is tender and almost all liquid is evaporated.

- Add cream and heat through. Add parsley and chives.

Serves 4

Per serving _____

Calories 596  Protein 36.7 g  Carbohydrates 16.4 g  Fat 39 g  Cholesterol 169 mg  Sodium 587 mg

# Wine Basted Chicken

Linda Uchiyama Kelley

4 pounds chicken pieces or 2
(2½ pound) whole chickens
2 teaspoons vegetable oil
½ teaspoon freshly ground black
pepper
½ teaspoon basil tarragon
½ cup white wine
½ cup chicken broth, fat removed

- Rinse chicken pieces or whole chickens and blot with paper towel. Brush with oil.

- Rub inside and out with seasonings.

- If using whole chickens, close and secure cavity with kitchen twine. Place chicken on rack in roasting pan.

- Bake at 400° for 1 hour, basting frequently with mixture of wine and broth.

Serves 8

Per serving _____

Calories 291  Protein 52.8 g  Carbohydrates .342 g  Fat 6.5 g  Cholesterol 131 mg  Sodium 197 mg

# Orange Maple Chicken

Patti Shields

1½ pounds chicken legs, thighs
or breasts
1 tablespoon vegetable oil
1 teaspoon finely grated orange
peel
¼ cup orange juice
¼ cup water
¼ cup maple syrup
2 tablespoons prepared mustard
¼ teaspoon salt
Dash of black pepper
1 tablespoon water
2 teaspoons cornstarch

- Sauté chicken in oil in skillet over medium-low heat for about 10 minutes, turning to brown on both sides.
- Combine orange peel, juice, water, syrup, mustard, salt and black pepper.
- Remove chicken, drain excess grease and return chicken to skillet.
- Pour orange mixture over chicken. Simmer, covered, for 30 minutes or until chicken is done. Remove chicken to serving platter and keep warm.
- Combine water and cornstarch. Add to warm skillet and cook, stirring often, until thickened and bubbly; continue to cook, stirring often, for additional 10 minutes.
- Pour sauce over chicken and serve with rice.

Serves 4

Per serving _____

Calories 287  Protein 39.8 g  Carbohydrates 16.9 g  Fat 6 g  Cholesterol 98.6 mg  Sodium 344 mg

# Sweet and Sour Barbecued Chicken

Kathi Mann

1 large onion, chopped
1 tablespoon butter or margarine
2 (12 ounce) bottles chili sauce
⅓ cup water
2 tablespoons lemon juice
1 teaspoon salt
1 teaspoon paprika
1 pound package brown sugar
4 pounds chicken, cut up, or 8 skinless chicken breast halves

- In large heavy saucepan, sauté onion in butter until tender.

- Add chili sauce, water, lemon juice, salt, paprika and brown sugar to onion. Simmer, uncovered, for 45 minutes, stirring occasionally.

- Place chicken, bone side up, in large baking pan in single layer. Pour sauce over chicken.

- Bake, uncovered, at 350° for 30 to 35 minutes or until nearly done.

- Transfer chicken to grill and cook, bone side down, over low heat for 10 to 15 minutes. Baste frequently with sauce from baking pan to build up a thick glaze; do not turn chicken as sauce burns easily.

*Chicken may be baked in sauce, then frozen. When ready to use, bake at 300° for 1 hour or until chicken is thawed and sauce is warm. Grill as directed.*

Serves 8

Per serving _____

Calories 346  Protein 29.7 g  Carbohydrates 50.9 g  Fat 3 g  Cholesterol 68.4 mg  Sodium 1509 mg

# Classic Chicken Cacciatore
Barbara Stromberg Boyd

1 *tablespoon vegetable oil*
1 *(3 pound) broiler-fryer, cut up*
1 *medium-sized onion, sliced*
2 *cloves garlic, minced*
1 *(16 ounce) can tomatoes*
1 *(8 ounce) can tomato sauce*
¾ *teaspoon salt*
¼ *teaspoon black pepper*
1 *teaspoon dried basil*
1 *teaspoon dried oregano*
½ *teaspoon celery seed*
2 *bay leaves*
¼ *cup dry white wine*

- Heat oil in a non-stick skillet. Sauté chicken until brown on both sides. Remove from skillet.

- Add onion and garlic to skillet and sauté until tender but not browned. Drain off excess oil. Return chicken to skillet.

- Combine tomatoes, tomato sauce and seasonings, mixing well. Pour over chicken.

- Simmer, covered, for 30 minutes. Add wine and simmer, uncovered, for 15 minutes more or until chicken is tender, turning occasionally.

*Serve over your favorite pasta.*

Serves 8

Per serving _____

Calories 344  Protein 36.7 g  Carbohydrates 7.16 g  Fat 17.5 g  Cholesterol 109 mg  Sodium 572 mg

## Chicken Cacciatore with Artichokes   Mary Francis

1 (6 ounce) jar marinated
artichokes
2 tablespoons olive oil
4 chicken breast halves
2 tablespoons all-purpose flour
1 (16 ounce) can tomatoes
2 cloves garlic, minced
1 teaspoon sugar
1 teaspoon salt
½ teaspoon black pepper
½ teaspoon basil
½ teaspoon oregano
½ cup sherry
½ pound fresh mushrooms,
sliced
Minced parsley for garnish

• Drain artichokes, reserving marinade. Combine marinade liquid and oil in skillet.

• Dredge chicken in flour. Sauté chicken in oil mixture, turning to brown on both sides. Drain chicken and place in casserole.

• Combine tomatoes, garlic, sugar, salt, black pepper, basil and oregano. Pour mixture over chicken.

• Bake, covered, at 350° for 45 minutes.

• Add sherry, mushrooms and artichokes to chicken. Bake for additional 10 minutes.

• Garnish with parsley.

*Serve with pasta or rice.*

Serves 4

Per serving _____

Calories 439  Protein 34.1 g  Carbohydrates 18.2 g  Fat 24 g  Cholesterol 92.8 mg  Sodium 1040 mg

## Aunt Sophia's Cheesy Chicken Casserole

*Cheryl Briggs Patton*

1 (4 to 5 pound) chicken or 6
chicken breast halves
2 (10 ounce) packages frozen
broccoli
2 cups milk
1 (8 ounce) package cream
cheese
1 teaspoon salt
¾ teaspoon garlic salt
1 cup (4 ounces) grated
Parmesan cheese, divided

- Cook chicken in water to cover until tender. Drain, let stand until cool, remove skin and bones and discard. Chop meat and set aside.

- Prepare broccoli according to package directions. Drain and place in 13x9x2-inch baking dish.

- In top of double boiler, blend milk, cream cheese, salt and garlic salt. Stir in ¾ cup Parmesan.

- Pour ½ of sauce over broccoli. Add chicken and top with remaining sauce. Sprinkle with remaining Parmesan.

- Bake at 350° for 45 minutes.

Serves 6

Per serving _____

Calories 534  Protein 45.5 g  Carbohydrates 10.6 g  Fat 34.5 g  Cholesterol 159 mg  Sodium 934 mg

## Clay Pot Chicken

Gwen Walden Irwin

3 pounds chicken pieces
¾ teaspoon salt
Dash of black pepper
½ teaspoon marjoram
½ teaspoon basil
½ cup brandy, white wine or
chicken broth
6 green onions, chopped
1 cup (4 ounces) grated cheese
6 large mushrooms, sliced
2 tablespoons parsley flakes
1 pound broccoli, cut lengthwise
or into bite-sized pieces
1 to 2 teaspoons arrowroot

- Presoak clay pot cooker in water for 15 minutes or as directed by manufacturer. Drain.

- Place chicken in clay pot. Sprinkle salt, black pepper, marjoram and basil on chicken. Add brandy and onions. Sprinkle with cheese, then top with mushrooms and parsley.

- Place covered clay pot in oven. Set temperature at 480° (do not preheat) and bake for 45 minutes.

- Add broccoli and bake, covered, for additional 15 minutes.

- Drain cooking liquid into a saucepan. Heat liquid, add arrowroot and stir until thickened. Serve sauce with chicken and broccoli.

Serves 6

Per serving _____

Calories 541  Protein 54.7 g  Carbohydrates 8.08 g  Fat 27 g  Cholesterol 162 mg  Sodium 534 mg

# Tamales Vera Cruz

Jeanne Cassidy

12 chicken, pork or beef tamales, cut in 2-inch pieces
4 cups chopped cooked chicken
2 cups fresh, frozen or canned corn, drained
2 cups canned tomatoes
½ cup raisins
½ cup sliced green olives
3 slices bacon, cooked and crumbled
1 cup chicken broth
1 tablespoon chili powder
½ teaspoon salt
1 tablespoon Worcestershire sauce
1 cup (4 ounces) grated sharp Cheddar cheese

- Combine tamales, chicken, corn, tomatoes, raisins, olives and bacon.

- Blend broth, chili powder, salt and Worcestershire sauce together. Add to tamale mixture, mixing lightly. Pour into greased 4-quart casserole.

- Bake at 350° for 40 to 45 minutes. Sprinkle cheese on tamale mixture and continue baking until cheese is melted and lightly browned.

- Serve with black beans.

Serves 12

Per serving _____

Calories 488  Protein 36.6 g  Carbohydrates 29 g  Fat 25.5 g  Cholesterol 103 mg  Sodium 1156 mg

# Mary Ann's Light Chicken Enchiladas

*Barbara Stromberg Boyd*

4 *chicken thighs*
1 *sprig celery leaves*
¾ *cup (3 ounces) grated Monterey Jack cheese, divided*
¼ to ⅓ *cup sour cream*
1 *clove garlic, minced*
3 *green onions, chopped*
2 *tablespoons vegetable oil*
1 *(4 ounce) can chopped green chilies, undrained*
1 *(16 ounce) can chopped tomatoes, undrained*
*Salt and black pepper to taste*
10 *corn tortillas*
⅛ *teaspoon ground cumin*
¼ *teaspoon dried oregano*

- In a 10-inch covered skillet, cook chicken and celery leaves in ½-inch water until chicken is tender. Skin and bone chicken and shred meat. Reserve broth.

- Combine chicken, ½ cup cheese and sour cream.

- Sauté garlic and onion in oil until soft but not browned.

- Add chilies, tomatoes and ¼ cup reserved broth to onion. Season with salt and black pepper. Simmer for 5 to 10 minutes.

- Dip each tortilla in sauce to soften. Spoon portion of chicken mixture on each tortilla, roll up and place in shallow 1½-quart casserole. Pour remaining sauce over rolled tortillas.

- Sprinkle with cumin, oregano and ¼ cup cheese.

- Bake, uncovered, at 350° for 15 minutes or until thoroughly heated.

Serves 5

Per serving _____

Calories 457  Protein 21.9 g  Carbohydrates 33.4 g  Fat 27 g  Cholesterol 85 mg  Sodium 830 mg

# Parmesan Chicken Baked Potatoes Nanci Norin Jordt

6 medium (about 2 pounds) baking potatoes
2 tablespoons butter or margarine
1 (10¾ ounce) can cream of chicken soup, undiluted
½ cup (2 ounces) grated Parmesan cheese
2 tablespoons minced parsley
1 cup cubed cooked chicken
Grated Parmesan cheese

- Bake potatoes until tender. Cut in halves lengthwise and remove pulp, leaving thin shell.
- Using electric mixer, mash potato pulp with butter. Gradually add soup, cheese and parsley, beating until light and fluffy. Fold chicken into potato mixture.
- Spoon potato mixture into shells and sprinkle with cheese. Place stuffed shells in 13x9x2-inch baking dish.
- Bake at 450° for 15 minutes or until hot.

*This is a great way to use leftover chicken.*

Serves 6

Per serving _____

Calories 232  Protein 17.6 g  Carbohydrates 15.5 g  Fat 11 g  Cholesterol 40.4 mg  Sodium 892 mg

# Cornish Hens Rosé

Vicki Ashley Atkins

*For more intense herb flavor, cover and refrigerate 2 to 3 hours before baking*

4 Cornish game hens, split lengthwise
2 cups light rosé wine, divided
½ teaspoon black pepper
½ teaspoon garlic powder
½ teaspoon onion powder
½ teaspoon celery seeds
½ teaspoon poultry seasoning
½ teaspoon paprika
½ teaspoon dried basil

- Place hen halves, cavity side up, in 9x9x1½-inch baking dish. Pour 1½ cups wine over hens.

- Combine seasonings and sprinkle ½ of mixture over hens.

- Bake, uncovered, at 350° for 1 hour. Turn hens over. Pour ½ cup wine over hens and sprinkle with remaining seasoning mixture. Bake for additional 30 minutes, basting every 10 minutes with pan juices.

*Combine 1 tablespoon of each seasoning in a tightly-covered spice jar for future use.*

Serves 8

Per serving

Calories 157  Protein 36 g  Carbohydrates 0 g  Fat 9 g  Cholesterol 110 mg  Sodium 394 mg

# Herb Roasted Turkey and Potatoes Nanci Norin Jordt

1½ pounds boneless turkey
breast
1 clove garlic, thinly sliced
4 red potatoes, quartered
2 tablespoons margarine, melted
¾ teaspoon onion salt
¾ teaspoon dried oregano
Paprika

- Cut slits in surface of turkey and insert garlic slices. Place turkey, skin side up, in 13x9x2-inch baking pan.
- Place potatoes around turkey. Drizzle potatoes with margarine.
- Combine onion salt and oregano. Sprinkle over turkey and potatoes.
- Season potatoes with paprika.
- Bake at 350° for 1½ hours or until internal temperature of turkey is 170°. Let stand 5 minutes before slicing.

Serves 6

Per serving _____

Calories 297  Protein 34.2 g  Carbohydrates 9.32 g  Fat 13 g  Cholesterol 81.7 mg  Sodium 412 mg

# Not Your Everyday Meatloaf Kari J. Tobias

1 pound ground turkey
3 carrots, shredded
1 cup low-fat cottage cheese
1 egg white
1 small onion, chopped
1 teaspoon salt
¼ teaspoon black pepper
½ teaspoon basil

- Combine all ingredients and mix thoroughly.
- Place in a 9x5x3-inch loaf pan.
- Bake at 300° for 50 minutes.
- Remove from pan, let stand for a few minutes and cut into slices to serve.

Serves 4

Per serving _____

Calories 291  Protein 41.1 g  Carbohydrates 9 g  Fat 9 g  Cholesterol 87.5 mg  Sodium 872 mg

# Chili Cheese Pie

Martha Rife

1 cup chopped onion
½ cup chopped red or green bell pepper
½ pound ground turkey, cooked and crumbled
1 (4 ounce) can chopped green chilies
1½ tablespoons tomato paste
2 teaspoons chili powder
Salt and black pepper to taste
½ teaspoon garlic powder
½ cup (2 ounces) shredded Cheddar cheese
¾ cup all-purpose flour
¼ teaspoon baking soda
¼ teaspoon salt
½ cup buttermilk
2 eggs
2 teaspoons margarine, melted

- Sauté onion and bell pepper in non-stick skillet prepared with vegetable cooking spray until onions are translucent.
- Add turkey, chilies, tomato paste, chili powder, salt, black pepper and garlic powder. Cook, stirring occasionally, for about 5 minutes.
- Pour turkey mixture into 9-inch pie pan. Sprinkle with cheese.
- Using blender or electric mixer, combine remaining ingredients, blending until smooth. Pour batter over meat mixture.
- Bake at 425° for about 30 minutes or until crust is browned.

Serves 6

Per serving _____

Calories 278  Protein 18.1 g  Carbohydrates 19.5 g  Fat 14 g  Cholesterol 120 mg  Sodium 887 mg

## Mexican Lasagna

Gwen Walden Irwin

1½ pounds ground turkey or
ground beef
1 (17 ounce) can whole kernel
corn, drained
1 cup picanté sauce
1 (15 ounce) can tomato sauce
or Italian style tomatoes
1 envelope taco seasoning
1 (16 ounce) carton cottage
cheese
2 eggs
1 teaspoon oregano
10 corn tortillas
1½ cups (6 ounces) shredded
Cheddar or Monterey Jack cheese

- In a 12-inch skillet, brown meat, stirring to crumble. Drain excess grease.

- Add corn, picanté sauce, tomato sauce and taco seasoning. Simmer for 5 minutes.

- Combine cottage cheese, eggs and oregano, mixing thoroughly.

- Place 5 tortillas in bottom of lightly-greased 13x9x2-inch baking dish, overlapping to fit.

- Layer, in order listed, ½ of meat mixture, cheese mixture, 5 tortillas and remaining meat mixture. Sprinkle with cheese.

- Bake, uncovered, at 375° for 30 minutes. Let stand 10 minutes before serving.

Serves 12

Per serving _____

Calories 386  Protein 29.4 g  Carbohydrates 25.7 g  Fat 19 g  Cholesterol 112 mg  Sodium 783 mg

# Veal Piccata

*Kathy Marsh*

¼ cup all-purpose flour
1 teaspoon salt
½ teaspoon black pepper
2 pounds veal, thinly sliced
¼ cup plus 2 tablespoons margarine, divided
1 cup white wine, divided
1 lemon, sliced paper thin
½ cup chopped parsley
2 egg yolks

- Combine flour, salt and black pepper. Dredge veal in seasoned flour, coating well. Sauté veal in ¼ cup margarine, turning to brown on both sides.

- Add ½ cup wine, lemon slices and parsley. Simmer, covered, for 10 minutes. Place veal on serving platter and keep warm. Discard lemon slices.

- Melt 2 tablespoons margarine in skillet over low heat. Beat egg yolks with ½ cup wine. Gradually add to melted butter, stirring constantly, and cook over low heat until thickened.

- Pour sauce over veal and serve.

Serves 8

Per serving _____

Calories 422  Protein 35.6 g  Carbohydrates 3.49 g  Fat 26.5 g  Cholesterol 202 mg  Sodium 421 mg

# Savory Meatballs and Rice

Nanci Norin Jordt

1½ cups uncooked regular rice
1 pound ground beef
¼ cup dried breadcrumbs
¼ cup minced onion
1 egg, lightly beaten
1 small clove garlic, minced
1 tablespoon vegetable shortening
1 (10¾ ounce) can golden mushroom soup, undiluted
½ cup chopped canned tomatoes, drained
2 tablespoons brown sugar
2 tablespoons vinegar
2 tablespoons soy sauce
Dash of black pepper

- Prepare rice according to package directions. While rice is cooking, prepare meatballs.
- Combine beef, breadcrumbs, onion, egg and garlic, mixing well. Shape into balls.
- Sauté meatballs in shortening, turning to brown on all sides. Drain excess grease from skillet.
- Add soup, tomatoes, brown sugar, vinegar, soy sauce and black pepper to meatballs. Simmer for 20 minutes or until done, stirring occasionally.
- Serve over rice.

Serves 6

Per serving _____

Calories 487  Protein 28.3 g  Carbohydrates 47.2 g  Fat 19.5 g  Cholesterol 111 mg  Sodium 699 mg

# Stroganoff Casserole

Barbara Stromberg Boyd

¼ cup chopped onion
1 clove garlic, minced
2 (3 ounce) cans mushrooms, drained
¼ cup margarine
1 pound ground beef
Salt to taste
1 (14½ ounce) can beef broth
3 tablespoons Burgundy wine
3 tablespoons lemon juice
1 (6 to 8 ounce) package noodles
1 cup sour cream

- Sauté onion, garlic and mushrooms in margarine until lightly browned. Add beef, season with salt and cook until beef is no longer pink.
- Add broth, wine and lemon juice to beef mixture. Simmer, uncovered, for 15 minutes.
- Stir in noodles and simmer, covered, just until noodles are tender. Add sour cream, stirring to blend, just before serving.

Serves 8

Per serving _____

Calories 277  Protein 20.1 g  Carbohydrates 10.8 g  Fat 16.5 g  Cholesterol 109 mg  Sodium 721 mg

# Stacked Enchiladas

Millie Skidmore

1 *pound extra lean ground beef*
2 *(8 ounce) cans tomato sauce*
2 *tablespoons chili powder*
2 *freshly roasted green chilies,*
*seeded and chopped*
1 *(8 ounce) can green chili sauce*
16 *corn tortillas*
1 *pound grated cheese*
1 *medium-sized onion, chopped*
½ *head lettuce, chopped*
2 *tomatoes, chopped*
*Fried eggs (optional)*

- Brown beef in skillet, stirring to crumble. Place in large saucepan.
- Discard skillet drippings. Combine tomato sauce, chili powder and green chilies in skillet. Simmer for 20 minutes.
- Prepare separate skillet with non-stick vegetable cooking spray. Heat each tortilla for 2 to 3 seconds on each side. Keep warm.
- For each serving, place 1 tortilla on plate, top with sauce, cheese, onions and beef. Repeat layer. Top each stack with lettuce, tomatoes and fried egg, if desired.

Serves 8

Per serving

Calories 591  Protein 36.7 g  Carbohydrates 40.5 g  Fat 32.5 g  Cholesterol 120 mg  Sodium 900 mg

# Low-Fat Swiss Steak

*Patti Shields*

1 *pound boneless beef round
steak, ¾-inch thick*
1 *(28-ounce) can tomatoes,
chopped, undrained*
1 *small onion, sliced in rings*
½ *cup sliced celery*
¼ *teaspoon salt*
⅛ *teaspoon black pepper*
1 *bay leaf*
1½ *teaspoons dried marjoram,
crushed*
1 *tablespoon cornstarch*
1 *tablespoon cold water*

- Trim fat from steak. Cut into 4 serving pieces. Preheat 12-inch skillet prepared with non-stick vegetable cooking spray. Sauté steak, turning to brown on both sides. Remove steak from skillet.

- Drain drippings and return steak to skillet. Add tomatoes, onion, celery, salt, black pepper, bay leaf and marjoram. Bring to a boil, reduce heat and simmer, covered, for about 1¼ hours.

- Remove steak from skillet. Skim off fat and discard bay leaf.

- Blend cornstarch and water until smooth. Add to tomato mixture. Heat until thickened and bubbly, stir and cook for 2 additional minutes.

- Serve steak and sauce over rice or fettuccine.

Serves 4

Per serving _____

Calories 266  Protein 38.2 g  Carbohydrates 13.5 g  Fat 16 g  Cholesterol 95.2 mg  Sodium 540 mg

# Peppered Tenderloin with Port-Ginger Sauce

Vicki Ashley Atkins

2 tablespoons black peppercorns
2 teaspoons green peppercorns in
brine, drained
4 (6 ounce) beef tenderloins
1 teaspoon olive oil
Salt to taste

**Port-Ginger Sauce**

1 cup ruby port wine
¼ cup minced shallots
1½ tablespoons minced fresh
ginger
1½ tablespoons butter
Salt to taste

- Crush peppercorns and rub on tenderloins. Season with salt.

- Sauté tenderloins in oil in heavy skillet over high heat, cooking to desired doneness (4 to 5 minutes per side for medium). Place on platter and tent with foil to keep warm.

- Add port, shallots and ginger to same skillet. Bring to a boil and cook, stirring frequently, for about 5 minutes or until reduced to thin syrup consistency.

- Strain sauce, pressing solids with back of spoon to release flavors. Discard solids and return liquid to skillet; boil until thickened (should measure about ½ cup). Whisk in butter and season with salt to taste.

- Spoon small amount of sauce on each tenderloin and serve remaining sauce on the side.

Serves 4

Per serving with 1 tablespoon sauce _____

Calories 326  Protein 50.19 g  Carbohydrates 1.57 g  Fat 11.5 g  Cholesterol 119.03 mg  Sodium 114.42 mg

# Beef and Broccoli

Julie Clark

¼ cup soy sauce
1 teaspoon sugar
1 pound sirloin steak, cut in 2-
inch strips
¼ cup olive oil
½ teaspoon ground ginger
1 clove garlic, chopped
2 cups chopped broccoli
1 tablespoon cornstarch
1 cup water

- Combine soy sauce and sugar. Pour mixture over steak and marinate for 1 hour.
- Combine oil, ginger and garlic in skillet and cook for 2 to 3 minutes. Add steak with marinade and sauté for 5 minutes. Stir in broccoli.
- Blend cornstarch and water until smooth. Add to steak and vegetables and cook for 5 minutes over low heat.

Serves 4

Per serving _____

Calories 383  Protein 36.8 g  Carbohydrates 7.1 g  Fat 23 g  Cholesterol 43.8 mg  Sodium 1116 mg

# Tex-Mex Roast

Dayna Beikirch

8 pounds rolled rump beef roast
or brisket
1 (16 ounce) package pinto
beans
2 (10 ounce) cans tomatoes with
green chilies
1 (8 ounce) can tomato sauce
1 (6 ounce) can green chilies
1 cup sliced mushrooms
1 onion, coarsely chopped
Salt and black pepper to taste

- Place roast in large roasting pan. Sort and rinse beans and place around roast.
- Add all remaining ingredients.
- Bake at 250° for 8 hours.

Serves 16

Per serving _____

Calories 448  Protein 74.8 g  Carbohydrates 11.3 g  Fat 16 g  Cholesterol 217.5 mg  Sodium 503 mg

## Beer Braised Beef

*Ann Bommarito Armstrong*

3 pounds beef chuck, cut in 1-
inch cubes
¼ cup all-purpose flour
¼ teaspoon salt
3 tablespoons vegetable oil
2 large onions, thinly sliced
1 clove garlic, minced
1 (8 ounce) can mushrooms,
drained
1 (10½ ounce) can condensed
beef broth, undiluted
1 (12 ounce) can beer
1 tablespoon vinegar
2 teaspoons sugar
1 teaspoon dried thyme, crushed
1 bay leaf
1 tablespoon all-purpose flour or
cornstarch
2 tablespoons water
1 tablespoon chopped parsley

- Coat beef cubes with mixture of flour and salt. Sauté beef in oil in Dutch oven, turning to brown on all sides.

- Add onion, garlic, mushrooms, broth, beer, vinegar, sugar, thyme and bay leaf to beef.

- Simmer, covered, for 1 1/2 to 2 hours or until beef is tender.

- Remove bay leaf. Blend flour with water to form a paste. Blend with pan juices, cooking until thickened slightly. Stir in parsley.

- Serve with buttered noodles or rice.

Serves 10

Per serving _____

Calories 555  Protein 38.5 g  Carbohydrates 7.59 g  Fat 39.5 g  Cholesterol 135 mg  Sodium 461 mg

# Italian Pot Roast

*Vicki Ashley Atkins*

2 *pounds boneless beef rump*
*roast*
4 *cloves garlic, minced*
2 *medium-sized onions, sliced*
1 *green bell pepper, sliced*
4 *stalks celery, cut in 2-inch*
*pieces*
6 *large carrots, cut in 2-inch*
*pieces*
12 *new potatoes*
1 *bay leaf*
1 *tablespoon Italian seasoning*
*Salt and black pepper to taste*
1 *tablespoon low-sodium soy*
*sauce*
1 *tablespoon Worcestershire*
*sauce*
1 *(28 ounce) can tomatoes,*
*undrained*
1 *(15 ounce) can tomato sauce*
½ *cup hearty red wine*

- Place meat in large roasting pan. Cover with minced garlic and slices of onion and bell pepper. Arrange remaining vegetables around roast.

- Add bay leaf, Italian seasoning, salt and black pepper.

- Combine soy sauce, Worcestershire sauce, tomatoes, tomato sauce and wine. Pour over vegetables and roast.

- Bake at 250° for 4 to 5 hours.

Serves 8

Per serving _____

Calories 367  Protein 40.1 g  Carbohydrates 31.5 g  Fat 8.5 g  Cholesterol 109 mg  Sodium 810 mg

## Fool Proof Roast Beef

Nanci Norin Jordt

*This roast, no matter what size, will be brown on the outside and rare on the inside. If less rare roast is preferred, increase final baking time slightly*

1 (5 pound) standing rib beef roast
1 tablespoon garlic powder
1 tablespoon black pepper

- Rub roast with garlic powder and black pepper. Let stand until room temperature. Place in roasting pan, rib side down.
- Bake at 375° for 1 hour. Turn oven off but do not open oven door; let roast stand in oven for 1 hour. Reset oven temperature to 375° and bake for 50 to 60 minutes.

*Wonderful served with Hot Mustard Sauce.*

Serves 10

Per serving _____

Calories 557  Protein 62.4 g  Carbohydrates 1.54 g  Fat 32 g  Cholesterol 181 mg  Sodium 164 mg

## Hot Mustard Sauce

Nanci Norin Jordt

1 (16 ounce) jar apple jelly
1 (18 ounce) jar orange marmalade or pineapple preserves
1 (5 ounce) jar cream-style horseradish
1 (6 ounce) jar prepared mustard
Salt and black pepper to taste

- Combine all ingredients in blender container. Blend until smooth.
- Serve hot or cold with beef or ham.

*Makes great gifts when bottled in small decorative jars.*

Makes 5½ cups

Per tablespoon _____

Calories 33  Protein .179 g  Carbohydrates 7.69 g  Fat .5 g  Cholesterol .696 mg  Sodium 34 mg

# Sausage and Rice Casserole

Vera Alexander Dufour

1 cup uncooked regular rice
1 cup chopped carrots
1 cup chopped celery
1 cup chopped onion
1 pound bulk pork sausage,
  cooked and crumbled
2 cups chicken broth

- Layer in casserole dish starting with rice, then carrots, celery, onion, finally sausage.
- Pour chicken broth over all. Cover with foil.
- Bake, in a 350° oven for 30 minutes.
- Uncover and mix well.
- Cover again and bake 30 minutes longer.

*Venison sausage may be used. Grated Monterey Jack cheese may be sprinkled on casserole during last 5 minutes of baking.*

Serves 8

Per serving _____

Calories 317  Protein 14.5 g  Carbohydrates 22.4 g  Fat 18.5 g  Cholesterol 47.1 mg  Sodium 945 mg

# Pork in Tomatillo Chili Sauce

Jennie Hentges

2 pounds boneless pork shoulder,
  cut in 1-inch cubes
¼ cup all-purpose flour
¼ cup vegetable oil
1 medium-sized onion, chopped
1 (13 ounce) can tomatillos,
  drained and mashed
1 cup chicken broth
½ cup chopped cilantro
½ cup chopped green chilies
1 teaspoon salt
¼ teaspoon black pepper
1 tablespoon dried oregano,
  crushed
½ cup sour cream for garnish

- Dredge pork in flour, coating all surfaces. Sauté pork in oil until no longer pink.
- Remove pork from skillet, drain excess grease and return pork to skillet. Stir in remaining ingredients, except sour cream. Bring to a boil, reduce heat and simmer, covered, for about 45 minutes or until pork is tender.
- Serve over hot steamed rice. Garnish individual servings with dollop of sour cream.

Serves 8

Per serving _____

Calories 279  Protein 25.9 g  Carbohydrates 6.05 g  Fat 16 g  Cholesterol 90.5 mg  Sodium 392 mg

## Cheese Stuffed Pork Chops
Linda Uchiyama Kelley

2 scallions
1 (4 ounce) package soft mild goat cheese
1 tablespoon white wine
2 tablespoons fresh lemon juice
½ teaspoon freshly ground black pepper
1 teaspoon dried thyme
4 (6 ounce) rib pork chops, 1-inch thick
Salt and black pepper to taste
2 tablespoons vegetable oil
½ cup dry white wine

- Thinly slice scallions, separating white and green portions.
- Combine cheese, wine, white portion of scallions, lemon juice, black pepper and thyme, beating until well blended. Chill for 15 minutes or until firm.
- Cut a small slit along bone into center of each chop, being careful not to cut through to other side. Spoon cheese mixture into each chop cavity, secure open edge with wooden picks and season with salt and black pepper.
- Cook chops in single layer in oil in large skillet over medium heat, covered, for 20 to 25 minutes or until browned and done. Place chops on serving platter and keep warm.
- Drain excess grease from skillet. Add wine and green part of scallions. Simmer, covered, for 20 to 25 minutes or until sauce is reduced to ¼ cup. Pour sauce over chops and serve immediately.

*Commercially prepared flavored soft cheese may be substituted. If so, omit first step.*

Serves 4

Per serving _____

Calories 660  Protein 34.2 g  Carbohydrates 2.56 g  Fat 54 g  Cholesterol 129 mg  Sodium 332 mg

# Pork Italiano

Jennie Hentges

4 boneless pork chops
1 tablespoon vegetable oil
¼ pound Italian bulk sausage
½ cup chopped onion
1 (8 ounce) can tomato sauce
¾ cup apple juice or cider
⅛ teaspoon black pepper
½ teaspoon garlic salt
½ teaspoon dried oregano, crushed
1 teaspoon cornstarch
2 tablespoons cold water

- Sauté chops in oil in skillet, turning to brown on both sides. Remove chops from pan and set aside.
- Sauté sausage and onion in skillet until sausage is cooked, stirring to crumble. Drain excess grease.
- Add tomato sauce, apple juice, black pepper, garlic salt and oregano to sausage mixture. Bring to a boil. Add chops and simmer, covered, for 10 minutes.
- Remove chops from skillet and keep warm. Blend cornstarch and water until smooth. Add to sauce and cook, stirring often, until bubbly and thickened.
- Pour sauce over chops and serve with your favorite pasta.

Serves 4

Per serving _____

Calories 404  Protein 35.9 g  Carbohydrates 12.3 g  Fat 23 g  Cholesterol 109 mg  Sodium 1069 mg

# *Pork Piquante*

Nancille Sewell Willis

8 large boneless pork loin chops,
trimmed
Salt to taste
Black pepper to taste
1 (15 ounce) can crushed
pineapple, drained and juice
reserved
½ cup water
¼ cup vinegar
2 tablespoons lemon juice
2 tablespoons Worcestershire
sauce
¼ cup firmly-packed brown
sugar
2 tablespoons prepared mustard
2 tablespoons cornstarch
2 tablespoons cold water
1 (29 ounce) can sweet potatoes,
drained
2 medium-sized onions

- Sear chops in skillet, turning to lightly brown on both sides. Drain on paper towel. Arrange chops in 13x9x2-inch baking dish. Season with salt and black pepper to taste. Set aside.

- Combine pineapple juice, water, vinegar, lemon juice, Worcestershire sauce, brown sugar and mustard in skillet. Blend cornstarch and cold water until smooth and add to sauce. Simmer until slightly thickened, stirring constantly.

- Arrange sweet potatoes around chops. Thinly slice onions, separate into rings and layer over sweet potatoes and chops. Season with salt and black pepper to taste.

- Pour sauce over vegetables and chops.

- Bake, covered, at 350° for about 1 hour or until pork and onions are fork-tender. Spread pineapple on chops and vegetables. Bake, uncovered, for additional 15 minutes.

Serves 8

Per serving

Calories 620  Protein 30.3 g  Carbohydrates 30.7 g  Fat 41.5 g  Cholesterol 116 mg  Sodium 614 mg

# Pork Roast Supreme

Jane Miller Sanders

1 (4 pound) boneless pork loin,
rolled and tied
½ teaspoon salt
½ teaspoon garlic salt
1½ teaspoons chili powder,
divided
1 cup apple jelly
1 cup ketchup
2 tablespoons vinegar
½ cup crushed corn chips

- Season pork with salt, garlic salt and ½ teaspoon chili powder, rubbing evenly on all surfaces. Place, fat side up, on rack in shallow baking pan.

- Bake at 325° for 2 hours or until internal temperature of pork is 165°.

- Combine apple jelly, ketchup, vinegar and 1 teaspoon chili powder in saucepan. Bring to a boil, reduce heat and simmer for 2 minutes. When pork is done, generously brush sauce over top and sides; reserve remaining sauce and keep warm. Sprinkle pork with chips.

- Bake for additional 10 to 15 minutes or until internal temperature of pork is 170°.

- Serve pork with remaining sauce.

Serves 10

Per serving _____

Calories 471  Protein 55.6  Carbohydrates 28.9 g  Fat 14 g  Cholesterol 142 mg  Sodium 616 mg

# Pork Roast

Shermette Naumann

1 (4 pound) boneless pork roast
½ cup browning sauce
1 tablespoon celery salt
1 tablespoon garlic salt
Salt and black pepper to taste

- Coat all sides of roast with browning sauce. Sprinkle celery salt, garlic salt, salt and black pepper on all surfaces of roast. Place roast on rack in baking pan.
- Bake at 350° for 30 minutes per pound or to desired doneness. Let stand for a few minutes before slicing.

Serves 10

Per serving _____

Calories 513  Protein 60.9 g  Carbohydrates 3.35 g  Fat 26.5 g  Cholesterol 191 mg  Sodium 1328 mg

# Pork Tenderloin with Mustard Sauce

Linda Cook Uhl

¼ cup soy sauce
¼ cup bourbon
2 tablespoons brown sugar
3 pounds pork tenderloin

**Mustard Sauce**

⅔ cup sour cream
⅔ cup mayonnaise
2 tablespoons dry mustard
3 or 4 green onions, chopped

- Combine soy sauce, bourbon and brown sugar in 11x7x1½-inch baking dish. Add tenderloin. Marinate in refrigerator for at least 2 hours, turning tenderloin occasionally.
- Prepare sauce by combining sour cream, mayonnaise, mustard and onion. Chill for at least 1 hour.
- Remove tenderloin from marinade and place on rack in shallow roasting pan.
- Bake at 325° for 45 minutes or until internal temperature of tenderloin is 160°.
- Serve with Mustard Sauce.

Serves 8

Per serving of pork _____

Calories 477  Protein 56.1 g  Carbohydrates 1.29 g  Fat 25 g  Cholesterol 179 mg  Sodium 256 mg

Per tablespoon sauce _____

Calories 62  Protein .527 g  Carbohydrates .865 g  Fat 6.5 g  Cholesterol 6.45 mg  Sodium 38.5 mg

# Pork Medallions with Burgundy

Jeanne Cassidy

½ cup dried cranberries
¾ cup boiling water
1 pound pork tenderloin
Salt and black pepper to taste
2 teaspoons vegetable oil
1 shallot, minced
¾ cup Burgundy wine
1 tablespoon plus 1 teaspoon
honey
¼ cup balsamic vinegar
1 cup beef consommé
½ teaspoon dried thyme
1 teaspoon cornstarch
1 tablespoon water

- Soak cranberries in boiling water. Set aside.

- Trim tenderloin and cut into 12 medallions.

- Season medallions with salt and black pepper. Sauté medallions in oil in large non-stick skillet over medium heat, cooking for 3 to 4 minutes on each side. Place on serving platter and keep warm.

- In same skillet, cook shallot, stirring constantly, for 1 minute. Add burgundy, honey and vinegar. Bring to a boil and cook for 3 to 5 minutes or until volume is reduced by ½.

- Drain cranberries, reserving liquid. Add liquid, consommé and thyme to sauce. Bring to a boil and cook for 5 minutes.

- Blend cornstarch and water until smooth. Whisk into sauce. Cook, stirring frequently, until slightly thickened. Add cranberries and cook for 1 minute.

- Ladle sauce over medallions and serve.

Serves 4

Per serving _____

Calories 427  Protein 41.3 g  Carbohydrates 14.4 g  Fat 19 g  Cholesterol 119 mg  Sodium 744 mg

# Desserts

As the holiday season approaches, members of Austin Junior Forum transform the historic Daniel H. Caswell House into a Christmas wonder. And what would this time of year be without special desserts? Top off a holiday buffet with an array of sweets including **Clara's Italian Cream Cake**, **Lacey's Old-Fashioned Raspberry Bars**, cinnamony **Apple Dumplings**, **Quickie Chocolate Mousse**, and **Chocolate Dipped Fruit**. Who would realize that preparation for many of these favorites has been streamlined? For instance, instead of made-from-scratch, prepared pie crust can be used for the apple dumplings, and in place of homemade filling, store-bought preserves fill the raspberry bars.

*Photo taken in the dining room of Austin Junior Forum's Daniel H. Caswell House, Austin, Texas.*

# Almond Amaretto Cake

*Barbara Stromberg Boyd*

½ cup sliced almonds
1 tablespoon butter
1 (18½ ounce) package yellow cake mix
4 eggs
½ cup amaretto liqueur
½ cup water
½ cup vegetable oil

**Glaze**

½ cup sugar
¼ cup margarine
2 tablespoons amaretto liqueur
¼ cup water

- Lightly brown almonds in butter in small saucepan. Pour almonds and butter into greased and floured 10-inch bundt pan.
- Combine cake mix, eggs, amaretto, water and oil, blending well.
- Pour batter over almonds.
- Bake at 325° for 45 minutes. Place pan on wire rack to cool while preparing glaze.
- Prepare glaze by combining sugar, margarine, amaretto and water in saucepan. Cook over medium heat, stirring until sugar is dissolve.
- Invert cake on serving plate. Pour glaze over cake.

Serves 16

Per serving _____

Calories 318  Protein 3.62 g  Carbohydrates 35.6 g  Fat 17 g  Cholesterol 55.6 mg  Sodium 270 mg

# Banana Applesauce Cake

Ann Bommarito Armstrong

2½ cups all-purpose flour
2 cups sugar
½ teaspoon baking powder
½ teaspoon baking soda
¾ teaspoon salt
1 teaspoon cinnamon
½ teaspoon ground cloves
½ teaspoon ground allspice
½ cup water
½ cup vegetable shortening
1 cup canned applesauce
1 cup mashed bananas
2 eggs
½ cup chopped nuts
¾ cup raisins

- Combine flour, sugar, baking powder, baking soda, salt, cinnamon, cloves and allspice in large mixing bowl.
- Add water, shortening, applesauce and bananas to dry ingredients. Using electric mixer, beat until creamy. Add eggs and beat at medium speed for 2 minutes. Stir nuts and raisins into batter.
- Pour batter into 13x9x2-inch baking pan lined on bottom with wax paper.
- Bake at 350° for 45 minutes. Invert on wire rack, remove wax paper and turn, right side up, while still warm.
- Sift powdered sugar on cake just before serving.

Serves 24

Per serving _____

Calories 196  Protein 2.29 g  Carbohydrates 33.3 g  Fat 6.5 g  Cholesterol 17.7 mg  Sodium 41 mg

★

Don't discard very ripe bananas. They can be frozen whole, in their peel, for later use in breads or cakes.

# Blackberry Wine Cake

*Cheryl Briggs Patton*

1 (18½ ounce) package white
cake mix
1 (3 ounce) package blackberry
or black cherry gelatin
4 eggs
½ cup vegetable oil
1 cup blackberry wine

**Glaze**

1 cup powdered sugar
½ cup blackberry wine
½ cup margarine or butter,
softened

- Combine cake mix and gelatin in large mixing bowl.
- Add eggs, oil and wine to dry ingredients. Using electric mixer, beat at low speed until moistened, then beat at medium speed for 2 minutes, scraping bowl frequently.
- Pour batter into well-greased 10-inch bundt pan.
- Bake at 325° for 45 to 50 minutes. Place pan on wire rack.
- Prepare glaze by mixing sugar and wine in saucepan. Bring to a boil. Add margarine and stir.
- Pour ½ of glaze over warm cake in pan and let stand for 30 minutes. Invert cake on serving pan and drizzle with remaining glaze.

Serves 12

Per serving

Calories 441  Protein 4.27 g  Carbohydrates 47.1 g  Fat 23 g  Cholesterol 91.4 mg  Sodium 395 mg

# Vi's Super Carrot Cake

*Ginny Ashley*

2 cups all-purpose flour
2 teaspoons baking soda
1 tablespoon cinnamon
1 teaspoon salt
4 eggs, beaten
2 cups sugar
1½ cups vegetable oil
3 cups grated carrots
1 cup yellow raisins (optional)

## Icing

½ cup margarine, softened
1 (8 ounce) package cream cheese, softened
2 teaspoons vanilla
1 (16 ounce) package powdered sugar
½ cup chopped pecans, toasted (optional)

- Sift flour, baking soda, cinnamon and salt.

- In large mixing bowl, combine eggs, sugar, oil and carrots. Mix well.

- Gradually add dry ingredients to wet ingredients and mix well. (Add raisins if desired.)

- Pour batter into 3 greased and floured 8-inch round baking pans.

- Bake at 350° for approximately 20 to 25 minutes or until wooden pick inserted in middle of cake comes out clean. Let cake cool and remove from pans.

- Using electric mixer, cream margarine and cream cheese. Add vanilla. Mix well. Gradually add powdered sugar, mixing well after each addition.

- Place icing between cake layers and on top and sides of cake. Sprinkle toasted pecans on sides of cake if desired.

Serves 16

Per serving _____

Calories 575  Protein 4.54 g  Carbohydrates 68.2 g  Fat 32 g  Cholesterol 68.6 mg  Sodium 369 mg

## Cappuccino-Chocolate Cheesecake   *Barbara Bump*

½ (9 ounce) package chocolate
wafers, crushed
⅛ teaspoon cinnamon
1 (8 ounce) package low-fat
cream cheese, softened
1 cup sugar
1 cup cocoa
½ cup egg substitute or 2 eggs
2½ cups non-fat sour cream
substitute, divided
2 tablespoons coffee liqueur
1 teaspoon vanilla

- Combine wafer crumbs and cinnamon. Firmly pat mixture in bottom of 9-inch springform pan.

- Using electric mixer, beat cream cheese until light and fluffy. Add sugar and cocoa, beating well. Add egg substitute, blending thoroughly.

- Stir 2 cups sour cream substitute, coffee liqueur and vanilla into cream cheese mixture.

- Spread batter in prepared pan.

- Bake at 350° for about 30 minutes or until cake is firm. Spread ½ cup sour cream substitute on top of cake. Bake for 1 additional minute to glaze.

- Cool at room temperature. Chill before serving.

Serves 16

Per serving _____

Calories 185  Protein 7.46 g  Carbohydrates 32.5 g  Fat 4 g  Cholesterol 2.96 mg  Sodium 219 mg

# Chocolate Truffle Cake

*Vicki Ashley Atkins*

*Must chill at least 4 hours*

3 (8 ounce) packages semisweet
chocolate
3 (1 ounce) squares unsweetened
baking chocolate
3 cups whipping cream
½ cup unsalted butter, softened
4 egg yolks
2 cups chocolate wafer cookie
crumbs
¼ to ½ cup butter, melted

- Place semisweet and unsweetened chocolate in large bowl.
- Heat cream to boiling point. Pour over chocolate and whisk until chocolate is melted.
- Add softened butter and whisk to blend. Whisk in egg yolks, 1 at a time. Set chocolate mixture aside to cool to room temperature.
- Combine cookie crumbs and melted butter. Pat crumbs firmly in bottom of 10-inch springform pan lined with parchment paper.
- Pour cooled chocolate mixture into pan. Cover and refrigerate for at least 4 hours or overnight.

*Delicious served with raspberry or vanilla sauce.*

Serves 24

Per serving _____

Calories 399  Protein 3.94 g  Carbohydrates 33.6 g  Fat 30.5 g  Cholesterol 92 mg  Sodium 146 mg

————— ★ —————

Try dusting your pans with cocoa instead of flour
when baking chocolate cakes.

# Chocolate Vienna Cheesecake   Tamra Beasley Bashaw

*Chill at least 12 hours*

| | |
|---|---|
| 1 *cup graham cracker crumbs*<br>2 *tablespoons sugar*<br>½ *teaspoon cinnamon*<br>¼ *cup butter*<br>1 (8 *ounce*) *package semisweet*<br>*chocolate squares*<br>1 *teaspoon espresso coffee powder*<br>¼ *cup hot water*<br>3 (8 *ounce*) *packages cream*<br>*cheese, softened*<br>2 *tablespoons whipping cream*<br>¾ *cup sugar*<br>3 *eggs*<br>1 *cup sour cream*<br>¼ *cup coffee liqueur*<br>2 *teaspoons vanilla* | • Combine graham cracker crumbs, sugar, cinnamon and butter, mixing well. Press crumbs in bottom of buttered 10-inch springform pan.<br>• Melt chocolate.<br>• Combine espresso and hot water. Set aside to cool.<br>• Beat cream cheese with whipping cream, sugar and eggs.<br>• Add sour cream, coffee liqueur, vanilla and diluted espresso to cream cheese mixture. Fold in melted chocolate.<br>• Pour batter into pan.<br>• Bake at 350° for 45 minutes. Refrigerate for at least 12 hours. Center may be soft but will become firm with chilling. |

Serves 15

Per serving _____

Calories 409  Protein 6.42 g  Carbohydrates 31.8 g  Fat 29 g  Cholesterol 110 mg  Sodium 237 mg

## Cookie Cake

Gwen Walden Irwin

2 (16 ounce) packages
refrigerated chocolate chip cookie
dough
2 (8 ounce) packages cream
cheese, softened
2 eggs
1 cup sugar
1 teaspoon vanilla

- Place cookie dough packages in the freezer for about 30 minutes before beginning. (This makes handling easier.)
- Flour and grease 13x9x2-inch baking pan.
- Remove 1 package of dough from freezer and slice in ¼-inch thick slices. Use the slices to "pave" the bottom of the pan.
- Mix cream cheese, eggs, sugar and vanilla together well. Spread mixture over the layer of cookie dough in the pan.
- Remove the second package of dough from the freezer and slice into ¼-inch thick slices. Place slices on top of the cream cheese mixture.
- Bake 30 to 35 minutes at 350°.

Serves 24

Per serving _____

Calories 273  Protein 3.61 g  Carbohydrates 32.1 g  Fat 14.5 g  Cholesterol 47.5 mg  Sodium 140 mg

# Glazed Poppy Seed Cake

Liza Fox-Mills

3½ cups all-purpose flour
2½ cups sugar
3 eggs
1¼ cups vegetable oil
1½ teaspoons baking powder
1½ cups milk
1½ teaspoons salt
1½ teaspoons vanilla extract
1½ teaspoons almond extract
1½ teaspoons butter flavoring
3 tablespoons poppy seeds

**Glaze**
¾ cup sifted powdered sugar
¼ cup orange juice
1½ teaspoons butter flavoring
1½ teaspoons vanilla extract
1½ teaspoons almond extract
¼ cup sliced almonds (optional)

- Mix ingredients for cake in large bowl until batter is smooth and pour into a greased bundt pan (2 loaf pans may be substituted).
- Bake 55 to 60 minutes at 350°.
- Stir together glaze ingredients and pour over warm cake/loaves and garnish with almonds if desired.

Also makes approximately 2 dozen cupcakes—cook for only 30 to 35 minutes at 350°.

Serves 16

Per serving _____

Calories 440  Protein 5.4 g  Carbohydrates 59.4 g  Fat 20.5 g  Cholesterol 42.9 mg  Sodium 225 mg

# Piña Colada Cake

Donna Earle Crain

1 (18½ ounce) package white cake mix (without pudding)
1 (16 ounce) can cream of coconut
1 (20 ounce) can crushed pineapple
1 (8 ounce) carton frozen whipped topping
¼ cup flaked coconut

- Prepare cake according to package directions. Pour batter into greased and floured 13x9x2-inch baking pan. Bake as directed.
- Pour cream of coconut over warm cake. Spoon pineapple on cake.
- Spread whipped topping on cooled cake and sprinkle with coconut. Refrigerate.

Serves 24

Per serving _____

Calories 150  Protein 1.63  Carbohydrates 19.8 g  Fat 7.5 g  Cholesterol 0  Sodium 119 mg

# Clara's Italian Cream Cake

*Chez Z Café*

*All ingredients should be at room temperature*

½ cup margarine, softened
½ cup vegetable shortening
2 cups sugar
5 eggs, separated
2 cups all-purpose flour (before
sifting)
1 teaspoon baking soda
1 cup buttermilk
2 teaspoons vanilla extract
½ teaspoon coconut extract
(optional)
6 ounces angel flake coconut
1 cup pecan pieces

- Using electric mixer, cream margarine and shortening together. Gradually add sugar and beat until fluffy. Add egg yolks, 1 at a time, beating until all is incorporated.
- Sift flour and baking soda together. Set aside.
- Combine buttermilk and extracts. Add to creamed mixture.
- Add flour and buttermilk mixture alternately to creamed mixture, beginning and ending with flour, beating after each addition only until incorporated.
- Fold in coconut and pecans.
- In separate bowl and with clean beaters, beat egg whites until stiff peaks form. Carefully fold egg whites into mixture in 2 or 3 small additions.
- Pour batter into 2 greased and floured 8 or 9-inch round baking pans, smoothing batter with spatula; do not tap pan to level.
- Bake on middle shelf at 350° for 30 to 45 minutes. Do not open oven during first 25 minutes of baking or cakes will fall.
- Cool 10 minutes in pan, remove and cool completely on racks. Refrigerate for at least 2 hours before frosting.

**Clara's Italian Cream Cake** (continued)

### Frosting

1 (8 ounce) package cream
cheese, softened
6 tablespoons butter, softened
3 cups powdered sugar
1 tablespoon vanilla

- Beat cream cheese and butter together until smooth. Add powdered sugar and vanilla and beat until fluffy. (In warm weather, add a little more powdered sugar to stiffen frosting.)
- Spread frosting between layers and decorate sides and top of cake.

Serves 16

Per serving _____

Calories 570  Protein 6.18 g  Carbohydrates 67.3 g  Fat 32 g  Cholesterol 94 mg  Sodium 268 mg

# Earthquake Cake

Patsy Eppright

1 cup chopped pecans
1 cup flaked coconut
1 (18¼ ounce) package German
chocolate cake mix
½ cup margarine
1 (8 ounce) package cream
cheese
1 (16 ounce) package powdered
sugar

- Sprinkle pecans in greased 13x9x2-inch baking pan. Sprinkle coconut over pecans.
- Prepare cake mix according to package directions. Pour batter over coconut.
- Melt margarine, cream cheese and powdered sugar together, stirring until smooth. Pour evenly over cake batter.
- Bake at 350° for 45 minutes.

Serves 24

Per serving _____

Calories 280  Protein 2.51 g  Carbohydrates 37.2 g  Fat 15 g  Cholesterol 10.4 mg  Sodium 258 mg

# Prune Cake

Debby Jenson

1 cup vegetable oil
2 cups sugar
3 eggs
2 cups all-purpose flour
1 teaspoon cinnamon
1 teaspoon salt
1 teaspoon nutmeg
¼ teaspoon allspice
1 cup buttermilk mixed with 1 teaspoon baking soda
¼ cup rum (optional)
1 cup chopped pecans
1 cup stewed prunes, drained

### Icing

1 stick margarine or butter, softened
1 (16 ounce) box powdered sugar
4 tablespoons hot coffee
1 tablespoon peanut butter

- Mix oil and sugar until fluffy. Add eggs 1 at a time, beating well after each addition.

- Combine flour, salt, nutmeg, cinnamon and allspice. Combine buttermilk and rum. Add dry and wet ingredients alternately to egg mixture, stirring well after each addition.

- Stir pecans and prunes into cake mixture; mix thoroughly. Pour batter into greased, floured tube cake pan.

- Bake 65 to 70 minutes at 300° until inserted toothpick is clean.

- Cool cake on rack. Spread cake with icing made as follows: Beat margarine and powdered sugar until smooth. Add coffee and peanut butter, blending thoroughly.

Serves 16

Per serving _____

Calories 530  Protein 4.53 g  Carbohydrates 71.4 g  Fat 26.5 g  Cholesterol 53.5 mg  Sodium 286 mg

# Pumpkin Cake

*Ginny Ashley*

1 (16 ounce) can pumpkin
3 eggs
¾ cup vegetable oil
½ cup water
2½ cups all-purpose flour
2¼ cups sugar
1½ teaspoons baking soda
1¼ teaspoons salt
1 teaspoon nutmeg
1 teaspoon cinnamon
1 cup yellow raisins

**Frosting**

½ (8 ounce) package cream
cheese, softened
3 tablespoons butter or
margarine, softened
1 teaspoon vanilla
½ (16 ounce) package powdered
sugar

- Combine pumpkin, eggs, oil and water, beating until smooth.

- Combine flour, sugar, baking soda, salt, nutmeg and cinnamon. Add dry ingredients to pumpkin mixture, mixing until smooth. Stir in raisins.

- Pour batter into greased and floured bundt pan.

- Bake at 350° for 1¼ hours. Cool cake in pan for approximately 20 minutes, then invert on wire rack to cool completely.

- Prepare frosting by blending cream cheese, butter or margarine, vanilla and powdered sugar, beating until smooth. Spread frosting on cooled cake.

Serves 16

Per serving _____

Calories 426  Protein 4.42 g  Carbohydrates 68.1 g  Fat 16 g  Cholesterol 53.4 mg  Sodium 302 mg

## Annie's Pumpkin Pie Cake
Gwen Walden Irwin

1 (16 ounce) can pumpkin
4 eggs, beaten
1 (12 ounce) can evaporated milk
1¾ cups sugar
1 tablespoon pumpkin pie spice
1 (18½ ounce) package yellow cake mix
1 cup margarine, melted
¾ cup chopped pecans
Whipped cream (optional)

- Combine pumpkin, eggs, milk, sugar and pie spice, blending well.
- Pour batter into ungreased 13x9x2-inch baking pan.
- Sprinkle cake mix evenly on batter. Drizzle margarine over cake mix and sprinkle with pecans.
- Bake at 350° for 1¼ hours.
- Place pan on wire rack to cool. Cut into squares and serve with whipped cream.

Serves 24

Per serving _____

Calories 281  Protein 3.55 g  Carbohydrates 35.3 g  Fat 14.5 g  Cholesterol 39.9 mg  Sodium 258 mg

## White Texas Sheetcake
Mary Lauderman Tavcar

2 cups sugar
2 eggs
2 cups all-purpose flour
2 teaspoons baking soda
1 teaspoon vanilla
1 (20 ounce) can crushed pineapple, undrained
1 cup chopped walnuts

**Frosting**
1 (8 ounce) package cream cheese, softened
½ cup margarine, softened
1 teaspoon vanilla
1½ cups powdered sugar

- Cream sugar and eggs together until smooth.
- Combine flour and baking soda. Add dry ingredients to egg mixture, mixing well. Stir in vanilla, pineapple and walnuts.
- Spread batter on greased and floured 18x12x1-inch jelly roll pan.
- Bake at 350° for 25 to 30 minutes. Let cake cool.
- Prepare frosting by blending cream cheese, margarine, vanilla and powdered sugar, beating until smooth. Spread frosting on cooled cake.

Serves 16

Per serving _____

Calories 371  Protein 4.75 g  Carbohydrates 53.8 g  Fat 16 g  Cholesterol 42.1 mg  Sodium 221 mg

# Chocolate Mousse Pie

Vicki Ashley Atkins

1 (8 ounce) package bittersweet
chocolate, chopped
¼ cup rum
¼ cup plus 2 tablespoons
unsalted butter, softened
1 envelope unflavored gelatin
¼ cup cold water
4 egg whites
½ cup sugar
1 cup whipping cream, whipped

**Crust**
2 cups graham cracker crumbs
½ cup unsalted butter, melted
2 tablespoons sugar

- Prepare crust by mixing graham cracker crumbs, butter and sugar. Press crumbs in bottom and along sides of deep 9-inch pie plate.
- Bake at 350° for 8 minutes. Set aside.
- Combine chocolate and rum in top of double boiler over boiling water. Stir until melted and smooth. Remove from heat and add butter, whisking to blend.
- Dissolve gelatin in cold water in small saucepan. Stir over low heat until clear. Blend into chocolate mixture. Set aside to cool.
- Beat egg whites to soft peaks. Add sugar and beat until stiff.
- Drizzle chocolate mixture over egg whites, folding to incorporate evenly. Fold in whipped cream, blending well.
- Spoon chocolate filling in cooled crust. Chill for several hours or overnight.

*For an elegant dessert without the crust, mousse may be piped into individual dessert dishes before chilling.*

Serves 10

Per serving _____

Calories 504  Protein 5.99 g  Carbohydrates 42.3 g  Fat 36.5 g  Cholesterol 76.1 mg  Sodium 179 mg

## Mud Pie

Ann Bommarito Armstrong

½ gallon coffee ice cream, softened
1 (18 ounce) bottle fudge ice cream topping
1 cup nuts
Whipped cream

**Crust**

2 (1 ounce) semisweet chocolate squares
2 cups corn flakes

- Melt chocolate squares and let partially cool. Coat corn flakes and press into 9-inch pie plate.
- Put ½ ice cream on crust, cover with ½ fudge, then repeat layers and top with nuts and whipped cream.
- Store in freezer until ready to serve.

Serves 8

Per serving _____

Calories 644  Protein 9.65 g  Carbohydrates 80.2 g  Fat 36 g  Cholesterol 65.7 mg  Sodium 253 mg

## Walnut Raisin Pie

Donna Earle Crain

1 cup broken walnuts
1 cup raisins
½ cup toasted coconut
1 (9 inch) unbaked pie shell
5 eggs
1½ cups sugar
3 tablespoons lemon juice
3 tablespoons milk
¾ teaspoon cinnamon
¾ teaspoon nutmeg
¾ teaspoon allspice

- Scatter walnuts, raisins and coconut in bottom of pie shell.
- Beat eggs. Add, beating well after each addition, in order listed: sugar, lemon juice, milk, cinnamon, nutmeg and allspice.
- Pour egg liquid into pie shell.
- Bake at 350° for 45 minutes or until center is set. Place on wire rack to cool completely before cutting.

Serves 8

Per serving _____

Calories 566  Protein 9.39 g  Carbohydrates 76.9 g  Fat 26.5 g  Cholesterol 133 mg  Sodium 251 mg

# Gooey Fudge Tart

Vicki Ashley Atkins

½ cup butter or margarine, softened
¾ cup firmly-packed brown sugar
3 eggs
1 (12 ounce) package semisweet chocolate morsels, melted
2 teaspoons instant coffee granules
1 teaspoon vanilla extract
½ cup all-purpose flour
1 cup coarsely chopped pecans or walnuts

**Crust**
1¼ cups chocolate wafer cookie crumbs
⅓ cup butter or margarine, melted

- Prepare crust by mixing cookie crumbs and butter or margarine. Firmly press crumbs in bottom and along sides of 9-inch tart pan or pie plate.
- Bake at 350° for 6 to 8 minutes. Set aside.
- Cream butter until smooth. Using electric mixer at medium speed, gradually beat in brown sugar. Add eggs, 1 at a time, beating well after each addition.
- Add melted chocolate, coffee granules, vanilla, flour and nuts to creamed mixture, stirring to blend.
- Pour chocolate filling into prepared crust.
- Bake at 375° for 25 minutes. Cool on wire rack.

Serves 10

Per serving

Calories 590  Protein 6.94 g  Carbohydrates 60.5 g  Fat 39 g  Cholesterol 64.2 mg  Sodium 371 mg

# Norwegian Pie

Mary Lauderman Tavcar

1 cup unsifted all-purpose flour
1½ cups sugar
2 teaspoons baking powder
½ teaspoon salt
1½ teaspoons cinnamon
2 eggs
1 teaspoon vanilla
2 cups diced or sliced canned or fresh apples
1 cup walnuts

- Mix all ingredients together well and put in two well greased and floured 8-inch pie pans.
- Bake at 325° for 25 to 30 minutes.

Serves 8

Per serving

Calories 336  Protein 5.38 g  Carbohydrates 57.2 g  Fat 11 g  Cholesterol 53 mg  Sodium 152 mg

# Pignolata

*Martha Rife*

1 cup sugar
¼ cup water
3 egg yolks
1 (8 ounce) package cream
cheese, softened and cubed
¼ cup amaretto liqueur
¾ cup pine nuts

**Crust**

¾ cup unsalted butter
2 cups all-purpose flour
¼ cup sugar
½ cup crushed amaretti cookies

- Prepare crust by melting butter in small saucepan over medium heat. Combine flour and sugar in large mixing bowl. Make well in center and gradually add butter, mixing with hands. Flour will be moistened by butter but will not be ball of dough.
- Press dough into 9-inch tart pan with removable bottom, moistening fingertips with water to prevent sticking. Press from center, working to edges and up sides. Place pan on baking sheet.
- Bake, on bottom shelf of oven, at 400° for 12 minutes or until golden brown. Remove from oven and set aside.
- Combine sugar and water in small saucepan. Bring to a boil, brushing down sides with brush dipped in water; do not stir or syrup will crystallize. Boil for 2 to 3 minutes or until slightly thickened.
- Place egg yolks in mixing bowl. Briskly whisk yolks, gradually adding hot syrup in very slow steady stream. Add cream cheese, beating well after each addition until there are no lumps. Stir in amaretto.
- Pour cookie crumbs into baked crust to form thin layer.
- Pour cheese filling into crust. Sprinkle with pine nuts. Place pan on baking sheet.
- Bake, on top shelf of oven, at 375° for 25 minutes or until filling is set and pine nuts are golden. Place pan on wire rack to cool slightly before cutting. Serve at room temperature or cold.

Serves 8

Per serving
Calories 615  Protein 8.09 g  Carbohydrates 69.3 g  Fat 33.5 g  Cholesterol 170 mg  Sodium 140 mg

# Pineapple Cream Cheese Custard Pie

*Carol Darilek*

⅓ cup plus ½ cup sugar, divided
1 tablespoon cornstarch
1 (9 ounce) can crushed pineapple, undrained
1 (8 ounce) package cream cheese, softened
2 eggs
½ cup milk
½ teaspoon vanilla
1 (9 inch) unbaked pastry shell
½ cup finely chopped pecans (optional)

- Blend ⅓ cup sugar and cornstarch in small saucepan. Add pineapple. Cook, stirring constantly, until mixture is thickened and clear. Set aside to cool.

- Combine cream cheese and ½ cup sugar, beating until smooth. Add eggs, 1 at a time, beating well after each addition. Blend in milk and vanilla.

- Spread cooled pineapple mixture in bottom of pie crust. Cover with cream cheese mixture.

- Bake at 400° for 10 minutes, then reduce temperature to 325° and bake for 50 minutes.

- Top with pecans.

Serves 8

Per serving _____

Calories 419  Protein 6.61 g  Carbohydrates 45.2 g  Fat 24 g  Cholesterol 86.2 mg  Sodium 300 mg

★

Egg yolks and whites will separate easiest when taken directly from the refrigerator.

## Pumpkin Pie Special

Wanda Rich

2 eggs, lightly beaten
1 (16 ounce) can pumpkin
¾ cup sugar
½ teaspoon salt
1 teaspoon cinnamon
½ teaspoon ground ginger
¼ teaspoon ground cloves
1 (14 ounce) can sweetened
condensed milk
1 (9 inch) unbaked pie crust

**Streusel Topping**
½ cup firmly-packed brown
sugar
¼ cup all-purpose flour
¼ cup chopped pecans
¼ cup butter

- Combine filling ingredients in order given.
- Pour into pie crust.
- Mix streusel topping ingredients with fork until crumbly. Sprinkle on pie.
- Bake at 400° for 15 minutes. Reduce temperature to 350° and bake an additional 40 to 50 minutes or until knife inserted near center comes out clean. (If necessary, cover edge of crust with aluminum foil to prevent excessive browning.)
- Cool and garnish if desired.

*Bake pie on preheated heavy-duty baking sheet only when using metal or foil pie pan.*

Serves 10

Per serving _____

Calories 466  Protein 7.33 g  Carbohydrates 64 g  Fat 21 g  Cholesterol 68.2 mg  Sodium 376 mg

★

Streusel Topping added to most any pie makes it special. For a quick and simple "homemade" dessert, add a can of your favorite fruit pie filling to a prepared pie crust and sprinkle with streusel topping. No one will guess that it didn't take hours!

# Rum Pie

*Debby Jenson*

1 envelope unflavored gelatin
½ cup cold water
½ cup egg substitute
¾ cup sugar
2 cups whipped cream
½ cup rum
1 (10 inch) baked pastry shell or vanilla wafer crust
Chocolate curls or slivered almonds (optional)

- Soften gelatin in cold water. Pour into top of double boiler over boiling water and cook, stirring until dissolved. Cool.

- Beat egg substitute until light. Add sugar, a small amount at a time, beating after each addition.

- Gradually add gelatin liquid to egg mixture in a steady stream, beating constantly. Fold in whipped cream and rum.

- Spread cream filling in crust. Chill until firm.

- Garnish with chocolate curls or almonds.

*Ground almond crust or cookie crumb crust with chocolate wafers can be used.*

Serves 10

Per serving _____

Calories 336  Protein 3.6 g  Carbohydrates 33.6 g  Fat 18.5 g  Cholesterol 42.7 mg  Sodium 165 mg

———— ★ ————

Basic Formula for a 9" pie crust: Combine 1½ cups flour with ¼ teaspoon salt. Cut in ½ cup shortening with a fork or pastry cutter until mixture resembles crumbs. Add 3-4 tablespoons ice water, one at a time, until dough holds together. Form into a ball, wrap loosely in plastic wrap, and chill for 20 minutes. Roll out and place gently into your pie pan.

# Strawberry Devonshire Tart

Janet Henegar

2 (3 ounce) packages cream
cheese, softened
1 cup sugar, divided
¼ cup sour cream
1½ quarts fresh strawberries,
hulled
Water
1 tablespoon cornstarch
Whipped cream

**Crust**
1½ cups all-purpose flour
½ teaspoon salt
¼ cup sugar
½ cup vegetable oil
2 tablespoons milk

- Prepare crust by combining flour, salt, sugar, oil and milk, blending well. Press dough into bottom and along sides of 10-inch pie plate. Flute edges and prick bottom and sides of pastry with fork tines.

- Bake at 400° for about 10 minutes. Set aside to cool.

- Beat cream cheese until fluffy. Add 1 teaspoon sugar and sour cream, beating until smooth. Spread cream cheese mixture in pastry shell and refrigerate.

- Force 1 rounded cup of strawberries through sieve. Add enough water to measure 1 cup.

- Combine remaining sugar and cornstarch in small saucepan. Mix ½ cup water with sieved berries and stir into cornstarch mixture. Cook over medium heat, stirring often, until thickened and clear, then boil for 1 minute.

- Remove from heat, stirring to cool slightly. Add small amount of red food coloring if necessary.

- Place remaining berries, tips up, on cream cheese layer in pastry shell. Pour glaze over berries. Chill for 1 hour or until set.

- Garnish with whipped cream.

Serves 8

Per serving _____

Calories 452  Protein 4.84 g  Carbohydrates 58.7 g  Fat 23 g  Cholesterol 26.3 mg  Sodium 336 mg

# Butterscotch Oatmeal Thins
*Kathy Marsh*

1 *cup uncooked regular oats*
1 *cup sugar*
½ *cup butter, melted*
1 *egg*
½ *teaspoon vanilla*
3 *tablespoons all-purpose flour*
¼ *teaspoon salt*
¼ *teaspoon baking powder*

- Combine ingredients.
- Drop by half teaspoon on cookie sheet covered with parchment paper. Space 3 inches apart.
- Bake 5 to 10 minutes at 350°.
- Cool and peel off paper.

Makes 4 dozen

Per cookie
Calories 43  Protein .472 g  Carbohydrates 5.69 g  Fat 2 g  Cholesterol 9.59 mg  Sodium 32.1 mg

# Chocolate Chip Charmers
*Wanda Rich*

1 *cup butter or margarine, softened*
¼ *cup sugar*
¾ *cup firmly-packed brown sugar*
1 *(4 ounce) package instant chocolate pudding mix*
2 *eggs*
1 *teaspoon vanilla extract*
2¼ *cups all-purpose flour*
1 *teaspoon baking soda*
1 *(12 ounce) package semisweet chocolate morsels*
1 *cup chopped pecans*

- Using electric mixer at medium speed, beat butter until creamy. Gradually beat in sugar, brown sugar and pudding mix.
- Add eggs and vanilla to creamed mixture, beating thoroughly.
- Combine flour and baking soda. Gradually add to creamed mixture, mixing thoroughly.
- Stir in chocolate morsels and pecans.
- Drop dough by rounded teaspoonfuls onto ungreased cookie sheets.
- Bake at 375° for 8 to 10 minutes. Cool on cookie sheets for 3 minutes, then transfer cookies to wire rack to cool completely.

*May be frozen in airtight containers for up to 8 months.*

Makes 3 dozen

Per cookie
Calories 172  Protein 1.93 g  Carbohydrates 19.4 g  Fat 10.5 g  Cholesterol 11.8 mg  Sodium 128 mg

## Melissa's Coconut Crispies

*Jeanne Cassidy*

¾ cup butter or margarine,
softened
1 cup sugar
1 egg
1 teaspoon vanilla
2 cups all-purpose flour
¾ teaspoon baking powder
¼ teaspoon salt
1½ cups shredded coconut

- Using electric mixer, beat butter, sugar, egg and vanilla together until fluffy.
- Combine flour, baking powder and salt. Add dry ingredients to creamed mixture and beat at low speed just until moistened. Stir in coconut, mixing by hand.
- Drop tablespoonfuls of dough onto ungreased cookie sheet, pressing each to ¼-inch thickness. Use back of fork tines, dipped in flour, to press ridges in each cookie.
- Bake at 375° for 10 to 12 minutes or until edges are golden. Cool on wire rack.

Makes 3 dozen

Per cookie

Calories 103  Protein 1.04 g  Carbohydrates 12.8 g  Fat 5.5 g  Cholesterol 5.89 mg  Sodium 71.6 mg

## Mrs. Mosse's Fudge Balls

*Nanci Norin Jordt*

1 (12 ounce) package semisweet
chocolate morsels
¾ cup sweetened condensed milk
Few grains salt
1 teaspoon vanilla
Chopped nuts or finely grated
coconut

- Melt chocolate in top of double boiler over very hot (not boiling) water or in microwave, stirring until smooth.
- Add condensed milk, salt and vanilla to chocolate, stirring to blend. Let stand until cool.
- Shape chocolate mixture into ¾-inch balls. Dip each in nuts or coconut.

Makes 18 balls

Per ball

Calories 154  Protein 2.06 g  Carbohydrates 19.6 g  Fat 9 g  Cholesterol 4.29 mg  Sodium 24.2 mg

# Fudge Cookies to Die For

*Donna Earle Crain*

6 tablespoons butter
1 (12 ounce) package semisweet
chocolate morsels
1 (14 ounce) can sweetened
condensed milk
1 cup all-purpose flour
2 cups chopped pecans

- Combine butter, chocolate and milk in heavy saucepan. Cook over low heat, stirring often, until chocolate is melted and mixture is smooth.
- Stir flour and pecans into chocolate mixture.
- Drop dough by teaspoonfuls onto lightly greased cookie sheet.
- Bake at 300° for about 10 minutes or until light glaze forms on cookies.

*Cookies will not appear done but do not overbake. Cool on wire rack.*

Makes 3 dozen

Per cookie

Calories 154  Protein 2.16 g  Carbohydrates 15.8 g  Fat 10 g  Cholesterol 8.89 mg  Sodium 34.7 mg

# Love Bites

*Nanci Norin Jordt*

1 (12 ounce) package semisweet
chocolate morsels
1 (14 ounce) can sweetened
condensed milk
1 (8½ ounce) package chocolate
wafers, crushed
1 cup chopped nuts, divided

- Melt chocolate in top of double boiler over very hot (not boiling) water or in microwave, stirring until smooth.
- Add condensed milk, wafer crumbs and ½ cup chopped nuts to chocolate. Stir to blend well.
- Press mixture into foil-lined 8x8x2-inch baking pan. Press remaining nuts into chocolate layer.
- Let stand at room temperature until firm. Cut into 2-inch squares.

Makes 16 squares

Per square

Calories 296  Protein 4.43 g  Carbohydrates 39.2 g  Fat 15.5 g  Cholesterol 8.65 mg  Sodium 121 mg

## German Fruit Cake Cookies   Ann Bommarito Armstrong

1 (8 ounce) package pitted dates
1 (12 ounce) package candied pineapple
1 (12 ounce) package candied red and green cherries
1 cup margarine, softened
1½ cups sugar
3 eggs
1 teaspoon baking soda
2 tablespoons hot water
3 cups all-purpose flour
½ teaspoon nutmeg
1½ teaspoons cinnamon
2 pounds pecans, halved or chopped

- Chop dates, pineapple and cherries into quarters. Set aside.
- Cream margarine and sugar together until smooth. Add eggs, beating thoroughly.
- Dissolve baking soda in hot water. Add to creamed mixture.
- Add flour, nutmeg, and cinnamon to creamed mixture, mixing well. Fold in pecans and fruit.
- Drop dough by rounded teaspoonfuls onto greased cookie sheet.
- Bake at 300° for 25 minutes. Cool on wire rack.

Makes 12 dozen

Per cookie _____

Calories 91  Protein .943 g  Carbohydrates 10.2 g  Fat 5.5 g  Cholesterol 4.42 mg  Sodium 35.8 mg

# Grandma's Rice Crispy-Oatmeal Cookies

Sherrie Smith

1 cup butter or margarine, softened
1 cup vegetable oil
1 cup sugar
½ cup firmly-packed brown sugar
1 egg
3½ cups all-purpose flour
1 teaspoon baking soda
1 teaspoon cream of tartar
1 teaspoon salt
1 cup crispy rice cereal
1 cup regular oats
1 cup chopped nuts

- Cream butter, oil, sugar and brown sugar together until smooth. Add egg and beat well.
- Sift flour, baking soda, cream of tartar and salt together. Add dry ingredients to creamed mixture, blending well.
- Fold cereal, oats and nuts into dough.
- Drop dough by teaspoonfuls onto lightly greased cookie sheet.
- Bake at 375° for 12 to 15 minutes. Cool on wire rack.

Makes 4 dozen

Per cookie

Calories 156  Protein 1.61 g  Carbohydrates 14.7 g  Fat 10.5 g  Cholesterol 14.8 mg  Sodium 110 mg

# LBJ'S Favorite Macaroons

Vera Alexander Dufour

2 egg whites
Pinch of salt
½ cup sugar
1 cup shredded coconut
½ teaspoon vanilla extract
½ teaspoon almond extract

- Using electric mixer, beat egg whites well. Add salt and beat until peaks form. Gradually add sugar, beating until glossy.
- Stir coconut, vanilla and almond extract into egg whites.
- Drop dough by mounded table-spoonfuls 2 inches apart onto lightly greased cookie sheets.
- Bake at 325° for 20 minutes. Cool on cookie sheets for 5 to 6 min-utes, then place on wire rack to cool completely.

Makes 3 dozen

Per cookie

Calories 25  Protein .269 g  Carbohydrates 4.03 g  Fat 1 g  Cholesterol 0  Sodium 40.3 mg

## Krystin's "Mankiller" Cookies    Donna Earle Crain

1 (8 ounce) package semisweet
chocolate
½ cup unsalted butter
2 eggs
¾ cup sugar
½ teaspoon vanilla
1½ cups all-purpose flour
½ teaspoon baking powder
½ teaspoon salt
8 chocolate covered peanut butter
candy cups (not miniature), cut
in chunks

- Melt chocolate and butter together in top of double boiler or using microwave. Set aside to cool slightly.

- Using electric mixer, beat eggs. Add sugar and vanilla and beat until light and fluffy. Add cooled chocolate and mix well.

- Stir flour, baking powder and salt together. Add dry ingredients to creamed mixture, mixing just until moistened.

- Fold peanut butter candy chunks into dough.

- Drop dough by large spoonfuls onto ungreased cookie sheet.

- Bake at 350° for 10 to 12 minutes or until firm. Cool on cookie sheets for 1 minute, then place on wire rack to cool completely.

Makes 2 dozen large cookies

Per cookie _____

Calories 175  Protein 2.59 g  Carbohydrates 21.9 g  Fat 9.5 g  Cholesterol 29.1 mg  Sodium 73.3 mg

# Nanu's Molasses Crinkles

Vicki Ashley Atkins

¾ cup vegetable shortening
1 cup firmly-packed brown sugar
1 egg, beaten
½ cup sorghum molasses
2¼ cups all-purpose flour
2 teaspoons baking soda
¼ teaspoon salt
½ teaspoon ground cloves
1 teaspoon cinnamon
½ teaspoon ginger
Sugar

- Thoroughly mix together shortening, brown sugar, egg and molasses.
- Sift together the dry ingredients and stir into the shortening mixture.
- Pinch off pieces of dough and shape into balls the size of a walnut. Flatten top slightly and dip in white sugar (this makes the cookies crinkle).
- Bake for 10 to 12 minutes at 375°, just until set but not hard.

*These cookies get better as they age, if you can keep them around long enough!*

Makes 3 dozen

Per cookie

Calories 101  Protein .986 g  Carbohydrates 14.5 g  Fat 4.5 g  Cholesterol 5.89 mg  Sodium 65.7 mg

## Nut Spritz Cookies

Kelley Brumley Pickens

1 cup butter or margarine,
softened
¾ cup sugar
1 egg
1 egg yolk
1 tablespoon vanilla or almond
flavoring
2½ cups all-purpose flour
1½ teaspoons baking powder
1 cup chopped pecans

- Cream butter and sugar together until smooth. Add eggs and vanilla or almond flavoring, beating until light and fluffy.
- Combine flour and baking powder. Add dry ingredients to creamed mixture, mixing well. Stir pecans into dough.
- Chill dough until firm enough to shape into rolls. Wrap rolls in wax paper and freeze.
- Cut dough into ½-inch thick slices and place on ungreased cookie sheet or form into small balls, approximately the size of a quarter. Place on ungreased cookie sheet and flatten.
- Bake at 350° for 8 to 12 minutes or until lightly browned. Cool on wire rack.

Makes 3 dozen

Per cookie _____

Calories 120  Protein 1.46 g  Carbohydrates 11.7 g  Fat 7.5 g  Cholesterol 11.8 mg  Sodium 61.9 mg

# Orange Pecan Delight

Nancille Sewell Willis

¾ cup butter, softened
½ cup sugar
1 cup firmly-packed brown sugar
2 eggs
1 tablespoon grated orange peel
½ cup sour cream
3 cups sifted all-purpose flour
2 teaspoons baking powder
½ teaspoon baking soda
½ teaspoon salt
1 cup chopped pecans

**Icing**
2 cups sifted powdered sugar
2 teaspoons grated orange peel
⅛ teaspoon salt
2 to 3 tablespoons frozen orange
juice concentrate
Water
5 dozen pecan halves

- Cream butter until light. Gradually add sugar and brown sugar, beating until smooth. Add eggs and orange peel, beating well. Stir in sour cream.
- Sift flour, baking powder, baking soda and salt together. Gradually add dry ingredients to creamed mixture, mixing well. Add pecans.
- Drop dough by rounded teaspoonfuls onto greased cookie sheet.
- Bake at 375° for 10 to 14 minutes. Place on wire rack.
- Prepare icing by combining powdered sugar, orange peel and salt. Add orange juice and water, if necessary, to make icing consistency to spread.
- Ice tops of each warm cookie and top with pecan half.

Makes 5 dozen

Per cookie

Calories 93  Protein 1.11 g  Carbohydrates 12.9 g  Fat 4.5 g  Cholesterol 14.1 mg  Sodium 56.9 mg

# Texas Cow Patties

*Wendy Coffin*

2 cups margarine, softened
2 cups sugar
2 cups firmly-packed brown
sugar
4 eggs
2 teaspoons vanilla
2 cups quick-cooking oats
2 cups corn flakes
4 cups all-purpose flour
2 teaspoons baking powder
2 teaspoons baking soda
1 (6 ounce) package semisweet
chocolate morsels
2 cups chopped broken pecans

- Cream margarine, sugar and brown sugar together until light and fluffy. Add eggs, 1 at a time, beating well after each addition. Stir in vanilla.
- Add oats and corn flakes to creamed mixture, mixing thoroughly.
- Sift flour, baking powder and baking soda together. Gradually add to creamed mixture, beating slowly to mix. Stir in chocolate morsels and pecans.
- Drop by rounded tablespoons onto cookie sheets.
- Bake on top rack of oven at 325° for 17 minutes. Cool on wire rack.

Makes 2 dozen

Per cookie

Calories 470  Protein 5.68 g  Carbohydrates 57.4 g  Fat 25.5 g  Cholesterol 35.3 mg  Sodium 286 mg

# Texas Trail Busters

*Carol Willis*

¾ *cup butter, softened*
1 *cup vegetable shortening*
2 *cups sugar*
2 *cups firmly-packed dark brown sugar*
4 *eggs*
2 *teaspoons vanilla*
3 *cups all-purpose flour*
2 *teaspoons baking soda*
2 *teaspoon salt*
3 *cups regular oats*
2 *cups coconut*
2 *cups raisins*
1 *(6 ounce) package semisweet chocolate morsels*
1 *cup chopped nuts*

- Cream butter, shortening, sugar and brown sugar together until light and fluffy. Add eggs, 1 at a time, beating well after each addition. Stir in vanilla.
- Combine flour, baking soda and salt. Add dry ingredients to creamed mixture, mixing thoroughly.
- Add oats, coconut, raisins, chocolate morsels and nuts, kneading to blend.
- Drop dough by heaping teaspoonfuls 2 inches apart onto greased cookie sheet.
- Bake at 350° for 8 minutes or until cookies are golden brown. Cool on wire rack.

*For best results, shape dough into rolls, wrap in wax paper and chill for several hours. Cut in slices and bake as directed.*

Makes 7 dozen

Per cookie

Calories 148  Protein 1.7 g  Carbohydrates 20.3 g  Fat 7.5 g  Cholesterol 14.5 mg  Sodium 97.1 mg

# Banana Pecan Squares

Barbara Hoover McEachern

½ cup butter or margarine,
softened
¾ cup sugar
1 egg
1 teaspoon vanilla
1 cup mashed banana
1½ cups all-purpose flour
½ teaspoon baking soda
½ teaspoon salt
½ cup chopped pecans
Pecan halves (optional)

- Cream butter and sugar together until light and fluffy. Add egg, vanilla and banana, beating until smooth.

- Combine flour, baking soda and salt. Add dry ingredients to creamed mixture, blending well. Stir in chopped pecans.

- Spread batter in greased 9x9x2-inch baking pan. Arrange pecan halves on batter.

- Bake at 350° for 25 minutes. Cool. Cut into squares to serve.

Makes 1¼ dozen

Per square

Calories 180  Protein 2.17 g  Carbohydrates 24.1 g  Fat 9 g  Cholesterol 13.3 mg  Sodium 164 mg

# Chess Squares

Janet Henegar

1 (18½ ounce) package butter
cake mix
½ cup butter, melted
1 egg
1 (8 ounce) package cream
cheese, softened
3 eggs
1 (16 ounce) package powdered
sugar

- Combine cake mix, butter and egg, mixing well. Press mixture into bottom of 13x9x2-inch baking pan.

- Using electric mixer, beat cream cheese, eggs and powdered sugar together until creamy. Pour over crust in pan.

- Bake at 325° for 50 minutes. Let stand until cool before cutting into squares.

Makes 2 dozen

Per square

Calories 246  Protein 2.78 g  Carbohydrates 36.2 g  Fat 10.5 g  Cholesterol 56.1 mg  Sodium 223 mg

# Caramel Apple Squares

*Dolly Brown*

1¾ cups all-purpose flour
½ teaspoon baking soda
1 cup quick-cooking oats
½ cup firmly-packed brown sugar
1 cup margarine, chilled
1 cup chopped walnuts
20 caramels
1 (14 ounce) can sweetened condensed milk
2 (21 ounce) cans apple pie filling

- Combine flour, baking soda, oats and brown sugar. Cut in margarine until crumbly.

- Reserving 1½ cups crumb mixture, press remaining crumbs in bottom of 13x9x2-inch baking pan.

- Bake at 375° for 15 minutes.

- While crust is baking, add walnuts to reserved crumbs.

- Combine caramels and milk in heavy saucepan. Cook over low heat, stirring frequently, until caramels are melted and mixture is smooth.

- Spoon apple filling over prepared crust. Top with melted caramel and sprinkle with reserved crumbs.

- Bake at 375° for 20 minutes. Cool. Cut into squares.

*Serve with ice cream, if desired.*

Makes 2 dozen

Per square

Calories 286  Protein 3.95 g  Carbohydrates 40.3 g  Fat 13 g  Cholesterol 6.03 mg  Sodium 168 mg

# Chocolate Praline Squares
Vicki Ashley Atkins

¾ cup graham cracker crumbs
¾ cup finely chopped pecans
¼ cup firmly-packed brown sugar
¼ cup butter or margarine, melted
1 (12-ounce) jar caramel topping
1 cup plus 3 tablespoons all-purpose flour, divided
1 cup butter or margarine
4 (1 ounce) squares unsweetened chocolate
1½ cups sugar
4 eggs, beaten
1 teaspoon vanilla extract

### Chocolate Frosting
1 tablespoon butter or margarine
2 tablespoons cocoa
2 tablespoons water
1 cup sifted powdered sugar
¼ teaspoon vanilla extract
Sifted powdered sugar (optional)

- Combine graham cracker crumbs, pecans, brown sugar and melted butter, mixing well. Press mixture into bottom of greased 9x9x2-inch baking pan.
- Bake at 350° for 6 to 8 minutes. Set aside to cool slightly.
- Combine caramel topping and 3 tablespoons flour, mixing well. Spoon caramel onto crust, spreading to within ¼ inch of edges. Set aside.
- Combine butter and chocolate in saucepan. Cook over low heat, stirring to blend, until melted. Remove from heat.
- Stir sugar, 1 cup flour, eggs and vanilla into chocolate mixture. Pour over caramel layer in pan.
- Bake at 350° for 50 minutes. Set aside to cool slightly.
- Prepare frosting by combining butter, cocoa and water in small saucepan. Cook over medium heat, stirring often, until thickened. Remove from heat. Stir in powdered sugar and vanilla.
- Spread frosting on warm praline layers. Lightly sift powdered sugar over frosting, if desired.

Makes 16 small squares

Per square _____

Calories 446  Protein 4.69 g  Carbohydrates 56.3 g  Fat 24.5 g  Cholesterol 53.2 mg  Sodium 302 mg

# Lacey's Old Fashioned Raspberry Bars

*Jeanne Cassidy*

2¼ cups all-purpose flour
1 cup sugar
1 cup margarine, softened
1 egg
1 cup chopped pecans
1 (10 ounce) jar seedless
raspberry preserves

- Combine flour, sugar, margarine, egg and pecans. Using electric mixer at low speed, beat for 2 to 3 minutes or until well blended, scraping sides of bowl often.

- Reserving 1½ cups of mixture, spread remainder in bottom of greased 8x8x2-inch baking pan.

- Spoon preserves on mixture in pan, spreading to within ½ inch of edges. Crumble reserved mixture and sprinkle on preserve layer; crumbs will not completely cover preserves.

- Bake at 350° for 45 minutes. Cool completely before cutting into bars.

Makes 1 dozen

Per bar _____

Calories 415  Protein 4.04 g  Carbohydrates 51.7 g  Fat 22.5 g  Cholesterol 17.7 mg  Sodium 194 mg

# Thunder Clouds

Nanci Norin Jordt

2 *egg whites*
⅛ *teaspoon cream of tartar*
⅛ *teaspoon salt*
1 *teaspoon vanilla*
¾ *cup sugar*
1 *(6 ounce) package semisweet chocolate morsels*
¼ *cup ground pecans (optional)*

- Combine egg whites, cream of tartar, salt and vanilla. Using electric mixer, beat until soft peaks form.
- Add sugar, 2 tablespoons at a time, to egg whites, until all is incorporated and stiff peaks form.
- Fold chocolate morsels and pecans into meringue.
- Drop by teaspoonfuls onto cookie sheet covered with brown paper bag.
- Bake at 300° for 25 minutes. Cool before removing from cookie sheet.

*May be frozen.*

Makes 2 dozen

Per cookie

Calories 68   Protein .686 g   Carbohydrates 11 g   Fat 3 g   Cholesterol 0   Sodium 17 mg

# Fat Ladies

Donna Earle Crain

1 *(16 ounce) package refrigerated chocolate chip cookie dough*
1 *(6 ounce) package semisweet chocolate morsels*
32 *caramels*
¼ *cup half and half*
1 *cup chopped pecans*

- Spread cookie dough evenly into the bottom of 13x9x2-inch baking pan.
- Bake for 15 to 20 minutes at 350°.
- Sprinkle with chocolate chips while hot. They will melt and form a layer of chocolate.
- Melt together the caramels and half and half. Pour over the chocolate layer.
- Sprinkle with chopped pecans.
- Cool and cut into small bars.

Makes 2 dozen

Per bar

Calories 113   Protein 1.27   Carbohydrates 14 g   Fat 6.5 g   Cholesterol 1.8 mg   Sodium 29 mg

## Tropical Cream

*Mary Lauderman Tavcar*

2 cups orange juice
2 bananas, cut in chunks
1 cup vanilla ice cream

- Combine all ingredients in blender. Blend until smooth. Refreeze to desired consistency.
- Serve in tall glasses or freeze and serve as a popsicle.

Serves 4

Per serving

Calories 174  Protein 2.61 g  Carbohydrates 34.1 g  Fat 4 g  Cholesterol 14.5 mg  Sodium 28.2 mg

## Clara Jo's Ice Cream

*Vicki Ashley Atkins*

6 eggs
2½ cups sugar
2½ teaspoons vanilla extract
Dash of salt
2 cups whipping cream
4 cups half and half
1½ cups milk (may vary with ice cream freezer size)

- Using electric mixer, beat eggs until light and fluffy.
- Add sugar to eggs and beat for 10 minutes.
- Stir vanilla, salt, whipping cream and half and half into egg mixture.
- Pour into container of 1-gallon ice cream freezer. Add milk to fill line.
- Freeze according to freezer manufacturer's directions.

Serves 16

Per serving

Calories 331  Protein 5.07 g  Carbohydrates 35.4 g  Fat 19.5 g  Cholesterol 141 mg  Sodium 77.9 mg

# Velvet Hammer

Nanci Norin Jordt

1 quart vanilla ice cream
2 tablespoons Cointreau liqueur
1 tablespoon cognac or brandy
1 tablespoon white crème de cacao
Chocolate shavings or curls

- Combine all ingredients in blender. Blend until smooth.
- Refreeze mixture. To serve, spoon into individual dessert cups and garnish with chocolate shavings or curls.

Serves 4

Per serving ─────────────────────────────

Calories 321  Protein 4.81 g  Carbohydrates 36.4 g  Fat 15.5 g  Cholesterol 58 mg  Sodium 107 mg

# Peach Cobbler Supreme

Ginny Ashley

¼ cup butter or margarine
1 cup sifted all-purpose flour
1 cup sugar
1 tablespoon baking powder
⅛ teaspoon salt
⅔ cup milk
1 (29 ounce) can sliced peaches, undrained
¼ teaspoon nutmeg
¼ teaspoon cinnamon
½ teaspoon grated lemon peel

- Melt butter in 8x8x2-inch baking dish.
- Sift flour, sugar, baking powder and salt together. Add milk and mix well. Pour batter into baking dish; do not stir.
- Top with peaches, including juice. Sprinkle with nutmeg, cinnamon and lemon peel; do not stir.
- Bake at 350° for 40 minutes or until golden brown.

*Serve warm with ice cream.*

Serves 10

Per serving ─────────────────────────────

Calories 236  Protein 2.25 g  Carbohydrates 47.3 g  Fat 5.5 g  Cholesterol 2.19 mg  Sodium 93.6 mg

## Hill Country Peach Cobbler    Rhonda Copeland Gracely

2 to 3 cups sliced peaches
1¾ cups sugar, divided
3 tablespoons butter or
  margarine, softened
½ cup milk
1 cup all-purpose flour
1 teaspoon baking powder
½ teaspoon salt, divided
1 tablespoon cornstarch
1 cup boiling water

- Place peaches in 9x9x2-inch baking pan.
- Combine ¾ cup sugar and butter, beating until smooth.
- Add milk, flour, baking powder and ¼ teaspoon salt to creamed mixture and mix until smooth. Pour batter over peaches.
- Combine 1 cup sugar, ¼ teaspoon salt and cornstarch. Sprinkle over batter. Pour boiling water over batter.
- Bake at 375° for 1 hour.

Serves 9

Per serving _____

Calories 267  Protein 2.26 g  Carbohydrates 56.3 g  Fat 4.5 g  Cholesterol 1.84 mg  Sodium 172 mg

## Frozen Strawberry Mousse    Sherrie Smith

1 cup all-purpose flour
½ cup firmly-packed brown
  sugar
½ cup chopped pecans
½ cup butter
2 egg whites
1 cup sugar
1 (10 ounce) package frozen
  sliced strawberries, thawed
2 tablespoons lemon juice
1 cup whipping cream, whipped

- Mix together flour, brown sugar, pecans and butter.
- Spread in a shallow pan and bake at 350° for 20 minutes, stirring often.
- Beat egg whites until peaks form. Then gently fold in sugar, strawberries, lemon juice, then whipped cream.
- Spread ⅔ of nut mixture in 9x9x2-inch baking pan.
- Spoon beaten mixture over and sprinkle with remaining nut mixture.
- Freeze for 8 hours.

Serves 12

Per serving _____

Calories 272  Protein 2.44 g  Carbohydrates 34 g  Fat 15 g  Cholesterol 34.3 mg  Sodium 94. 3 mg

# Quickie Chocolate Mousse

Cheryl Briggs Patton

1 (12 ounce) package semisweet
chocolate morsels
½ cup sugar
3 eggs
1 cup hot skim milk
2 to 4 tablespoons amaretto
liqueur or brandy
Frozen whipped topping
(optional)

- Combine chocolate morsels, sugar and eggs in blender. Blend briefly to combine.
- Gradually blend in hot milk and amaretto or brandy. Continue blending at medium speed until mixture is smooth.
- Pour into demitasse cups. Chill for 1 hour.
- Garnish with frozen whipped topping.

Serves 8

Per serving _____

Calories 303  Protein 5.17 g  Carbohydrates 42.8 g  Fat 14.5 g  Cholesterol 80.1 mg  Sodium 44.4 mg

# Apple Dumplings

*Vicki Ashley Atkins*

2 cups all-purpose flour
2 teaspoons baking powder
1 teaspoon salt
⅔ cup vegetable shortening
½ cup milk
6 whole apples
6 tablespoons sugar
6 teaspoons cinnamon
6 teaspoons nutmeg
6 teaspoons butter

**Syrup**

1 cup sugar
1 cup water
⅛ teaspoon cinnamon
⅛ teaspoon nutmeg
2 drops red food coloring
2 tablespoons butter

- Sift together flour, baking powder and salt. Cut in shortening until crumbly. Add milk all at once and stir until moistened.

- Roll out into a rectangle ¼-inch thick and cut into 6-inch squares.

- Peel and core apples. Place one whole apple in center of each square and sprinkle each apple generously with sugar, cinnamon and nutmeg. Dot with butter.

- Fold corners of pastry up to top of apples and pinch edges together to seal.

- Prepare a 13x9x2-inch glass baking dish with non-stick vegetable spray. Place apples at least 1 inch apart in pan.

- In a saucepan, combine sugar, water, cinnamon, nutmeg and food coloring. Bring to a boil and add butter, stirring well to combine.

- Spoon syrup over dumplings in pan and sprinkle with sugar.

- Bake for 35 minutes at 375°.

*Serve warm with vanilla sauce or ice cream. Garnish with mint leaves.*

Serves 6

Per serving _____

Calories 705  Protein 5.31 g  Carbohydrates 94.2 g  Fat 36 g  Cholesterol 33.8 mg  Sodium 448 mg

# Baklava

*Pam Bommarito*

2 (24 sheet) packages filo dough
1½ cups butter, clarified
6 cups ground pecans
(approximately 2 pounds ground
in food processor)
1 cup sugar
1 to 1½ tablespoons lemon
extract

## Syrup

4 cups sugar
3 cups water
Juice of 2 small lemons

- Cut filo dough with scissors to fit two 13x9x2-inch baking pans.
- Spray each sheet with butter and layer approximately 20 sheets on the bottom of each pan.
- Mix pecans with sugar and lemon extract in the bowl. Place pecan mixture on top of filo.
- Add the top 20 layers of filo, spraying butter on each sheet and on top.
- Cut through all layers with a sharp knife, creating diagonal shapes.
- Bake at 350° for 25 to 30 minutes. Remove from oven when slightly brown.
- While baklava is baking, bring syrup ingredients to boil and cook for 10 minutes or to a soft ball stage. While the baklava is still hot, pour syrup on top. Use all syrup.
- Let the baklava cool before removing from pan.

*Store in tight tins. Can be frozen.*

Makes 72

Per serving ──────────────────────────────
Calories 192  Protein 1.71  Carbohydrates 22.4 g  Fat 11 g  Cholesterol 10.3 mg  Sodium 100 mg

# *Chocolate Dipped Fruit*

Ada Smyth

1 (12 ounce) package semisweet chocolate morsels
¼ cup vegetable shortening
Washed and dried fresh strawberries or mandarin orange slices, drained or pineapple chunks, drained, or maraschino cherries

- Over hot (not boiling) water, combine chocolate morsels and shortening. Stir until morsels melt and mixture is smooth. Remove from heat, but keep chocolate over hot water. If chocolate begins to set, return to heat and add one to two teaspoons shortening.

- Dip pieces of desired fruit into chocolate mixture, shaking off excess chocolate. Place on foil-lined cookie sheets.

- Chill in refrigerator for 10 to 15 minutes until chocolate is set. Gently loosen fruit from foil.

Serves 18

Per serving _____

Calories 123  Protein .94 g  Carbohydrates 13.7 g  Fat 8.5 g  Cholesterol 0  Sodium 2.32 mg

———————— ★ ————————

For an almost fat-free chocolate dipping sauce: Using a candy thermometer, heat ½ cup low calorie maple syrup to 240 degrees; beat 3 egg whites until stiff peaks form, then gradually beat in hot syrup; add ¼ cup cocoa and ½ teaspoon vanilla and beat for three minutes longer. Serve with fresh fruit for dipping.

# Chocolate Espresso Flan with Vanilla Pecans

Word of Mouth Fine Catering

*Must chill at least 6 hours after baking*

¾ cup sugar, divided
3 tablespoons water
3 eggs
3 egg yolks
2 cups half and half
1 cup whipping cream
6 ounces semisweet chocolate, coarsely chopped
1½ teaspoons instant espresso powder
2 teaspoons vanilla extract

• Combine ½ cup sugar and water in small saucepan. Over moderate heat, bring to a boil, stirring occasionally to dissolve sugar. Boil without stirring until a dark golden caramel forms, about 10 minutes. Immediately pour caramel into individual ramekins or 9x5x3-inch glass loaf pan, quickly tilting pan to coat the bottom. Caramel will quickly harden.

• In a large bowl, lightly beat the whole eggs with egg yolks and set aside.

• Combine half and half, whipping cream and ¼ cup sugar in heavy saucepan. Over moderately high heat, scald cream mixture. Remove from heat and add chocolate, espresso powder and vanilla, stirring until smooth.

• Whisk chocolate mixture into eggs until incorporated. Pour custard through a strainer onto caramel in ramekins or loaf pan.. Place ramekins or loaf pan in shallow roasting pan in middle of oven. Pour hot water into roasting pan to 1-inch depth around the dishes of custard.

• Bake at 325° for approximately 35 minutes for ramekins (may vary with size of ramekins) or 1 hour for loaf pan; custard should be set but slightly soft in center. Let stand in water bath for 20 minutes. Remove from roasting pan

**Chocolate Espresso Flan with Vanilla Pecans** (continued)

**Vanilla Pecans**
1 *tablespoon vanilla extract*
2½ *tablespoons vegetable oil*
1 *pound pecan halves*
*Boiling water*
½ *cup sugar*
¼ *teaspoon salt*
⅛ *teaspoon black pepper*
¼ *teaspoon ground coriander*
¼ *teaspoon cinnamon*
¼ *teaspoon nutmeg*
¼ *teaspoon allspice*

and let cool until room temperature. Chill, covered, for 6 hours or overnight.

• To prepare Vanilla Pecans, begin by blending vanilla and oil.

• Blanch pecans for 1 minute in boiling water and drain well. Combine hot pecans, sugar and vanilla oil. Let stand for 10 minutes. Place pecans on baking sheet with rim.

• Bake at 325° for 30 to 35 minutes, turning every 5 to 10 minutes, until nuts are lightly browned and crisp.

• Combine salt, black pepper, coriander, cinnamon, nutmeg and allspice. Toss hot pecans with spice mixture, coating thoroughly. Spread pecans in single layer to cool. Store in airtight container.

• Serve flan directly from ramekins or use knife tip to loosen around edges and invert on serving plate. If using loaf pan, invert and slice into individual servings. Sprinkle top with Vanilla Pecans.

*For added indulgence, serve with sweetened whipped cream, flavored with vanilla.*

Serves 8

Makes 4 cups pecans

Per serving of flan _____

Calories 410  Protein 6.7 g  Carbohydrates 36.4 g  Fat 28 g  Cholesterol 222 mg  Sodium 64. 7 mg

Per ¼ cup pecans _____

Calories 235, Protein 2.21 g, Carbohydrates 11.8 g, Fat 21.5 g, Cholesterol 0, Sodium 33.7 mg

# Sugar-Honeyed Pecans

*Laura Pankonien*

1½ cups sugar
¼ teaspoon salt
¼ cup honey
½ cup water
½ teaspoon vanilla extract
3 cups pecans

- Combine sugar, salt, honey and water in saucepan. Cook over medium heat, stirring constantly, until sugar is dissolved. Continue cooking without stirring until syrup will form a firm ball in cold water. Remove from heat.

- Add vanilla and pecans to syrup, stirring gently until mixture is creamy.

- Pour pecans on wax paper. Separate with fork and let stand until dry.

Serves 16

Per serving _____

Calories 224  Protein 1.59 g  Carbohydrates 26.8 g  Fat 13.5 g  Cholesterol 0  Sodium 33.9 mg

# Coconut Amaretto Fluff

*Kathy Marsh*

1 (8 ounce) package cream cheese, softened
¼ cup plus 2 tablespoons amaretto liqueur
1 (8 ounce) carton frozen whipped topping, thawed
½ pound crisp macaroon cookies, crumbled (approximately 16)

- Beat cream cheese until smooth. Add amaretto and beat well.

- Fold whipped topping and cookie crumbs into cream cheese mixture.

*Serve with assorted fruit or pieces of angel food cake.*

Makes approximately 2½ cups

Per tablespoon _____

Calories 72  Protein .847 g  Carbohydrates 6.3 g  Fat 4.5 g  Cholesterol 11.2 mg  Sodium 38.2 mg

# Brunch and Breads

The rich heritage and warm hospitality of the Texas Governor's Mansion beckons, as a Sunday morning brunch is presented in its parlor. On this occasion, the menu includes **Sue's Club Soda Waffles**, a colorful **Fruit Rainbow**, **Cinnamon Tea Rolls**, and a healthy and refreshing **Texas Sunrise**.

*We are proud to share with you a glimpse into the parlor of the Texas Governor's Mansion. The State's official china, crystal, silver and linen made an elegant addition to this very special photo setting.*

# Jamaican Baked Bananas

Michelle Just-Linder

2 bananas, peeled and halved
lengthwise
1 tablespoon brown sugar
⅛ teaspoon cinnamon
Pinch of allspice
¼ orange, peeled and sliced
(optional)
1½ teaspoons dark rum
3 tablespoons lemon or orange
juice

- Arrange banana halves in baking pan prepared with vegetable cooking spray.
- Sprinkle brown sugar, cinnamon and allspice on bananas. Top with orange slices.
- Combine rum and juice. Pour over fruit.
- Bake at 350° for 25 minutes.

Serves 4

Per serving _____

Calories 72  Protein .741 g  Carbohydrates 18 g  Fat .5 g  Cholesterol 0  Sodium 1.65 mg

# Curried Fruit Bake

Cheryl Briggs Patton

Prepare one day prior to serving

1 (16 ounce) can cling peach
halves, drained
1 (16 ounce) can pineapple
slices, drained
1 (16 ounce) can pear halves,
drained
5 maraschino cherries with stems
⅓ cup butter, melted
¾ cup firmly-packed brown
sugar
4 teaspoons curry powder

- Drain and towel dry fruit. Place in 1½-quart casserole.
- Combine butter, brown sugar and curry powder, mixing well. Spoon mixture over fruit.
- Bake, uncovered, at 325° for 1 hour. Let stand until room temperature, then chill, covered, overnight.
- About 30 minutes before serving, reheat at 350° for 30 minutes. Serve warm.

Serves 12

Per ½ cup serving _____

Calories 139 g  Protein .682 g  Carbohydrates 24.2 g  Fat 5 g  Cholesterol 13.8 mg  Sodium 59.4 mg

# Yogurt Ambrosia

Michelle Just-Linder

½ cup chopped orange
½ cup sliced banana
½ cup seedless grapes
1 cup non-fat vanilla yogurt
5 teaspoons toasted shredded coconut

- Combine fruit with yogurt.
- Spoon mixture into 5 individual serving dishes. Sprinkle 1 teaspoon coconut on each serving.
- Serve chilled or at room temperature.

Serves 5

Per ½ cup serving

Calories 78  Protein 3.41 g  Carbohydrates 15.3 g  Fat 1 g  Cholesterol .882 mg  Sodium 38.3 mg

# Fruit Rainbow

Linda Cook Uhl

For enhanced flavor, chill overnight

½ cup honey
2 tablespoons lemon juice
1 tablespoon finely snipped candied ginger
1 teaspoon finely grated orange peel
4 oranges, peeled and sliced crosswise
1½ cups blueberries
2 cups cubed honeydew melon
1½ cups strawberry halves
Whole strawberries for garnish

- Combine honey, lemon juice, ginger and orange peel.
- Place orange slices in bowl. Add honey dressing and toss gently to coat. Chill, covered, for several hours or overnight.
- Chill remaining fruit.
- Drain oranges, reserving dressing. Arrange orange slices in bottom of glass serving dish. Layer blueberries, honeydew and strawberry halves over oranges.
- Pour reserved dressing over fruit and garnish with whole strawberries, if desired.

This is lovely served in individual dessert dishes.

Serves 10

Per ½ cup serving

Calories 112  Protein 1.09 g  Carbohydrates 29.3 g  Fat .5 g  Cholesterol 0  Sodium 5.86 mg

# Hill Country Peach Delight

Michelle Just-Linder

3 large ripe peaches
Boiling water
2 tablespoons orange flavored
liqueur
2 tablespoons chopped almonds,
lightly toasted
6 fresh strawberries, sliced

- Immerse peaches in boiling water for 1 minute, drain and rinse under cold water. Peel skin from peaches, cut in halves and remove pits.
- Place peach halves in individual serving dishes. Spoon liqueur into each peach cavity, sprinkle with chopped almonds and garnish with strawberry slices.
- Chill before serving.

*Pretty served in stemmed glass dishes.*

Serves 6

Per serving _____

Calories 74  Protein 1.21 g  Carbohydrates 13.1 g  Fat 1.5 g  Cholesterol 0  Sodium .743 mg

# Your Basic Omelet

Beverly Woldhagen James

4 eggs, separated
¾ teaspoon salt
⅛ teaspoon black pepper
¼ cup water
1 tablespoon butter

- Beat egg yolks until thickened. Stir in salt and black pepper.
- In separate bowl and with clean beaters, beat egg whites until foamy. Add water and beat until stiff. Fold egg whites into yolk mixture.
- Melt butter in skillet. Pour egg mixture into skillet and cook over low heat until well puffed. Fold and serve immediately.

*Vegetables such as green bell pepper, onion, asparagus or spinach may be added to omelet. Chop and sauté in butter before adding to omelet mixture.*

Serves 2

Per serving _____

Calories 200  Protein 12.6 g  Carbohydrates 1.31 g  Fat 16 g  Cholesterol 440 mg  Sodium 985 mg

# Potato Omelet

Nanci Norin Jordt

2 tablespoons butter or margarine
1 medium potato, thinly sliced
1 small onion or 3 green onions, thinly sliced
1 tablespoon chopped green bell pepper
⅛ teaspoon salt
⅛ teaspoon black pepper
⅛ teaspoon paprika
2 eggs, lightly beaten

- Melt butter in oven-proof 9-inch skillet. Add potato, onion and bell pepper. Cook until browned on all sides.
- Season vegetables with salt, pepper and paprika. Add eggs.
- Bake at 350° for 15 to 20 minutes.

Serves 2

Per serving _____

Calories 307  Protein 9.87 g  Carbohydrates 30.5 g  Fat 17 g  Cholesterol 243 mg  Sodium 323 mg

# Macaroni Relleno

Ada Smyth

1 (7 ounce) package elbow macaroni (2 cups uncooked)
1 egg, beaten
½ cup skim milk
¼ teaspoon ground cumin
1 (4 ounce) can chopped green chilies, drained
1 (4 ounce) can diced pimiento, drained
1 (15 ounce) can pinto beans, heated and drained
1 cup (4 ounces) shredded Monterey Jack cheese
1 medium tomato, peeled, seeds removed and chopped
1 medium-sized green bell pepper, chopped
¼ cup sliced green onion

- Prepare macaroni according to package directions. Drain well.
- Blend egg, milk and cumin. Stir in hot macaroni, chilies and pimiento.
- Prepare 9-inch skillet with vegetable cooking spray and heat.
- Add macaroni mixture to skillet. Cook, covered, over low heat for about 15 minutes or until macaroni mixture is set. Using rubber spatula, loosen edges and invert on warm platter.
- Top with beans, cheese, tomato, bell pepper and green onion. Let stand for 15 minutes before cutting.

Serves 8

Per serving _____

Calories 221  Protein 11.2 g  Carbohydrates 31.6 g  Fat 5.5 g  Cholesterol 39.4 g  Sodium 319 mg

# Potato and Leek Frittata

Jeanne Cassidy

*May be served at room temperature as an appetizer*

1 tablespoon butter
1 tablespoon olive oil
1 cup cubed peeled potatoes
1 cup thinly sliced white portion of leeks, rinsed and dried
6 eggs, beaten, or 1½ cups egg substitute
½ cup half and half
¼ teaspoon salt
Freshly ground black pepper to taste
½ cup (2 ounces) freshly grated Gruyère or Swiss cheese
1 tablespoon minced parsley

- Heat butter and oil in non-stick skillet. Add potatoes and leeks and cook until tender and very lightly browned.
- Combine eggs, half and half, salt, black pepper, cheese and parsley, mixing thoroughly. Pour over potatoes and leeks.
- Cook over low heat, gently lifting bottom and edges until eggs begin to set. Cook, covered, over low heat for 2 to 3 minutes or until firm. To lightly brown top of frittata, place under broiler.
- Cut into wedges to serve.

*For delicious variations, top with ½ cup chopped artichoke hearts, chopped spinach, chopped tender asparagus or thin tomato slices.*

Serves 8

Per serving _____

Calories 154  Protein 7.76 g  Carbohydrates 6.4 g  Fat 11 g  Cholesterol 176 mg  Sodium 161 mg

---

★

---

To test an egg for freshness, place it in a bowl of water. If it tips upward in the bowl, or floats, toss it out - it is too old to use.

# Chicken Spinach Quiche
Mary Francis

1 (10 inch) unbaked pastry shell
1 tablespoon Dijon mustard
1 green onion, minced
1 tablespoon margarine
1½ cups half and half
4 eggs or 1 cup egg substitute
1 teaspoon salt
⅛ teaspoon black pepper
1 cup (4 ounces) shredded Swiss cheese
1 (10 ounce) package frozen chopped spinach, thawed and squeezed dry
1 (6 ounce) can chunk chicken, drained and flaked

- Spread pastry shell with mustard.
- Sauté green onion in margarine until tender.
- Combine onions with half and half, eggs, salt, black pepper, cheese, spinach and chicken. Pour mixture into pastry shell.
- Bake at 425° for 15 minutes, reduce temperature to 325° and bake for 20 minutes longer.

Serves 8

Per serving _____

Calories 362  Protein 14.8 g  Carbohydrates 20.4 g  Fat 25 g  Cholesterol 146 mg  Sodium 717 mg

# Classic Quiche Lorraine
Randi deVos Barrentine

A fool-proof recipe, great every time

10 slices bacon, cooked and crumbled
½ cup plus 2 tablespoons (2⅓ ounces) grated Swiss cheese
½ cup plus 2 tablespoons (2⅓ ounces) grated Cheddar cheese
1 (9 inch) baked deep dish pastry shell
4 eggs, beaten
1 cup whipping cream
Salt to taste (optional)

- Sprinkle bacon and cheese in bottom of pastry shell.
- Combine eggs and cream. Pour over bacon and cheese.
- Season with salt.
- Bake at 325° for 40 minutes or until custard appears firm when gently shaken.

For variation, substitute ham, shrimp, chopped olives, mushrooms or asparagus for bacon.

Serves 8

Per serving _____

Calories 371  Protein 12.2 g  Carbohydrates 12.3 g  Fat 30.5 g  Cholesterol 171 mg  Sodium 401 mg

# Shrimp and Crab Quiche
*Lillian Alexander*

1 (6 ounce) can crab meat, drained
1 (6 ounce) can tiny shrimp, drained
1 cup (4 ounces) shredded Swiss cheese
⅓ cup minced onion
1 (9 inch) unbaked pastry shell
4 eggs, lightly beaten
1½ cups half and half
1 teaspoon salt
¼ teaspoon black pepper
⅛ teaspoon cayenne pepper

- Sprinkle crab meat, shrimp, cheese and onion in bottom of pastry shell.
- Combine eggs, half and half, salt, black pepper and cayenne pepper. Pour over crab meat mixture.
- Bake at 425° for 15 minutes, reduce temperature to 300° and bake for additional 30 minutes or until center is firm. Let stand for 10 minutes before cutting in wedges.

Serves 6

Per serving _____

Calories 415  Protein 21.1 g  Carbohydrates 21 g  Fat 27 g  Cholesterol 230 mg  Sodium 785 mg

# Individual Cheese Soufflé
*Beverly Woldhagen James*

1 egg yolk
⅓ cup (1⅓ ounces) grated Cheddar cheese
¼ cup milk
¼ teaspoon salt
⅛ teaspoon black pepper
⅛ teaspoon cayenne pepper
2 egg whites

- Beat egg yolk, cheese, milk, salt, black pepper and cayenne pepper together.
- Beat egg whites until stiff. Fold into cheese mixture.
- Pour mixture into greased individual baking dish.
- Bake at 450° for 12 minutes.

Serves 1

Per serving _____

Calories 221  Protein 11.2 g  Carbohydrates 31.6 g  Fat 5.5 g  Cholesterol 39.4 mg  Sodium 319 mg

# Florentine Crêpe Cups

Joyce Moeller

3 eggs, lightly beaten
⅔ cup all-purpose flour
½ teaspoon salt
1 cup milk
1½ cups (6 ounces) shredded
sharp Cheddar cheese
3 tablespoons all-purpose flour
3 eggs, lightly beaten
⅔ cup mayonnaise
1 (10 ounce) package frozen
chopped spinach, thawed and
drained
1 (4 ounce) can sliced
mushrooms, drained
6 slices bacon, cooked and
crumbled
⅛ teaspoon black pepper

- Combine eggs, flour, salt and milk, mixing until smooth. Let stand.
- Pour 2 tablespoons batter into hot lightly greased 8-inch skillet. Cook until under side of crêpe is lightly browned. Remove and fit into greased muffin pan.
- Repeat, using remaining batter to make total of 12 crêpe cups.
- Toss cheese and flour together.
- Combine eggs, mayonnaise, spinach and mushrooms. Pour over cheese.
- Spoon into crêpe cups.
- Bake at 350° for approximately 40 minutes.
- Garnish with bacon bits.

Serves 6

Per serving _____

Calories 507  Protein 20.5 g  Carbohydrates 20.6 g  Fat 38.5 g  Cholesterol 267 mg  Sodium 797 mg

# Brunch Casserole
Linda Uchiyama Kelley

½ cup butter or margarine,
melted
3 medium baking potatoes,
grated
2 pounds bulk pork sausage
2 cups (8 ounces) grated
Cheddar cheese
1 cup (4 ounces) grated
mozzarella cheese
8 eggs
1 cup milk

- Pour margarine into 13x9x2-inch baking pan. Line pan with grated potatoes.
- Bake at 450° for 20 minutes.
- Fry sausage, stirring to crumble. Drain excess grease. Pour sausage over browned potatoes. Sprinkle with cheese.
- Combine eggs and milk. Pour over the top.
- Bake at 350° for 30 minutes.

Serves 24

Per serving _____

Calories 272  Protein 13.8 mg  Carbohydrates 5.55 g  Fat 21.5 g  Cholesterol 116 mg  Sodium 641 mg

# Cheesy Broccoli Squares
Gayle Williamson

⅔ cup chopped onion
1 tablespoon margarine
2 (10 ounce) packages frozen
chopped broccoli, thawed
3 cups (12 ounces) shredded
Cheddar cheese, divided
1⅓ cups milk
3 eggs
¾ cup buttermilk baking mix
¼ teaspoon black pepper

- Sauté onion in margarine until tender.
- Rinse broccoli and drain well.
- Combine onion, broccoli and 2 cups cheese. Spread mixture in greased 8x8x2-inch baking dish.
- Beat milk, eggs, baking mix and black pepper together until smooth. Pour over broccoli mixture.
- Bake at 400° for 25 to 30 minutes. Sprinkle with 1 cup cheese and bake for additional 1 to 2 minutes. Let stand for 5 minutes before cutting.

Serves 8

Per serving _____

Calories 351  Protein 18.3 g  Carbohydrates 21.1 g  Fat 22 g  Cholesterol 130 mg  Sodium 612 mg

# Green Chili Eggs

Gwen Walden Irwin

*Freezes well for a make-ahead dish*

| | |
|---|---|
| 10 *eggs* | • Beat eggs until fluffy. |
| ½ *cup all-purpose flour* | • Add flour, baking powder, salt, butter, and cheeses to eggs, mixing lightly but thoroughly. Fold in chilies. |
| 1 *teaspoon baking powder* | |
| ½ *teaspoon salt* | |
| ¼ *cup butter, melted* | |
| 2 *cups small curd cottage cheese* | • Pour mixture into greased 13x9x2-inch baking pan. |
| 4 *cups (16 ounces) shredded Monterey Jack cheese* | • Bake at 350° for 35 minutes. |
| 2 *(4 ounce) cans chopped green chilies, drained* | *If making ahead freeze before baking. When ready to serve remove from freezer and bake 45 minutes or until firm.* |

Serves 10

Per serving _____

Calories 356  Protein 23.5 g  Carbohydrates 8.4 g  Fat 25.5 g  Cholesterol 271 mg  Sodium 896 mg

# Sausage Puff

Janet Nash

*May be prepared in advance*

| | |
|---|---|
| 1 *pound bulk pork sausage* | • Fry sausage, stirring to crumble. Drain excess grease. |
| 6 *eggs, beaten* | |
| 2½ *cups (10 ounces) grated Monterey Jack cheese* | • Combine eggs, all cheeses, flour, baking powder, salt and milk, mixing well. Stir in sausage. |
| 1½ *cups (6 ounces) grated sharp Cheddar cheese* | |
| 1 *cup cottage cheese* | • Pour into lightly greased 13x9x2-inch baking pan. |
| 1 *(3 ounce) package cream cheese, cubed* | |
| ½ *cup all-purpose flour* | • Bake, uncovered, at 350° for 35 minutes. |
| 1 *teaspoon baking powder* | |
| ⅛ *teaspoon salt* | *Casserole may be prepared and stored in refrigerator until ready to bake.* |
| 1 *cup milk* | |
| 1 *green onion, chopped (optional)* | Serves 12 |

Per serving _____

Calories 398  Protein 24 g  Carbohydrates 7 g  Fat 30 g  Cholesterol 187 mg  Sodium 865 mg

# Eggs Woldhagen

Beverly Woldhagen James

*May be assembled and refrigerated the night before*

6 slices day-old wheat bread
3 tablespoons butter, softened
1 cup (4 ounces) shredded sharp
Cheddar cheese
¼ cup pimiento strips or ½ cup
sliced pimiento-stuffed green
olives
3 eggs, beaten
2 cups milk, scalded and cooled
½ teaspoon salt
⅛ teaspoon black pepper

- Spread bread with butter. Trim crusts and discard. Cut bread into cubes.
- Layer bread cubes, cheese and pimiento strips or olives in greased 13x9x2-inch baking dish.
- Combine eggs and milk. Pour over layered ingredients. Season with salt and black pepper.
- Bake at 325° for 50 minutes.

*Can be doubled to serve a crowd. Add a touch of hot pepper sauce for extra flavor.*

Serves 6

Per serving _____

Calories 282  Protein 12.9 g  Carbohydrates 17.6 g  Fat 18 g  Cholesterol 152 mg  Sodium 561 mg

# Scrambled Egg Quesadillas

*Kelly Brumley Pickens*

1 *tablespoon butter or margarine, melted*
8 *(6 to 8 inch) flour tortillas*
1 *medium-sized ripe avocado*
*Lemon or lime juice*
1 *tablespoon butter or margarine*
8 *eggs, well beaten*
*Salt and black pepper to taste*
1 *cup (4 ounces) cubed Monterey Jack cheese*
½ *cup chopped cilantro*
*Salsa*

- Using melted butter, brush both sides of each tortilla, stack and wrap in aluminum foil.

- Warm tortillas in oven at 350° for 15 minutes.

- Peel avocado, remove pit and cut into 16 slices. Sprinkle with lemon juice to prevent darkening.

- Heat 1 tablespoon butter in skillet over medium heat. Add eggs and stir to scramble. Add cheese.

- Place equal amount of egg mixture on ½ of each warm tortilla. Fold tortilla over egg, place on individual plate and garnish with 2 avocado slices and cilantro. Serve with salsa.

*Diced cooked potatoes, sausage or chorizo can be added to egg mixture.*

Serves 8

Per serving _____

Calories 628  Protein 27.2  Carbohydrates 47.4 g  Fat 37 g  Cholesterol 465 mg  Sodium 913 mg

# Sunshine Eggs

*Beverly Woldhagen James*

4 *hard-cooked eggs*
2 *tablespoons margarine*
2 *tablespoons all-purpose flour*
*Salt and black pepper to taste*
1 *cup milk*
4 *slices Canadian bacon, broiled*
4 *slices toast*

- Separate yolks and egg whites. Crumble each and set aside separately.
- Melt margarine in saucepan over low heat. Stir in flour, salt and black pepper. Gradually add milk, stirring constantly until smooth.
- Add chopped egg white to cream sauce.
- Place 1 slice bacon on each toast slice, top with ¼ cup creamed sauce and sprinkle with crumbled egg yolk.

Serves 4

Per serving _____

Calories 299 Protein 16.9 g Carbohydrates 20.9 g Fat 16 g Cholesterol 235 mg Sodium 664 mg

# Belgian Brunch Sandwiches

*Vicki Ashley Atkins*

3 *tablespoons low-fat mayonnaise*
2 *teaspoons Dijon mustard*
1 *teaspoon honey*
8 *slices reduced-calorie wheat bread*
4 (¾ *ounce*) *slices Canadian bacon*
4 (¾ *ounce*) *slices low-fat Cheddar cheese*
4 *thin slices tomato*

- Combine mayonnaise, mustard and honey. Spread on 4 slices of bread.
- Top each with 1 slice bacon, cheese and tomato. Cover with remaining bread slices.
- Cook sandwiches in Belgian waffle iron or grill on griddle prepared with butter-flavored vegetable cooking spray, cooking until lightly browned and cheese is melted. Gently apply pressure to top of waffle iron if necessary.

*Serve with fresh fruit kabobs.*

Serves 4

Per serving _____

Calories 283 Protein 16.8 g Carbohydrates 37.9 g Fat 8.5 g Cholesterol 17.9 mg Sodium 766 mg

# Stuffed French Toast

Jeanne Cassidy

¼ cup chopped pecans (or walnuts)
4 ounces cream cheese, softened and whipped
6 slices firm textured wheat or white bread, crusts trimmed
2 eggs, well beaten
½ cup milk
1 teaspoon vanilla
Pinch of nutmeg
1 tablespoon margarine
Strawberry jam, slightly warmed, optional

- Combine pecans and cream cheese. Spread mixture on 3 slices of bread and cover with remaining bread to form 3 sandwiches.

- Combine eggs, milk, vanilla and nutmeg, mixing thoroughly.

- Dip sandwiches into egg mixture. Grill in melted margarine in non-stick skillet over medium heat, turning several times, until golden brown.

- Cut sandwiches in halves or quarters and serve with strawberry jam.

This recipe is inspired by a breakfast dish served at a bed and breakfast inn in Maine. It is especially good made with homemade bread or English toasting bread.

Serves 4

Per serving _____

Calories 376  Protein 10 g  Carbohydrates 30.5 g  Fat 23.5 g  Cholesterol 142 mg  Sodium 425 mg

# Sue's Club Soda Waffles

*Sue Creighton Ashley*

2 cups biscuit baking mix
1 egg, beaten
3 tablespoons vegetable oil
1½ cups club soda

- Combine all ingredients, adding more club soda if needed for thick but flowable batter.
- Bake batter in Belgian waffle iron until golden brown. Serve immediately.

*Serve with fresh strawberries, whipped cream and warm maple syrup.*

Makes 6 waffles

Per waffle _____

Calories 396  Protein 7.09 g  Carbohydrates 48 g  Fat 19.5 g  Cholesterol 36.1 mg  Sodium 988 mg

# Easy Whole Wheat Waffles

*Pamela Jones*

1 cup non-fat plain yogurt
1 cup skim milk
3 tablespoons butter, softened
2 cups whole wheat flour
2 teaspoons baking powder
1 teaspoon baking soda

- Combine yogurt, milk and butter, mixing well.
- Combine flour, baking powder and baking soda. Add yogurt mixture to dry ingredients, blending thoroughly.
- Bake batter in waffle iron until golden brown.

Serves 4

Per serving _____

Calories 337  Protein 13.9 g  Carbohydrates 52.2 g  Fat 10 g  Cholesterol 25.5 mg  Sodium 376 mg

# Corn Fritters

*Assorted Affairs*

4½ cups fresh or frozen corn, thawed
4 egg yolks
1 teaspoon sugar
Dash of kosher salt
1 cup all-purpose flour
1 tablespoon baking powder
Vegetable oil for frying

- If using fresh corn, cook to al dente stage. Reserving ½ cup, pour remaining corn in food processor and process until partially creamed.
- Combine reserved and creamed corn. Add egg yolks, sugar and salt, mixing well. Stir in flour and baking powder. Let stand for 10 minutes.
- Heat oil in a frying pan.
- Drop batter by heaping spoonfuls into hot oil and cook until golden brown, turning once to brown evenly.
- Serve with jalapeño jelly or mango chutney.

Makes approximately 2 dozen

Per fritter

Calories 98  Protein 1.85 g  Carbohydrates 9.53 g  Fat 6 g  Cholesterol 33.9 mg  Sodium 16.5 mg

# Apple Crunch Coffee Cake

*Kathy Marsh*

2 cups chopped peeled apples
2 cups all-purpose flour
2 cups sugar
1 cup vegetable oil
2 eggs
2 teaspoons cinnamon
2 teaspoons baking powder
½ teaspoon salt
1 cup chopped nuts

- Combine all ingredients in order listed and stir well. Batter will be thick.
- Spread batter in greased and floured 13x9x2-inch baking pan.
- Bake at 350° for 55 minutes.

*One of the most asked for recipes at our neighborhood coffees.*

Serves 16

Per serving

Calories 343  Protein 3.01 g  Carbohydrates 41.1 g  Fat 19.5 g  Cholesterol 26.5 mg  Sodium 75.7 mg

# Holiday Brunch Coffee Cake

Cheryl Briggs Patton

*May be prepared in advance and frozen*

1 cup margarine, softened
1 cup sugar
2 eggs
½ teaspoon almond extract
2 cups all-purpose flour
1 tablespoon baking powder
½ teaspoon salt
1 cup low-fat sour cream
1 (8 ounce) can whole cranberry sauce
½ cup slivered almonds

### Glaze

1 cup powdered sugar
2 tablespoons milk
½ teaspoon almond extract

- Cream margarine and sugar together until light and fluffy.
- Add eggs, 1 at a time, beating well after each addition.
- Alternately add almond extract, flour, baking powder and salt with sour cream to egg mixture.
- Pour batter into greased 13x9x2-inch baking pan. Spoon cranberry sauce over batter. Sprinkle with almonds.
- Bake at 350° for 35 to 40 minutes.
- Prepare glaze by blending powdered sugar, milk and almond extract. Drizzle glaze over warm coffee cake.

*This is great to serve the morning of Thanksgiving while waiting for the turkey to cook or on Christmas morning after Santa has arrived.*

Serves 24

Per serving

Calories 206  Protein 2.6 g  Carbohydrates 25.5 g  Fat 11 g  Cholesterol 21.7 mg  Sodium 148 mg

# Joan's Apple Kuchen

*Kathy Marsh*

1 (18½ ounce) package yellow
cake mix
½ cup butter, softened
½ cup flaked coconut
1 (20 ounce) can apple slices
½ cup sugar
1 teaspoon cinnamon
1 cup sour cream
1 egg

- Combine cake mix, butter and coconut, mixing thoroughly. Press mixture in bottom and along sides of ungreased 13x9x2-inch baking pan.
- Bake at 350° for 10 minutes.
- Arrange apple slices on partially baked crust.
- Combine sugar and cinnamon. Sprinkle on apples.
- Blend egg and sour cream. Drizzle over fruit.
- Bake at 350° for 25 minutes or until edges are lightly browned.

Serves 15

Per serving _____

Calories 288  Protein 2.58 g  Carbohydrates 38 g  Fat 14.5 g  Cholesterol 38.2 mg  Sodium 305 mg

# Overnight Coffee Cake

Ann Bommarito Armstrong

¾ cup butter, softened
1 cup sugar
2 eggs
1 cup sour cream
2 cups all-purpose flour
1 teaspoon baking powder
1 teaspoon baking soda
½ teaspoon salt
1 teaspoon nutmeg

**Topping**
¾ cup firmly-packed brown sugar
½ cup chopped pecans
1 teaspoon cinnamon

- Cream butter and sugar together until fluffy. Add eggs and sour cream, mixing well.
- Combine flour, baking powder, baking soda, salt and nutmeg. Add to creamed mixture, blending thoroughly.
- Pour batter into 13x9x2-inch baking pan.
- Combine brown sugar, pecans and cinnamon. Sprinkle mixture on batter.
- Chill, covered, overnight.
- Bake, uncovered, at 350° for 35 to 40 minutes.

Serves 12

Per serving _____

Calories 364  Protein 4.32 g  Carbohydrates 43.5 g  Fat 20 g  Cholesterol 74.9 mg  Sodium 300 mg

## Cinnamon Tea Rolls

*Linda Cook Uhl*

1 (8 count) package refrigerated
crescent rolls
2 tablespoons butter, melted
⅓ cup sugar
¼ teaspoon cinnamon
⅓ cup sifted powdered sugar
1 tablespoon frozen orange juice
concentrate
1 tablespoon water

- Unroll dough on lightly floured surface. Press perforations to seal.
- Brush dough with melted butter.
- Combine sugar and cinnamon. Sprinkle on dough.
- Roll up jelly roll fashion starting along the long side. Cut into 1-inch slices and place in lightly greased miniature muffin pans.
- Bake at 375° for 8 to 10 minutes.
- Combine powdered sugar, orange juice and water, blending until smooth. Drizzle over warm tea rolls.

Makes 12 rolls

Per roll _____

Calories 112  Protein 1.23 g  Carbohydrates 17.1 g  Fat 4.5 g  Cholesterol 5.18 mg  Sodium 229 mg

## Nutty Cheese Spread

*Sherrie Smith*

1 (8 ounce) package cream
cheese, softened
1 teaspoon vanilla
¼ cup sugar
½ cup firmly-packed brown
sugar
½ cup chopped nuts

- Combine all ingredients and blend well.
- Chill for at least 1 hour before serving.

*Serve with slices of apple, pear or banana or with English muffins or bagels.*

Makes 1½ cups

Per 1 tablespoon serving _____

Calories 70  Protein .905 g  Carbohydrates 5.77 g  Fat 5 g  Cholesterol 10.4 mg  Sodium 29.1 mg

# Skinny Sticky Buns

*Terre Churchill*

1 (8 count) *package refrigerated crescent rolls*
¼ *cup firmly-packed brown sugar*
2 *tablespoons plus 2 teaspoons low-fat margarine, melted, divided*
2 *tablespoons frozen apple juice concentrate, thawed*
2 *tablespoons water*
2 *tablespoons finely chopped pecans*
¼ *cup plus 2 tablespoons currants*
2 *tablespoons sugar*
½ *teaspoon cinnamon*

- Unroll dough on lightly floured surface. Press perforations to seal.

- Combine brown sugar, 2 tablespoons margarine, apple juice and water in saucepan. Bring to a boil, reduce heat and simmer for 5 minutes, stirring frequently.

- Pour syrup into 8x4x2½-inch loaf pan. Sprinkle pecans on syrup.

- Spread 2 teaspoons margarine on surface of dough.

- Combine currants, sugar and cinnamon. Sprinkle on dough.

- Beginning from long edge, roll up, jelly roll fashion. Pinch ends to close. Cut into 8 slices and place in syrup in loaf pan.

- Bake at 350° for 20 to 25 minutes. Cool in pan for 5 minutes, then invert on serving plate.

Serves 8

Per serving _____

Calories 180  Protein 2.21 g  Carbohydrates 27.2 g  Fat 7.5 g  Cholesterol 0  Sodium 340 mg

## Apple Pecan Muffins

Carol Willis

½ cup butter, softened
2 cups sugar
2 eggs
1 teaspoon vanilla
2½ cups all-purpose flour
1 teaspoon baking powder
¾ teaspoon baking soda
1 teaspoon salt
½ teaspoon nutmeg
1 teaspoon cinnamon
3 cups peeled finely diced apples
1 cup chopped pecans, toasted

- Cream butter and sugar together until smooth. Add eggs and vanilla and beat until fluffy.
- Combine flour, baking powder, baking soda, salt, nutmeg and cinnamon. Gradually add to creamed mixture, mixing just until moistened.
- Stir in apples and pecans.
- Spoon batter into greased and floured muffin pans (or paper lined), filling about ½ full.
- Bake at 350° for 25 minutes.

*Great for breakfast or morning meetings.*

Makes 18

Per muffin

Calories 261  Protein 3.09 g  Carbohydrates 40.1 g  Fat 10.5 g  Cholesterol 37.4 mg  Sodium 213 mg

## Morning Glory Muffins

Wendy Coffin

2 cups all-purpose flour
1 cup sugar
2 teaspoons baking powder
¼ teaspoon salt
2 teaspoons cinnamon
2 cups grated carrots
½ cup raisins
½ cup chopped nuts
½ cup coconut
1 apple, grated
3 eggs
¾ cup vegetable oil
2 teaspoons vanilla

- Combine flour, sugar, baking powder, salt and cinnamon.
- Add carrots, raisins, nuts, coconut and apple to dry ingredients.
- Beat eggs, oil and vanilla together. Add to dry ingredients, mixing just until moistened.
- Spoon batter into well-greased muffin pans, filling ⅔ full.
- Bake at 350° for 20 minutes.

*These muffins are wonderful served warm and fresh from the oven!*

Makes 18

Per muffin

Calories 244  Protein 3.1 g  Carbohydrates 29.9 g  Fat 13 g  Cholesterol 35.3 mg  Sodium 51.1 mg

# Bran Muffins

*Beverly Irick*

⅔ cup raisins
1 cup frozen apple juice concentrate, divided
¼ cup frozen orange juice concentrate
1½ cups whole wheat flour
½ cup wheat germ
1½ cups unprocessed bran
2 teaspoons baking soda
1 teaspoon cinnamon
½ cup chopped walnuts
1½ cups low-fat buttermilk
2 egg whites, lightly beaten
⅓ cup instant non-fat dry milk
2 tablespoons margarine, melted and cooled

- Combine raisins, ¼ cup apple juice concentrate and orange juice concentrate in saucepan. Simmer, stirring constantly, for about 5 minutes.

- Combine flour, wheat germ, bran, baking soda, cinnamon and walnuts, mixing thoroughly.

- Combine ¾ cup apple juice concentrate, buttermilk, egg whites, dry milk and margarine, beating well. Add dry ingredients, blending just until moistened.

- Fold in raisins and their cooking liquid.

- Spoon batter into muffin pans prepared with vegetable cooking spray, filling ⅔ full.

- Bake at 350° for 20 minutes. Remove from tins immediately to cool on wire rack.

Makes 18

Per muffin

Calories 150  Protein 5.01 g  Carbohydrates 26.7 g  Fat 4 g  Cholesterol .945 mg  Sodium 147 mg

# Orange Muffins

Ada Smyth

2 cups buttermilk baking mix
4 tablespoons sugar, divided
1 egg
⅔ cup orange juice
1 teaspoon grated orange peel
¼ teaspoon cinnamon
⅛ teaspoon nutmeg

- Combine baking mix and 2 table-spoons sugar.
- Add egg, orange juice and orange peel to dry ingredients. Beat for 30 seconds.
- Grease bottoms only of 12 muffin cups. Spoon in batter, filling ⅔ full.
- Mix 2 tablespoons sugar, cinnamon and nutmeg. Sprinkle on each muffin.
- Bake at 400° for 15 minutes.

Makes 1 dozen

Per muffin

Calories 191  Protein 3.65 g  Carbohydrates 29.6 g  Fat 6.5 g  Cholesterol 18 mg  Sodium 488 mg

# Sweet Potato Muffins

Jeanne Cassidy

½ cup margarine, softened
1¼ cups firmly-packed brown sugar
2 eggs
1¼ cups cooked, mashed sweet potatoes
1½ cups all-purpose flour
2 teaspoons baking powder
¼ teaspoon salt
1 teaspoon cinnamon
¼ teaspoon nutmeg
1 cup milk
¼ cup chopped pecans
½ cup raisins (optional)

- Cream margarine and sugar together until fluffy. Add eggs, mixing well. Blend in sweet potatoes.
- Combine flour, baking powder, salt, cinnamon and nutmeg. Add dry ingredients and milk alternately to creamed mixture, blending gently.
- Fold pecans and raisins into batter.
- Spoon batter into greased or paper-lined muffin pans, filling ⅔ full.
- Bake at 400° for 25 minutes.

Makes 2 dozen

Per muffin

Calories 136  Protein 2.18 g  Carbohydrates 20.2 g  Fat 5.5 g  Cholesterol 19.1 mg  Sodium 91 mg

## Apple Raisin Bread

Janet Henegar

3 cups all-purpose flour
1½ teaspoons baking soda
½ teaspoon baking powder
1½ teaspoons salt
2 teaspoons cinnamon
1 teaspoon ground cloves
2½ cups sugar
1¼ cups vegetable oil
4 eggs, beaten
1 tablespoon plus 1 teaspoon vanilla
3 cups chopped apples
⅔ cup raisins
½ cup chopped nuts

- Generously grease bottoms only of two 9x5x3-inch loaf pans.

- Beat all ingredients on low speed of mixer for one minute, scraping the bowl constantly. Increase to medium speed and beat 1 minute longer.

- Pour batter into pans and bake uncovered at 325° for 1 hour or until wooden pick inserted near center comes out clean. Cool 10 minutes in the pans.

- Cool completely before slicing. Store in the refrigerator.

Makes 2 loaves

Per ½-inch slice _____

Calories 225  Protein 2.29 g  Carbohydrates 31 g  Fat 10.5 g  Cholesterol 26.5 mg  Sodium 147 mg

## California Pistachio Date Nut Bread

*Nancille Sewell Willis*

1 cup chopped dates
1 cup boiling water
1¼ cups all-purpose flour
½ cup sugar
1 teaspoon baking powder
1 teaspoon baking soda
¼ teaspoon salt
½ cup chopped natural pistachios
2 eggs, beaten
2 tablespoons margarine, melted
1 teaspoon vanilla
1 teaspoon grated orange peel

• Soak dates in boiling water. Set aside to cool.

• Combine flour, sugar, baking powder, baking soda, salt and pistachios.

• Combine date mixture, eggs, margarine, vanilla and orange peel. Add to dry ingredients and mix just until moistened.

• Spread batter in greased 8x4x2½-inch loaf pan.

• Bake at 350° for 45 to 50 minutes. Cool on wire rack.

Makes 1 loaf

Per ½-inch slice _____

Calories 137  Protein 2.85 g  Carbohydrates 23.1 g  Fat 4 g  Cholesterol 26.5 mg  Sodium 111 mg

# Cream Cheese Bread

Ann Bommarito Armstrong

1 cup sour cream
½ cup sugar
1 teaspoon salt
½ cup butter, melted
2 packages active dry yeast
½ cup lukewarm (105 to 115°) water
2 eggs, beaten
4 cups all-purpose flour

**Cream Cheese Filling**
2 (8 ounce) packages cream cheese, softened
¾ cup sugar
1 egg, beaten
⅛ teaspoon salt
2 teaspoons vanilla extract

**Glaze**
2 cups powdered sugar
¼ cup milk
2 teaspoons vanilla extract

- Heat sour cream in saucepan over low heat. Add sugar, salt and butter. Let cool to lukewarm.
- Sprinkle yeast over warm water in large mixing bowl, stirring to dissolve. Add sour cream mixture, eggs and flour, mixing well.
- Chill dough, tightly covered, overnight.
- Divide dough into 4 equal portions. On well-floured surface, roll each portion into a 12x8-inch rectangle.
- Prepare filling by combining cream cheese, sugar, egg, salt and vanilla, blending until smooth.
- Spread ¼ of cream cheese filling on each rectangle of dough. Beginning at long edge, roll up, jelly roll fashion. Pinch seam to seal and tuck ends under.
- Place rolls, seam side down, on greased baking sheets. Cut slits about ⅔ of the way through roll at 2 inch intervals. Cover and let rise in a warm place, free from drafts, for about 1 hour or until doubled in bulk.
- Bake at 375° for 12 to 15 minutes.
- Prepare glaze by combining powdered sugar, milk and vanilla, blending until smooth. Spread glaze on warm loaves.

Makes 4 loaves

Per 2-inch slice

Calories 284  Protein 5.01 g  Carbohydrates 36.1 g  Fat 13.5 g  Cholesterol 62.2 mg  Sodium 210 mg

# Harvest Loaf Cake

Janet Henegar

1¾ cups all-purpose flour
1 teaspoon baking soda
½ teaspoon salt
1 teaspoon cinnamon
½ teaspoon nutmeg
¼ teaspoon ginger
¼ teaspoon ground cloves
½ cup butter, softened
1 cup sugar
2 eggs
¾ cup canned pumpkin
¾ cup semisweet chocolate morsels

**Glaze**

½ cup powdered sugar
⅛ teaspoon nutmeg
⅛ teaspoon cinnamon
1 to 2 tablespoons milk

• Combine flour, baking soda, salt, cinnamon, nutmeg, ginger and cloves.

• Cream butter and sugar together until fluffy. Add eggs and blend well.

• Alternately add dry ingredients and pumpkin to creamed mixture, beginning and ending with dry ingredients. Mix thoroughly. Stir in chocolate morsels.

• Pour batter into greased 9x5x3-inch loaf pan.

• Bake at 350° for 65 to 75 minutes. Cool in pan.

• Prepare glaze by combining powdered sugar, nutmeg and cinnamon. Add enough milk to form glaze consistency. Drizzle glaze over cake.

Makes 1 loaf

Per ½-inch slice _____

Calories 214  Protein 2.78 g  Carbohydrates 32.3 g  Fat 9 g  Cholesterol 42.2 mg  Sodium 187 mg

# Hawaiian Surprise Bread

Carol Willis

3 cups all-purpose flour
2 cups sugar
1 teaspoon baking powder
1 teaspoon baking soda
½ teaspoon salt
1 teaspoon cinnamon
½ teaspoon nutmeg
1 cup chopped nuts
3 eggs, beaten
1½ cups vegetable oil
1 cup shredded carrots
2 cups mashed banana
1 (8 ounce) can crushed pineapple, undrained
2 teaspoons vanilla

- Combine flour, sugar, baking powder, baking soda, salt, cinnamon, nutmeg and nuts.
- Combine eggs, oil, carrots, banana, pineapple and vanilla. Add dry ingredients and mix just until moistened.
- Spread batter in 2 greased and floured 9x5x3-inch loaf pans.
- Bake at 350° for 1 hour. Cool in pan for 10 minutes, then invert on wire rack to complete cooling.

*This is a very moist bread with a dark brown crust.*

Makes 2 loaves

Per ½-inch slice _____

Calories 154  Protein 2.04 g  Carbohydrates 24.1 g  Fat 6 g  Cholesterol 17.7 mg  Sodium 59.4 mg

# Honey Apricot Bread

Julie Strait

*Should be made a day ahead*

1½ cups non-fat vanilla yogurt
⅔ cup grape nut cereal
1¾ cups whole wheat flour
1¼ teaspoons baking powder
½ teaspoon baking soda
1 teaspoon salt
⅓ cup firmly-packed brown sugar
2 egg whites
1½ tablespoons vegetable oil
¼ cup honey
⅔ cup dried apricots

- Combine yogurt and cereal. Set aside.
- Combine flour, baking powder, baking soda, salt and brown sugar. Add yogurt mixture, egg whites, oil and honey, stirring just until moistened. Stir in apricots.
- Spread batter in greased 8x4x2½-inch loaf pan.
- Bake at 350° for 50 minutes. Cool in pan for 10 minutes, then invert on wire rack to complete cooling. Wrap and store overnight before slicing.

*A very moist, low-calorie bread with almost no fat.*

Makes 1 loaf

Per ½-inch slice _____

Calories 118  Protein 4.19 g  Carbohydrates 23.2 g  Fat 1.5 g  Cholesterol .41 mg  Sodium 217 mg

# Pear Bread with Half Hour Apple Butter

*Wanda Rich*

½ cup margarine, softened
1 cup sugar
2 eggs
2 cups all-purpose flour
1 teaspoon baking powder
½ teaspoon baking soda
½ teaspoon salt
½ teaspoon nutmeg
¼ cup plain yogurt
1 cup chopped unpeeled pears
1 teaspoon vanilla

**Apple Butter**
2 cups applesauce
½ cup sugar
1 teaspoon cinnamon
¼ teaspoon allspice
⅛ teaspoon ginger
⅛ teaspoon ground cloves

- Cream butter and sugar together until smooth. Add eggs, 1 at a time, beating after each addition.
- Combine flour, baking powder, baking soda, salt and nutmeg.
- Alternately add dry ingredients and yogurt to creamed mixture, mixing well. Stir in pears and vanilla.
- Pour batter into greased 9x5x3-inch loaf pan.
- Bake at 350° for 1 hour. Cool in pan for 10 minutes, then invert on wire rack to cool completely.
- Prepare apple butter by combining applesauce, sugar, cinnamon, allspice, ginger and cloves in large saucepan. Bring to a boil and cook for 30 minutes, stirring often. While still hot, spoon into a small canning jar and process according to canning directions.

*I put these loaves in Christmas gift baskets for family and friends.*

Makes 1 loaf and 1¼ cups apple butter

Per ½-inch slice _____

Calories 156  Protein 2.4 g  Carbohydrates 23.6 g  Fat 6 g  Cholesterol 23.8 mg  Sodium 152 mg

Per 1 tablespoon apple butter _____

Calories 30  Protein .049 g  Carbohydrates 7.86 g  Fat .25 mg  Cholesterol 0  Sodium .624 mg

# Pumpkin Date Nut Bread

Sue Kidwell

4 cups sugar
1 cup vegetable oil
2 eggs
3 cups canned pumpkin
5 cups all-purpose flour
1 tablespoon plus 1 teaspoon
baking soda
1 teaspoon salt
1 teaspoon cinnamon
1 teaspoon ground cloves
1 cup finely chopped dates
1 cup chopped pecans or walnuts
½ cup orange juice

- Combine sugar and oil. Beat several minutes until fluffy.
- Add eggs and beat thoroughly. Blend in pumpkin.
- Combine flour, baking soda, salt, cinnamon and cloves. Add dry ingredients, dates and pecans to pumpkin mixture, stirring to mix; do not overmix. Blend orange juice into batter.
- Pour batter into three 9x5x3-inch loaf pans, filling each ½ full.
- Bake at 350° for 1 hour. Cool in pans for 10 minutes.

Makes 3 loaves.

Per ½-inch slice _____

Calories 189  Protein 2.06 g  Carbohydrates 31.3 g  Fat 6.5 g  Cholesterol 8.83 mg  Sodium 117 mg

# Sausage Bread

Ann Bommarito Armstrong

1 cup raisins
1 pound hot bulk pork sausage,
uncooked
1½ cups sugar
1½ cups firmly-packed brown
sugar
2 eggs
1 cup chopped pecans
3 cups all-purpose flour
1 teaspoon baking powder
1 teaspoon ginger
1 teaspoon pumpkin pie spice
1 teaspoon baking soda
1 cup cold coffee

- Place raisins in saucepan with water to cover. Simmer for 5 minutes. Drain.
- Combine raisins, sausage, sugar, brown sugar, eggs and pecans, mixing well.
- Combine flour, baking powder, ginger and pumpkin pie spice.
- Dissolve baking soda in coffee. Add coffee and dry ingredients to sausage mixture, blending well.
- Pour batter into greased and floured 9-inch tube pan.
- Bake at 350° for 1½ hours.

Serves 24

Per serving _____

Calories 270  Protein 6.48 g  Carbohydrates 40 g  Fat 10 g  Cholesterol 33.4 mg  Sodium 289 mg

# Chocolate Zucchini Bread

*Gwen Walden Irwin*

2 cups sugar
1 cup vegetable oil
2 eggs
1 teaspoon vanilla
2¾ cups all-purpose flour
¼ cup cocoa
¼ teaspoon baking powder
1 teaspoon baking soda
1 teaspoon salt
3 cups grated zucchini squash
1 cup chopped nuts
1 cup miniature chocolate morsels
1 cup shredded coconut

- Combine sugar, oil, eggs and vanilla, blending well.
- Combine flour, cocoa, baking powder, baking soda and salt. Add to egg mixture, blending thoroughly.
- Stir in zucchini, nuts, chocolate morsels and coconut.
- Pour batter into 2 greased 9x5x3-inch loaf pans.
- Bake at 325° for 1 hour. Cool in pans for 10 minutes, then invert on wire rack to complete cooling.

Makes 2 loaves

Per ½-inch slice _____

Calories 215  Protein 2.37  Carbohydrate 25.9 g  Fat 12.5 g  Cholesterol 13.3 mg  Sodium 98.2 mg

# Zucchini Bread

*Rhonda Copeland Gracely*

2 cups sugar
1 cup oil
3 eggs
2 teaspoons vanilla
3 cups all-purpose flour
¾ teaspoon baking powder
2 teaspoons baking soda
1½ teaspoons salt
2 teaspoons cinnamon
2 cups shredded zucchini squash
1 (15 ounce) can crushed pineapple, drained
1 cup chopped pecans

- Combine sugar, oil and eggs. Beat until thickened. Stir in vanilla.
- Combine flour, baking powder, baking soda, salt and cinnamon. Add to egg mixture, blending thoroughly.
- Stir in zucchini, pineapple and pecans.
- Pour batter into 2 greased 9x5x3-inch loaf pans.
- Bake at 350° for 1 hour. Cool in pans for 10 minutes, then invert on wire rack to complete cooling.

Makes 2 loaves

Per ½-inch slice _____

Calories 192  Protein 2.24 g  Carbohydrates 24.4 g  Fat 10 g  Cholesterol 19.9 mg  Sodium 228 mg

# Rich Butterhorn Rolls

*Dee Dufour*

*Can be made in advance and frozen*

1 cup milk
½ cup vegetable shortening
1 package dry active yeast
½ cup sugar
1 teaspoon salt
3 eggs
4 cups all-purpose flour
3 tablespoons butter, melted

- Scald milk. Remove from heat. Add shortening and stir until melted.
- Combine yeast and sugar. Add to lukewarm milk mixture. Let stand for 5 minutes until bubbles form.
- Stir salt and eggs into milk mixture. Add flour, mixing until smooth. Place in well-oiled bowl, turning to coat. Let rise for 2 to 3 hours or until doubled in bulk.
- Divide dough into 3 portions. Place each portion on a floured surface and roll into a circle about ½ inch thick. Brush with melted butter.
- Cut each circle into 20 pie-shaped wedges. Beginning at wide edge, roll each wedge and place on greased baking sheet with narrow tip beneath roll. Brush with butter. Let rise until doubled in size.
- Bake at 400° for 15 minutes.

Makes 5 dozen

Per roll _____

Calories 63  Protein 1.36 g  Carbohydrates 8.28 g  Fat 3 g  Cholesterol 12.7 mg  Sodium 46.8 mg

## Sun-Dried Tomato Rolls  *Four Seasons Hotel - Austin, Texas*

2 ounces sun-dried tomato
4 cups bread flour
¼ cup plus 2 tablespoons sugar
1 tablespoon salt
3 tablespoons milk
3 tablespoons tomato puree
1 ounce active dry yeast
4 eggs
1 cup butter, softened
Kosher salt
Olive oil
Minced fresh garlic

- Place sun-dried tomato in bowl and add hot water to cover. Let stand for 2 to 3 hours or until soft. Coarsely chop and set aside.
- Sift flour, sugar and salt together.
- Combine milk, tomato puree and yeast.
- Using electric mixer with dough hook, blend dry ingredients and milk mixture until smooth. Add eggs, 1 at a time, mixing well after each addition. Knead dough at medium speed until very elastic. Add butter and blend until completely incorporated.
- Place dough in oiled bowl. Let rise, covered, until doubled in bulk. Punch down and place in refrigerator.
- When dough is chilled, divide in 2 dozen pieces, rolling each into a ball. Place in lightly greased muffin tins and lightly sprinkle tops with kosher salt. Using sharp knife, slash surface of rolls. Let rise in warm place until doubled in bulk.
- Bake at 400° until lightly browned and tops of rolls spring back when lightly pressed with fingertip. Remove rolls from pans. Combine fresh garlic with olive oil and brush on tops of rolls.

Makes approximately 2 dozen

Per roll

Calories 174  Protein 3.95 g  Carbohydrates 20.1 g  Fat 9 g  Cholesterol 56.3 mg  Sodium 376 mg

# Focaccia

Cookbook Committee

2 envelopes rapid-rise yeast
2 cups lukewarm (110-115°) water
2 tablespoons sugar
½ cup olive oil, divided
½ cup vegetable oil
1 teaspoon salt
5½ cups unbleached flour
3 cloves garlic, crushed
2 tablespoons fresh minced rosemary or 2 teaspoons dried rosemary
1 tablespoon kosher salt

- Dissolve yeast in water. Add sugar, ¼ cup olive oil, vegetable oil and salt.

- Add 3 cups flour and whip for about 10 minutes or until dough pulls away from sides of bowl. Mix in remaining flour by hand or with dough hook, kneading dough until it is smooth.

- Let dough rise in bowl until doubled in bulk, then punch down. Allow to rise again and punch down again.

- Brush oil on 2 baking sheets with rims. Divide dough between sheets. Using fingers, press dough to edges of each sheet. Let rise for 30 minutes.

- Combine garlic with ¼ cup olive oil. Brush on dough surface and sprinkle with rosemary and kosher salt.

- Bake at 375° for about 30 minutes.

Although focaccia is a popular item in many trendy restaurants today, it is actually a very old form of bread in Italy, going back hundreds of years. It may be used for sandwiches, pizza or simply as a very wonderful bread by itself or with a meal. Try it with a salad!

Makes 32 slices

Per slice _____

Calories 144  Protein 2.41 g  Carbohydrates 17.6 g  Fat 7 g  Cholesterol 0  Sodium 168 mg

# Norwegian Bread

Beverly Woldhagen James

5 cups milk
¾ cup sugar
1 teaspoon salt
1 cup margarine
3 envelopes dry active yeast
¾ cup molasses
5 pounds all-purpose flour
Butter

- Combine milk, sugar, salt and margarine in large saucepan. Bring to a boil. Remove from heat and let stand until cooled to 105 to 115°.
- Add yeast and molasses, mixing well.
- Gradually sift in flour, mixing until dough becomes thick enough to knead by hand. If using electric mixer with dough hook, mix until dough is smooth and satiny.
- Divide dough into 2 portions and place in well-oiled bowls, turning to coat. Let rise for about 1½ hours or until doubled in bulk.
- Knead dough, shape into 8 loaves and place in well-greased 9x5x3-inch loaf pans. Let rise for about 45 minutes or until doubled in bulk.
- Bake at 325° for 30 minutes. Remove loaves from pans, place on wire racks and brush top crust with butter.

May be varied by adding raisins or nuts to dough or by using ⅓ whole wheat flour.

Makes 8 loaves

Per ½-inch slice

Calories 93  Protein 2.22 g  Carbohydrates 16.5 g  Fat 2 g  Cholesterol 1.3 mg  Sodium 39.2 mg

## Seasoned French Bread

Vicki Ashley Atkins

1½ tablespoons low-fat
margarine, melted
1 teaspoon parsley flakes
¼ teaspoon basil
⅛ teaspoon garlic powder
½ teaspoon Worcestershire sauce
4 (1 inch) slices brown and serve
French bread

- Combine all ingredients except bread.
- Generously brush on each bread slice. Place, butter side up, on baking sheet.
- Bake at 400° for 5 minutes.

Serves 4

Per slice _____

Calories 122  Protein 3.17 g  Carbohydrates 18.5 g  Fat 4 g  Cholesterol 0  Sodium 247 mg

## Broccoli Cornbread

Tamra Beasley Bashaw

2 (8 ounce) packages cornbread
mix
4 eggs, beaten
1 cup cottage cheese
1 (10 ounce) package frozen
chopped broccoli, thawed and
drained
1 cup margarine, softened

- Combine all ingredients and mix well.
- Pour into greased 13x9x2-inch baking pan.
- Bake at 350° for 30 minutes.

Serves 16

Per serving _____

Calories 259  Protein 5.98 g  Carbohydrates 21.3 g  Fat 17 g  Cholesterol 55.1 mg  Sodium 526 mg

# Jalapeño Dressing

Nancille Sewell Willis

1 bunch green onions, chopped
½ stalk celery with leaves, chopped
½ cup bacon drippings
1 cup water
8 cups crumbled cornbread
4 cups crumbled day-old bread
3½ cups chicken broth
1 cup jalapeño pepper juice
½ teaspoon salt
⅛ teaspoon black pepper
1 to 3 jalapeño peppers, chopped

- Sauté onion and celery in bacon drippings. Add water and cook, covered, for about 7 minutes or until tender.

- Combine vegetables and liquid, breads, broth and jalapeño juice. Season with salt and pepper. Add jalapeño peppers to taste.

- Add water to bread mixture as needed to achieve a very moist consistency.

- Spoon dressing into cavity of 20 pound turkey, placing extra dressing in greased casserole.

- Bake casserole at 350° for 30 minutes.

*Family tradition at Thanksgiving—only in Texas! Mom always makes one pan of regular dressing for the weak at heart and one pan of jalapeño dressing.*

Makes approximately 12 cups

Per ½ cup serving

Calories 357  Protein 9.13 g  Carbohydrates 52.8 g  Fat 12 g  Cholesterol 38.4 mg  Sodium 926 mg

# Walnut and Oyster Dressing
Donna Earle Crain

½ pound sage-flavored bulk pork sausage
½ cup chopped parsley
1 tablespoon dried sage
2 cups raw oysters, rinsed and drained
1 cup broken walnuts
1 cup chopped onion
1 cup chopped celery
¾ cup unsalted butter, divided
4 cups crumbled cornbread
Salt and black pepper to taste
1 (15 ounce) can chicken broth
1 egg, well beaten
2 cups herb-seasoned stuffing mix

- Fry sausage in skillet, stirring to crumble, until browned. Drain sausage and place in large bowl. Add parsley, sage and oysters. Set aside.
- Toast walnuts at 350° for 9 minutes, stirring often. Add to sausage mixture.
- Sauté onion and celery in ½ cup butter until vegetables are tender. Stir into sausage mixture.
- Melt ¼ cup butter. Combine with cornbread, salt, black pepper, broth and egg, mixing well. Add stuffing mix.
- Combine cornbread mixture with sausage mixture. Pour into 13x9x2-inch baking pan.
- Bake at 350° for 30 minutes.

Makes approximately 10 cups

Per ½ cup serving

Calories 399  Protein 10.7 g  Carbohydrates 38.1 g  Fat 23 g  Cholesterol 71.5 mg  Sodium 896 mg

# Croutons
Mary Lauderman Tavcar

½ cup butter, melted
¼ teaspoon black pepper
1 teaspoon garlic powder
1¼ teaspoons onion salt
½ teaspoon paprika
½ teaspoon celery salt
1 teaspoon parsley
1 (24 ounce) loaf day-old bread, cubed

- Combine all ingredients except bread.
- Pour over bread cubes and toss to coat thoroughly. Spread in single layer on well-buttered rimmed baking sheet.
- Bake, stirring occasionally, at 325° for 10 minutes or until golden brown on all sides.

Makes approximately 1½ pounds croutons

Per 1 ounce serving

Calories 114  Protein 2.71 g  Carbohydrates 14.7 g  Fat 5 g  Cholesterol 11.5 mg  Sodium 202 mg

# Equivalents

| Ingredient | Equivalent |
|---|---|
| 3 medium apples | 3 cups sliced apples |
| 3 medium bananas | 2½ cups sliced, 2 cups mashed banana |
| 1 stick butter or margarine | ½ cup |
| 1 pound butter or margarine | 4 sticks; 2 cups |
| 1 medium lemon | 2 to 3 tablespoons juice and 2 teaspoons grated rind |
| 1 medium lime | 1½ to 2 tablespoons juice |
| 1 medium orange | ⅓ cup juice and 2 tablespoons grated rind |
| 4 medium peaches | 2 cups sliced peaches |
| 4 medium pears | 2 cups sliced pears |
| 1 quart strawberries | 4 cups sliced strawberries |
| 1 pound head cabbage | 4½ cups shredded cabbage |
| 2 medium corn ears | 1 cup whole kernel corn |
| 1 large green pepper | 1 cup diced green pepper |
| 1 pound head lettuce | 6¼ cups torn lettuce |
| 8 ounces raw mushrooms | 1 cup sliced cooked mushrooms |
| 1 medium onion | 1 cup chopped onion |
| 3 medium white potatoes | 2 cups cubed cooked or 1¾ cups mashed white potatoes |
| 1 medium sweet potato | 1 cup sliced sweet potatoes |
| 8 slices cooked bacon | ½ cup crumbled bacon |
| 1 pound American or Cheddar cheese | 4 cups shredded cheese |
| 4 ounces cheese | 1 cup shredded cheese |
| 4 large whole eggs | 1 cup eggs |
| 8 large eggs | 1 cup egg whites |
| 16 large eggs | 1 cup egg yolks |
| 1 cup quick-cooking oats | 1¾ cups cooked oats |
| 1 cup uncooked long grain rice | 3 to 4 cups cooked rice |
| 1 cup pre-cooked rice | 2 cups cooked rice |
| 1 pound coffee | 40 cups perked coffee |
| 1 pound pitted dates | 2 to 3 cups chopped dates |
| 1 pound all-purpose flour | 4 cups flour |
| 1 pound granulated sugar | 2 cups sugar |
| 1 pound powdered sugar | 3½ cups powdered sugar |
| 1 pound brown sugar | 2¼ cups firmly packed packed brown sugar |
| 1 cup (4 ounces) uncooked macaroni | 2 cups cooked macaroni |
| 4 ounces uncooked noodles | 2 cups cooked noodles |
| 8 ounces uncooked spaghetti | 4 cups cooked spaghetti |
| 1 pound shelled nuts | 4 cups chopped nuts |
| 1 cup whipping cream | 2 cups whipped cream |
| 1 cup soft bread crumbs | 2 slices fresh bread |
| 1 pound crab in shell | ¾ to 1 cup flaked crab |

| | |
|---|---|
| 1½ pounds fresh, unpeeled shrimp | 2 cups cooked, peeled deveined shrimp |
| 1 pound fresh small shrimp | 35 or more shrimp |
| 1 pound fresh medium shrimp | 26 to 35 shrimp |
| 1 pound fresh large shrimp | 21 to 25 shrimp |
| 1 pound fresh jumbo shrimp | less than 20 shrimp |
| 19 chocolate wafers | 1 cup crumbs |
| 14 graham cracker squares | 1 cup fine crumbs |
| 28 saltines | 1 cup finely crushed crumbs |
| 22 vanilla wafers | 1 cup finely crushed crumbs |

# Substitutions

| Recipe Ingredients | Substitution |
|---|---|
| 1 cup sour milk or buttermilk | 1 tablespoon vinegar or lemon juice plus sweet milk to make 1 cup |
| 1 cup commercial sour cream | 1 tablespoon lemon juice plus evaporated milk to equal 1 cup |
| 1 cup yogurt | 1 cup sour milk or buttermilk |
| 1 whole egg | 2 egg whites or ¼ cup egg substitute |
| 1 tablespoon cornstarch | 2 tablespoons all-purpose flour |
| 1 teaspoon baking powder | ½ teaspoon cream of tartar plus ¼ teaspoon soda |
| 1 cup cake flour | 1 cup all-purpose flour minus 2 tablespoons |
| 1 cup self-rising flour | 1 cup all-purpose flour plus 1 teaspoon baking powder and ½ teaspoon salt |
| 1 cup honey | 1¼ cups sugar plus ¼ cup liquid |
| 1 ounce unsweetened chocolate | 3 tablespoons cocoa plus 1 tablespoon butter or margarine |
| 1 pound fresh mushrooms | 6 ounces canned mushrooms |
| 1 tablespoon fresh herbs | 1 teaspoon ground or crushed dry herbs |
| 1 teaspoon onion powder | 2 teaspoons minced onion |
| 1 clove fresh garlic | 1 teaspoon garlic salt or ⅛ teaspoon garlic powder |
| Dry sherry | Dry vermouth |
| 1 cup cream | 1 cup skim milk plus 2 tablespoons nonfat dry milk; or ¾ cup milk plus ⅓ cup butter |

# Measurements to Remember

| | |
|---|---|
| 3 teaspoons | =1 tablespoon |
| 4 tablespoons | =¼ cup |
| 8 tablespoons | =½ cup |
| 16 tablespoons | =1 cup |
| 5 tablespoons plus 1 teaspoon | =⅓ cup |
| 4 ounces | =½ cup |
| 8 ounces | =1 cup |
| 16 ounces | =1 pound |
| 1 ounce | =2 tablespoons |
| 2 cups fat | =1 pound |
| 2 cups | =1 pint |
| 2 pints | =1 quart |
| 4 cups | =1 quart |

# The Metric System

| | |
|---|---|
| 2 cups | =474 milliliters |
| 1 cup | =237 milliliters |
| ¾ cup | =178 milliliters |
| ⅔ cup | =158 milliliters |
| ½ cup | =119 milliliters |
| ⅓ cup | =79 milliliters |
| ¼ cup | =59 milliliters |
| 1 tablespoon | =15 milliliters |
| 1 teaspoon | =5 milliliters |
| 1 fluid ounce | =30 milliliters |

# Measurement Conversion Formulas

**How to Convert:**

| | | | | | | | | |
|---|---|---|---|---|---|---|---|---|
| liters | x | 2.12 | = | pints | kilograms | x | 2.21 | = | pounds |
| liters | x | 1.06 | = | quarts | grams | x | .035 | = | ounces |
| pints | x | .472 | = | liters | pounds | x | .45 | = | kilograms |
| quarts | x | .946 | = | liters | ounces | x | 28.35 | = | grams |

**Temperatures:**

250 degrees Fahrenheit = 121 degrees Celsius
300 degrees Fahrenheit = 149 degrees Celsius
350 degrees Fahrenheit = 177 degrees Celsius
400 degrees Fahrenheit = 205 degrees Celsius
450 degrees Fahrenheit = 232 degrees Celsius

# *Index*

# Lone Star Legacy

## A Texas Cookbook

*Lone Star Legacy is more than just a cookbook - it is a keepsake! Its more than 800 recipes are seasoned with cooking tips, spiced with Texas trivia, and frosted with breathtaking photos of Texas landmarks and landscapes. It has sold over 180,000 copies and was the first Texas cookbook selected for the Walter S. McIlhenny Community Cookbook Hall of Fame.*

# and

# Lone Star Legacy II

## A Texas Cookbook

*Following in the tradition of Lone Star Legacy, Lone Star Legacy II will capture your heart and tantalize your tastebuds with over 800 new and exciting recipes. Plan your next fiesta with its "South of the Border" section, including everything from margaritas to sopaipillas. Or, try the Peppered Beef Flambe' and Pasta with Texas Pecan Sauce, followed by a slice of Apricot Brandy Cake!*

### Austin Junior Forum Publications
### P.O. Box 26628
### Austin, Texas  78755-0628

Please send me_____ copies of **Changing Thymes**      @ $17.95 *each* _____
Please send me_____ copies of **Lone Star Legacy**      @   17.95 *each* _____
Please send me_____ copies of **Lone Star Legacy** II      @   17.95 *each* _____
Postage and handling      @     2.50 *each* _____

Name _____

Address _____

City _____ State _____ Zip _____

*Make checks payable to AJF Publications*

---

### Austin Junior Forum Publications
### P.O. Box 26628
### Austin, Texas  78755-0628

Please send me_____ copies of **Changing Thymes**      @ $17.95 *each* _____
Please send me_____ copies of **Lone Star Legacy**      @   17.95 *each* _____
Please send me_____ copies of **Lone Star Legacy** II      @   17.95 *each* _____
Postage and handling      @     2.50 *each* _____

Name _____

Address _____

City _____ State _____ Zip _____

*Make checks payable to AJF Publications*

---

### Austin Junior Forum Publications
### P.O. Box 26628
### Austin, Texas  78755-0628

Please send me_____ copies of **Changing Thymes**      @ $17.95 *each* _____
Please send me_____ copies of **Lone Star Legacy**      @   17.95 *each* _____
Please send me_____ copies of **Lone Star Legacy** II      @   17.95 *each* _____
Postage and handling      @     2.50 *each* _____

Name _____

Address _____

City _____ State _____ Zip _____

*Make checks payable to AJF Publications*